GENDER & SEXUALITY

*To Richard,
with great thanks
and in solidarity*

TALKING RADICAL

GENDER & SEXUALITY

Canadian History Through the Stories of Activists

Scott Neigh

Fernwood Publishing
Halifax & Winnipeg

Copyright © 2012 Scott Neigh
All rights reserved. No part of this book may be reproduced or transmitted in any form by any means without permission in writing from the publisher, except by a reviewer, who may quote brief passages in a review.

Editing: Marianne Ward
Cover design: John van der Woude
Printed and bound in Canada by Hignell Book Printing

Published in Canada by Fernwood Publishing
32 Oceanvista Lane, Black Point, Nova Scotia, B0J 1B0
and 748 Broadway Avenue, Winnipeg, Manitoba, R3G 0X3
www.fernwoodpublishing.ca

Fernwood Publishing Company Limited gratefully acknowledges the financial support of the Government of Canada through the Canada Book Fund and the Canada Council for the Arts, the Nova Scotia Department of Communities, Culture and Heritage, the Manitoba Department of Culture, Heritage and Tourism under the Manitoba Publishers Marketing Assistance Program and the Province of Manitoba, through the Book Publishing Tax Credit, for our publishing program.

Library and Archives Canada Cataloguing in Publication

Neigh, Scott
  Gender and sexuality : Canadian history through the stories of
activists / Scott Neigh.

Includes bibliographical references and index.
ISBN 978-1-55266-521-3

1. Sex discrimination--Canada. 2. Gender identity--Canada. 3. Sexual minorities--Canada. 4. Sexism--Canada. 5. Sex--Social aspects--Canada. 6. Social movements--Canada--History. I. Title.

HQ1236.5.C3N45 2012   305.420971   C2012-903153-4

Contents

Acknowledgments / viii

Foreword
    Encounters with a Radical History From Below
    by Gary Kinsman / 1

Introduction / 6
    Approaches to History / 7
    Social Thinking / 9
    Power and Oppression / 10
    Standpoint and Struggle / 12
    Doing History Differently / 14
    Gender and Sexuality / 16
    Connection and Action / 19

1. Decolonize Your Mind: Doreen Spence and Donna MacPhee on the Plains Indian Cultural Survival School / 23
    Knowledge and Difference / 24
    Knowledge and Conquest / 27
    Knowledge, Gender, and Assimilation / 28
    Schools / 30
    Spence / 33
    MacPhee / 38

2. Against Company, Church, and State: Madeleine Parent and the Dominion Textile Strike of 1946 / 45
    People, Not Things / 46
    Origins / 49
    The Labour Movement in Canada / 51
    Parent / 54

3. Women Against Violence (Part I): Lee Lakeman on Feminist Anti-Violence Activism in Woodstock and Vancouver / 69
    Tea, Embodiedness, and Violence / 70
    Denying Violence Against Women / 72
    Women Resurgent / 76
    Lakeman / 78
    A Conference and a Lunch / 80
    The State / 82
    Vancouver / 86
    The Resurgent Right / 90
    Lakeman's Lessons / 94

4. Women Against Violence (Part II): Shree Mulay and Sadeqa Siddiqui on Feminist Anti-Violence Activism in Montreal / 97

    Seeing Difference / 98
    Understanding Difference / 100
    How It Matters / 103
    Working Against Violence / 105
    Mulay / 107
    Siddiqui / 109
    Barriers and Divisions / 111
    Making Change / 115

5. Living Rooms, Bedrooms, and the Streets: Chris Vogel and Richard North on Gay Liberation in Winnipeg / 123

    Sexuality Matters / 124
    Same-Gender Relationships in History / 127
    Vogel and North / 129
    Beyond Visibility: Resisting Punishment / 137
    Existing Together / 142

6. Women's Liberation and the Lord: Shelley Finson on Feminism in Christian Churches / 146

    Paying Attention to Religion / 147
    Religion and Social Analysis / 149
    The Substance of the Shift / 150
    Christianity, Gender, and Sexuality / 153
    Gender and the United Church of Canada / 154
    To Canada, Christianity, and Feminism / 156
    Friends of Hagar / 158
    The Movement for Christian Feminism / 160
    The Task Forces / 162
    Racism and Heterosexism / 165
    Relentless Persistence / 171

Conclusion / 174

    Implications / 175
    Canadian History Through the Stories of Activists / 178
    Nodes and Strands / 180
    Ordinary / 183

References / 186

Index / 196

For SAR and GLRN, with love.

For Ms. Henriques,
who asked me in third grade to dedicate my first book to her.
It has taken a while, but here you go.

And for all who have worked for justice and liberation
but whose stories are not recorded, not remembered.

Acknowledgments

First and foremost, my utmost gratitude to those individuals who were generous enough to give their time and share their stories with me. The volume of material collected has meant that many wonderful stories have not been published here, for which I apologize, but every one has contributed to shaping the project. Thank you so much to Lynn Brooks, Rosemary Brown, Roy Carless, Bridget Coll, Elsie Dean, Audi Dharmalingam, Muriel Duckworth, Rev. Shelley Davis Finson, John Friesen, Carolina Gajardo, Jojo Geronimo, Josephine Grey, Dorothy Groves, Ariel Harper, Richard Hudler, Lynn Jones, Rita Kohli, Lee Lakeman, Mel Lehan, Donna MacPhee, Kathy Mallett, Cindy McCallum, Theresa Meuse-Dallien, Christine Morrissey, Shree Mulay, Rev. David Nobu-tsune Murata, Greta Hofmann Nemiroff, Fo Niemi, Richard North, Roger Obonsawin, Brian O'Neill, Madeleine Parent, William Paterson, Daniel Paul, Betty Peterson, Ron Poynter, Charles Roach, Wey Robinson, Frank Showler, Isabel Showler, Eric Shragge, Sadeqa Siddiqui, Shahina Siddiqui, Robert Silverman, Doreen Spence, Leslie Spillett, Yvonne Stanford, Joan Thompson, Chris Vogel, and Don Weitz. Your stories have not only been the central pillar of this project, but they have taught me, challenged me, and, through the many years they have been a focus for my work and reflection, transformed me.

Thank you to Randy Kay for collaboration in doing the interviews with Frank and Isabel Showler and with Roy Carless, which gave me a taste for hearing these stories before I knew what I might do with them; to Matthew Behrens for collaboration in doing the interview with the Showlers as well, and for feedback and encouragement at various stages of the interview and writing process; to Ahmad Saidullah, Rabea Murtaza, Gary Kinsman, Ander Reszczynski-Negrazis, and Chris Dixon for their feedback on drafts of the book proposal and/or pieces of the manuscript at various stages; to Chris Dixon and Alexis Shotwell for consistent support of all kinds, but especially that which comes from regular opportunities to talk about a writing project of this magnitude with others who are at a similar stage in figuring out how to do similar work. I have benefited enormously from the chance to do activist work with all of the people in this paragraph, and to learn from them about politics and ideas and the living of life.

Many of the people already mentioned provided suggestions about whom to interview or what to do with the material. Many other people did as well, in forms covering the entire range from extended conversations with friends to single, brief e-mails from helpful souls out there on the Internet. My thanks to Vilma Rossi, Jane Mulkewich, Michelle Cho, Cole Gately, Andrew Loucks, Cindy Sue McCormack, David Jefferess, Chris Shannon, Suzanne Brown,

Jeff Wingard, Deirdre Pike, Mark Fraser, Kevin McKay, Hanna Schayer, the staff of *Outlook* magazine, Brian Burch, Mark Vorobej, Peter Archibald, Bob Wood, Graeme MacQueen, Joy Warner, Gary Warner, Raj Hathiramani, Peter Hutton, Don Maclean, the PAR-L e-mail list, Louise Marchand, Audra Estrones Williams, Catherine Laidlaw-Sly, Laura Briskin, Joyce Green, Robin Smith, Donna-lee Iffla, Lisa Sharik, Amy Nixon, Darlene Juschka, Philippe Duhamel, Angela Bischoff, the late Tooker Gomberg, Norman Nawrocki, William Carroll, Tom Langford, Alison R. Hall, Kerry Pither, Nancy Ruth, Tom Warner, Alina Chaterjee, Frank Saptel, Ron Garnett-Doucette, Si Transken, Greg Nepean, Carolyn van Gurp, Anne Clark, David Henry, Harold Shuster, Carroll Holland, Amy Goudie, Karen Lior, Carmon Henry, Janice Gairey, Terry St. Jacques, staff at the National Anti-Poverty Organization, Paulette Sadoway, the Student Christian Movement, Fiona Green, Brenda Savage, Peter Kulchyski, Janice Ristock, Zarqa Nawaz, Gord Christie, Bilbo Poynter, Linda Briskin, Shannon Folland, Ursule Christoph, Victoria Fenner, Renee Wetselaar, and, I'm sure, many others. And thank you to some on the above list and others too numerous to mention for your roles in my own political evolution — for hours spent working on the same activist projects, for support, for challenges, for arguments, for collaborations, for many beers consumed, and many opinions exchanged.

    Thank you to Janet Neigh and Joy Hartzler for places to stay during trips to do interviews. Thank you to Margaret Neigh for logistical support in the interview processing stage. Thank you to Janet, Margaret, David Neigh, David Scott, Kathryn Neigh, Edward Neigh, Dianne Ritz, and John Ritz for support of various kinds, including great patience and understanding for choices that I'm sure must sometimes seem strange and for my frequent reluctance to talk about the things that occupy the bulk of my time. Thank you to Debi Dawson for doing some of the transcription work. Thank you to the Social Planning and Research Council of Hamilton for the opportunity to earn income that supported the early stages of work on this project, and for use of their fax machine. Thank you to Marcia Ritz and Chris Cates for input into the project's initial website design and to Rachel Ellaway for the use of the infrastructure that allowed me to produce the audio clips referred to in the text. Thank you to Liz Cates for emotional support and undying patience in listening to endless repetitions of the same anxieties about the work, particularly during its earlier phases. Thank you to Errol Sharpe of Fernwood Publishing for his enthusiasm and support for this project, as well as Beverley Rach, Nancy Malek, Marianne Ward, and all of the rest at Fernwood whose hard work have made this book a reality.

    Finally, there are no words to describe my gratitude to Liam Ritz Neigh and to Stacey Ritz. I cannot point to specific phrases or ideas, but I am sure that if my path during the period of this work had not involved countless hours primarily focused on being with Liam as he grew from baby to kid, my thinking about the world and its reflection in this book would be much less rich. Certainly my life would have been much less rich. And without the love, the patience, the constant input, and the steadfast support of Stacey through all of these years, through moments of great joy and great challenge, through transitions that would once have been unimaginable, this book would not have been possible. Thank you.

Foreword

Encounters with a Radical History From Below
by Gary Kinsman

What a delight it was to be asked by Scott Neigh to write the Foreword for his companion books: *Gender and Sexuality* and *Resisting the State*, both with the subtitle, *Canadian History Through the Stories of Activists*. These books are powerful examples of historical work that pushes against the social organization of forgetting our histories of struggle for social justice through the resistance of remembering these struggles.[1] I am also profoundly committed to this perspective in my work. In the pages of these books history comes to life in popular and accessible ways allowing readers to make connections between past struggles, our present struggles, and possible futures. These books are not only about the important recovery of people's stories but are also very much about the creation and making of our social and historical memories. These books are history and social memory in the making.

Gender and Sexuality focuses our attention on gender and sexual political struggles, while *Resisting the State* draws our attention to struggles against state relations. Since these two books are so complexly interwoven, with *Gender and Sexuality* also dealing with struggles against state formation and *Resisting the State* engaging with gender and sexual politics, I have written a common Foreword to both.

When I first came out as a queer man in the early 1970s and got involved in the gay liberation movement we viewed those who had been active around lesbian and gay concerns in the 1960s and earlier (the homophile movement) as "self-oppressed" and extremely limited. It was only when I actually met, talked with, and learned from early activists like Jim Egan, Doug Sanders, and Bruce Somers that I realized how misguided this approach was. It not only distorted our views of past queer organizing but prevented us from learning from them for our struggles in the historical present.[2] It was these early activists who opened up spaces and helped lay the basis for the emergence of our later liberation movements. It is these struggles in the past that created the basis for what we have in the present — and often in the age of neoliberal capitalism we need to defend these gains from attack.

This impressed on me the need to both respect and learn from activists who have come before us. This is one of the main strengths of what Scott Neigh accomplishes in these books. We get to hear and learn from a number of our elder activists. This learning from our elders is not done often enough outside indigenous contexts. We are not always the first activists and organizers to take up particular struggles, and there is a lot to learn from the wisdom of those who have come before us. We do not need to always reinvent the wheel.

The stories Scott allows us to hear are from activists/organizers who have had long histories of being able to sustain their differently located activisms — or what Lynn Jones in *Resisting the State* calls "surviving" — over the long haul. There is also much to be learned here as present day activists often suffer from burn-out and overload and sometimes a falling away from the struggle. How do we stay committed to our struggles when gains are not always tangible and clear and when the possibilities for major victories may seem remote?

Some of these activists/organizers were known to me before I read this manuscript — including Madeleine Parent, Charles Roach, Isabel and Frank Showler, Lee Lakeman, Chris Vogel, Josephine Grey, and Don Weitz — although I got to know them a lot better through engaging with their narratives in these books. But there are also others whom I had never heard of before, and I am very glad I got a chance to meet them and learn from them through these books. Struggles get spoken of here that are not usually mentioned including the struggle of the psychiatrized with the story of Don Weitz. All of these people are extraordinary, but they also engage in very everyday and ordinary forms of resistance and rebellion. As the Zapatistas — an indigenous-based movement against neoliberal capitalism in southern Mexico — point out, to be a rebel is part of the ordinary fabric of life in an unjust and oppressive society that denies people their dignity.

Central to the project of this book is entering into an encounter with history through the narratives of these long-time activists, organizers, and survivors which is a crucial entry point. This is history that is directly about people's lives and struggles. This places us in the midst of indigenous struggles for justice and survival, feminist struggles against violence against women, various mobilizations against racism, union battles in the Duplessis era in Quebec, human rights battles against poverty, and gay rights struggles. We hear of the experiences of those who have fought for justice in the courts and through use of the law, of the radical sources and of the social gospel, and of feminist struggles in the churches.

These stories of long-time activists are historically and socially contextualized with illuminating commentary and analysis from Scott. This ties these stories into broader social and historical currents, linking these struggles together, pointing to tensions between different stories and movements, and making these stories relevant to all readers. Rather than this book being a monologue it has a very dialogical[3] and living texture with the various voices of the long-time activists and Scott's commentary existing in dialogue and mutually informing each other. In the politics of the writing of this book there has been careful attention paid listening to and learning from the long-time activists whose stories both drive the book forward and ground its analysis. This is a politics of writing that revolves around listening, asking and raising questions, making connections, and creating contexts.

These books are not the history of the elite or the official history of the Canadian nation-state. Indeed they provide a major counter-text to this. These books disrupt, undermine, and subvert official state and professional histories. They look at the world from the vantage point of these long-time activists. This is a history from below, a formulation derived from E.P. Thompson's important work on working class history,[4] which looks at the world from the diverse social standpoints of activists and organizers, the oppressed, exploited, and marginalized.

This involves Scott along with us as readers in challenging relations of social power and privilege. We come to learn about and to challenge relations of race, gender, class, sexuality, and much more. In this complex of relations Scott positions himself in a very up front, self-critical, and reflexive fashion, troubling and raising crucial questions about social privilege and especially about white and masculine privilege in his own social experiences and practices. In this regard he raises crucial questions and challenges about the need for a politics of becoming an ally with movements of the oppressed and for a politics of responsibility for those of us who are situated in positions of social privilege. How those of us within positions of power and privilege can learn from and listen to the voices of the oppressed and how we can challenge relations of power and oppression from our own locations within them is central here.

The colonizing project of Canadian state formation — that "Canada" is a colonial settler state — in relation to indigenous people, including the residential schools and the profound resistance to this racism and colonialism, is key to these books. In this regard it is crucial that *Gender and Sexuality* starts with the stories of Doreen Spence and Donna MacPhee on struggles for indigenous education and the need for a decolonizing pedagogy. Similarly, in *Resisting the State* we hear from Roger Obonsawin and Kathy Mallett on the struggles of indigenous people in urban areas. In this and other areas, reading this book rips open the fabric of the liberal, tolerant, humanitarian, multicultural mythologies of official Canadian history. This includes recognizing the depth and deep roots of racism in Canadian history and social organization, including the deportation of women domestic workers and clear and long-term experiences of racism in Canadian immigration policy. This critique resonates with the current struggles of No One Is Illegal activist groups and others for status for all migrants, refugees, and immigrants.

Scott highlights the importance of recognizing social differences between people and the autonomous character of many of our social movements, but this is not an autonomy that portrays our struggles as in any way separate and unrelated. He cuts across the tendency that can exist in some narrow forms of identity politics to remove social differences from the social relations and historical struggles in which they are made *and* resisted. Instead, through the many different entry points and narratives provided in these books, he allows us to see how we make social relations together that have very differential impacts on groups of people located differently in relations of social power. For instance, the social practices of those of us bound up with the colonial settler state project are directly related to the racialization and colonization experienced by indigenous peoples. These are common social relations experienced and lived very differently depending on where we are located in these relations. At the same time these social relations can be challenged from a number of different social locations within them.

The powerful and often inspiring narratives that Scott weaves together provide important moments of our social histories and are not only about the historical past, although often they allow us to view and feel the past in very different ways. They are also very much about the historical present that we find ourselves in today, how it has been made, and how it can be transformed.

I also really appreciate Scott's attempts to move away from the common problem we face in social and even historical analysis of giving far too much power to things like commodities and money. This prevents us from being able to grasp how it is people, through our own social doings, who make these things and objects and give them social value. By attempting to disclose the human social practices that lie behind the power of things Scott assists us in developing a way of doing historical and social analysis that does not participate in reification — transforming social relations between people into relations between things. We can then see how we have been active in making our social worlds and can collectively transform them.

In closing, we need more work like this, using people's stories as a way of building social histories and analysis. Scott's work, although impressive and important, is only a beginning. It is by no means the final word and I hope it initiates a new wave of social and historical inquiry that uses historical narratives to build critical social historical analysis. I hope these two books provide inspiration for others to take up similar historical projects.

As Scott himself points out, we need to be motivated by a politics of listening and asking questions. This book does not provide final answers and in my view it is important that it does not try to do this. As the Zapatistas have put it, walking we ask questions; it is only in moving together against oppression that the questions we need to address become clearer and the paths we need to walk become visible.

Gary Kinsman,
Sudbury, on the historical territories of the Atikameksheng Anishnawbek First Nation,
July 2, 2011

Notes

1. On the social organization of forgetting and the resistance of remembering see my book co-authored with Patrizia Gentile, *The Canadian War on Queers: National Security as Sexual Regulation* (Vancouver: UBC Press, 2010).
2. On some of this see Gary Kinsman, *The Regulation of Desire: Homo and Hetero Sexualities* (Montreal: Black Rose Books, 1996).
3. Dialogical is an expression used by Russian literary theorist Mikhail Bakhtin that is used to describe how the social is made up of multiple dialogues and discussions. See Mikhail Bakhtin, (Michael Holquist ed.), *The Dialogic Imagination: Four Essays by M.M. Bakhtin* (Austin: University of Texas Press, 1981).
4. See E.P. Thompson, *The Making of the English Working Class* (Harmondsworth: Penguin Books, 1968).

Introduction

The sense of connection blew me away.[1]

In 1998, not long after my final university exam, I was rumbling down Highway 403 on a bus sponsored by the Hamilton and District Labour Council. I was on my way to the St. Catherine's instalment of the Ontario Days of Action campaign against the anti-community, anti-worker, anti-environment, anti-anti-racist, anti-poor offensive of the Conservative provincial government of the day. As the miles rolled by, an older woman was making a progression from seat to seat, chatting with everyone and making sure they knew about the campaign against the Multilateral Agreement on Investment.[2]

Unfortunately, I don't recall her name, and I no longer remember what she had to say about international investment agreements, but the rest of our conversation has very much stuck in my mind: She reminisced about being a little girl in a working-class neighbourhood in Liverpool, England, and going door-to-door with her sister to collect money to support the Left's fight against Franco's fascists in the Spanish Civil War.[3]

She had begun working for radical social change in 1936, almost forty years before I was born. She talked about supporting a struggle that felt unbelievably distant and occurred in a world that, in my ink-and-paper mediated understanding of it, felt completely different from the one that I lived in. For me (and my budding anarchist imagination) the struggle between the anarchist/Communist/labour alliance and the fascists, the massacre at Guernica, the bad faith of the West in looking the other way as Hitler supported Franco, and the schemes of the Stalinists were a thing of myth; for her, they were all part of something real in which she, in a small way, took part. And here she was, so many decades later, still contributing to struggles for social justice.

Over the years as I have learned more about history I have often thought about the sense of connection that I felt that day — a sense of connection between present and past, between local and global, between individual and social. Most importantly, it was a sense of connection between History with a capital *H* and action by ordinary people. This book and its companion, *Resisting the State: Canadian History Through the Stories of Activists*, are one small attempt to address the absence of these connections in the version of Canadian history that most of us have the opportunity to learn. The two books do this by entering Canadian history through the words of long-time activists from diverse eras, identities, locations, and movements.

I first learned about Canadian history in grade school and high school classes. The details have faded with the years, but I still remember fragments and outlines. I remember names like Wolfe and Montcalm and Macdonald and Riel. I remember hearing about explorers and fur traders, railways and conscription crises. I remember stories of a great nation carved from the wilderness, of "two solitudes," of "peace, order, and good government." I remember this thing called Canada being presented as unquestionably great and good, as a historical project no sane person could doubt. I remember that, except for a few conflicts we were taught to see as being at the centre of present-day national identity — English/French and English/American, with indigenous peoples as sidekicks for different Europeans in the early years; Canadian/American; and the path to "responsible government" — everyone on this continent seemed to pretty much get along. In the sections on the twentieth century there was an additional brief mention of some workers who were momentarily unhappy during the Depression, and another of some women who got a bit miffed until they were allowed to vote and be regarded as legal persons, but on the whole Canada was shown as a country at peace within itself.

Some Canadians learn this country's history in other ways, of course; those who immigrate as adults may first encounter it when they go through the process to become citizens. A few years ago, after decades as a permanent resident, my mother finally took the plunge. The booklet provided by the government to guide her through the process proclaims in bold print, "You must also learn about voting procedures and Canada's history and geography," but its historical content is limited to an even shallower version of what I learned in high school — a few facts, like the dates that various provinces joined Confederation and the name of the first Prime Minister, and an emphasis on the claim that Canada is a happy and welcoming place for all (Citizenship and Immigration Canada 2002).

As an adult, I have learned some history from the mass media as well. Most television and newspaper content is fixated on an eternal present, but if you look there are spaces where information about the past is talked about explicitly, and more where we get hints about what supposedly matters about the past from the ways that the present gets talked about. But very little that I have found there goes beyond what I learned in school. In other words, most of the sources that most Canadians can easily access to learn about our history teach the same basic set of stories. And there are some pretty fundamental problems with what those stories say and what they leave out.

Approaches to History

A first step in thinking about what is wrong with conventional history is taking a look at who and what is omitted. In my school classes, for example, whole categories of people were largely left out. Almost everyone I heard about was white. Indigenous peoples were mentioned, but it is only through reading and listening in the last few years that I have come to appreciate how completely ignorant of their histories the school system left me. Communities of colour may have received passing mention, as with a few minutes spent on talking about how wonderful Canada was for accepting runaway slaves from the U.S. via the Underground Railroad, but mostly these communities were treated as peripheral to Canada's history. Token (mostly white) women appeared, like Laura Secord and Queen Victoria, but other than a few brief words the realities of women were mostly absent. The very idea that history could be about working people would have taken some explaining to get through to me, and in my extremely homophobic rural high school lesbian and gay people were never mentioned at all.

In retrospect, it was not just certain groups of people that were missing, it was stories, too — including stories that would have been very relevant to my life. Every time I went to the doctor's office, I benefited from socialized medical care, but I never got a sense of the legacy of struggle by workers and people of faith, the acts of political courage and sacrifice, that made that possible. At various times both of my parents and my partner have belonged to unions, but in school I learned nothing about how relentless struggle by generations of workers who never dreamed of a life as comfortable as mine made it unremarkable for my parents and partner to have collective agreements and the right to strike. I knew from my great aunt's work on family history that the first Neigh came to southern Ontario in 1839, but nothing in my schooling helped me really appreciate the significance of him being an early white settler on land that had belonged since time immemorial to Anishnabe peoples. And nothing explained to me that my mother, a white woman from Scotland who moved to Canada in the late 1960s, ended up in a country where the vast majority of people looked like her because of decades of deliberate effort by the Canadian state to make it so, and that around the time she arrived, Canada's racist immigration policies were being contested and changed in limited but still significant ways.

As I have learned more about the history of the country I live in from the spoken and written words of others, I have come to realize that it is not just a matter of people and stories being left out or of a basically useful framework for understanding history that happens to have a few holes in it that need to be filled. Rather, conventional history makes certain assumptions about how society works and what history should be, and the exclusion of people and stories and ideas flows from those assumptions. Approaching history with a different framework can result in a much different and much more useful picture of how the present was produced by the past, and how the future can be produced by the present. I remember many of the stories in high school making it sound like exceptional individuals — usually white men in positions of great power — determined the path of history. Since then, I've learned to think about past and present in much more social ways.

Social Thinking

The place that I start from is that the social world exists and that it matters.[4] This may seem obvious but it needs to be said because in so many ways we are encouraged to see ourselves purely as individuals who can shape our destinies solely by making individual choices and by sheer force of will. Individual choices matter, certainly, but we need to understand them in the context of our relationships to the people around us. And I don't just mean interpersonal relationships, but also the relationships we have with other people that we have never met through the ways that our lives are *socially organized*.

In each moment, all of us create the social world through what we do. As we do that, our space to act in our everyday lives is shaped and constrained by what the people around us are doing, and by what they might do. Our timing for walking across a street depends on the presence and timing of people driving down it. We choose not to eat the last piece of pie because it will make our lover happy if we save it for them. We show up to work at nine o'clock every morning, more or less, because our supervisor would likely fire us if we made a habit of drifting in at ten thirty. In each of these situations, we make choices, but the people around us shape the context in which we make them.

However, our actions are not just shaped by the actions of others in our own immediate, local context; human activity is also organized in ways that are *not* local. For instance, it is likely that every office in our company from the Arctic Circle to the Gulf of Mexico is governed by the same policy about the structure of the work day (though how it is taken up and put into practice will vary from manager to manager). It organizes when we arrive and it also organizes (along with various human resources policies and laws and regulation about employment) the capacity for supervisors in that company to fire people who ignore it. Those policies only mean anything because people acting in their own local situations take them up and act on them, but they organize different local circumstances across vast distances in similar ways. Not only written documents can have that effect, but also looser clusters of ideas can be propagated through popular culture and interpersonal interactions in ways that shape our lives. For instance, particular notions of what it means to be in the category "woman" organize the actions and reactions of enough people that often when a woman acts counter to those dominant notions, she faces responses from other people that amount to informal punishment for deviating from the norm.

That is how I understand the mechanics of how the social world is organized at the level of everyday life: people acting based on their immediate interactions with other people in their local environment in ways that are organized by written texts and by more amorphous but no less powerful discourses (which also come to exist and are given power by human beings

10 — Gender and Sexuality

acting in their own local circumstances). It is possible to investigate how this plays out in very detailed, rigorous ways. That is not the purpose of this book, however. The purpose of this book is to look at the larger scale patterns of social organization that are built from these elements and the ways in which people have historically struggled to change them.

Power and Oppression

A key feature of social organization is the organization of people into different groups with different ranges of experience of *power* and *oppression*. Those two ideas are central to the workings of what we call "Canada" today, and have been central to the ebb and flow of events throughout what we think of as "Canadian history."

At the simplest level, power is the ability to act, to do, to exert agency. I tie my shoes, I cook dinner, I make a picket sign, I write a book — these are all examples of me exerting power-to-do, to act in the world and shape my own life. Yet because of how our world is socially organized, different people and different groups of people do not have the same scope to use that capacity to act to shape their own lives. Moreover, that basic human capacity to do gets channelled by social organization into some groups exerting power in ways that dominate, cause harm to, put down other groups — that is, power-to-do is channelled into power-over.[5] Members of the dominant groups may actively and consciously participate in maintaining or expanding that power-over, but because it is a product of social organization and not individual malevolence, they may also remain oblivious of the ways in which their doing is premised on and reinforces the subordination of others. This is *privilege* — the idea that some people experience certain kinds of unearned advantages, which they may or may not be aware of, in ways that depend on and reinforce other people's lives being organized into disadvantage and oppression.

That relationship of power-over and how it shapes the experiences of those on the receiving end are what I mean by oppression. In her book *Becoming an Ally*, Nova Scotian writer and activist Anne Bishop (2002: 161) defines it as follows (where her use of "power" refers to "power-over"):

> Oppression/oppressor/oppressed: Oppression occurs when one group of people uses different forms of power to keep another group down in order to exploit them (or an individual keeps another down for the same purpose). The oppressor uses the power; the oppressed are exploited.

Power-over and the oppressions that it produces are relations — socially organized relations, or just *social relations* — between people and groups of people. Here are some key current examples of such social relations between groups with more power and groups with less power along various axes (adapted from Kivel 1999: 24).

More Powerful Groups	Less Powerful Groups
adults	young people and seniors
men	women
the rich	the poor
white people	people of colour and indigenous people
settlers[6]	indigenous people
owners[7]	workers
heterosexuals	lesbian, gay, bi, two-spirited, queer[8] people
cisgender[9] people	transgender, intersex, genderqueer,[10] gender non-conforming people
Christians	Jews, Muslims, Buddhists, Hindus
able-bodied people	people with disabilities
formally educated	not formally educated
born here	recent immigrants

Each of these relations — and it is important to point out that this list is not exhaustive, and that this book and its companion do not deal with all that are mentioned — is produced by different kinds of social organization, has different sorts of historical origins, and has changed over time in distinct ways. Racism and sexism, for example, are not organized in the same way, did not emerge historically in the same way, and are not experienced in the same ways. Nonetheless, the relations that organize racial groupings and gender never happen in isolation. Some activists and writers, especially radical women of colour, have long argued that racism and sexism are always shaping their experiences together, never just one or the other. This ensures that women of colour have experiences of sexism different from white women and experiences of racism different from men of colour. Similarly, my experiences of gender are never unconnected to the ways in which my life is organized into whiteness, and my experience of white privilege takes on a particular character because of the ways in which masculinity is socially organized. How this all happens in practice can be complicated, and most of us lead lives that are shaped by some mix of privilege and oppression.[11]

One crucial way in which all of these relations are organized is through the important institutions and organizations that shape society. An individual does not need to personally control an institution to benefit from the oppression of others, they just need to be a member of the dominant group. For example, very few people are high-ranking officials in the judicial system, but the socially organized relations that supposedly dispense "justice" are part of mainstream power relations that are white-dominated and straight-dominated. Throughout Canadian history, white people have not had to worry about being pulled over by the police just because of the social meaning historically attached to the colour of their skin, while people of colour and indigenous people still have to deal with the realities of racial profiling (Brown 2004; Smith 2004; Tator and Henry 2006). Straight people have not had to worry about bars that let them be open about their sexual identity being raided by the police just because of that identity, in contrast with lesbians and gay men (Warner 2002; G. Smith 2006).

At the level of individual and group experience, the impacts on oppressed groups can include less access to adequate income and other key resources; reduced personal safety and heightened likelihood of experiencing violence; less control over what happens to your own body; heightened surveillance, regulation, targeting by mainstream institutions, and barriers to using mainstream services; the ubiquity of stories and images about you that portray you as inferior or defective in some way; your people's historical way of relating to land treated as illegitimate; less access to, choice about, and control over work; lack of opportunity to learn and speak the language of your ancestors; erasure of your history; lack of visibility of your reality in the dominant media; inability to have your romantic relationships acknowledged; and various kinds of emotional harm.

Standpoint and Struggle

Another important concept for approaching history differently is the idea of *standpoint*.[12] Just as experience of Canada today varies a lot depending on who you are and how your experiences are organized by social relations of power and oppression, so the content and emphasis of the stories labelled "history" change depending on where in relation to power and oppression the text is situated — its "standpoint." What matters about a strike will be different for people working in a factory than for the owners, for example. You can extrapolate from that to appreciate that history told from the standpoint of workers will treat different stories as important than history that assumes the standpoint of owners, and that the former might treat certain things as victories that the latter would see as defeats and vice versa.

Conventional history has a standpoint but does not usually talk about it. It tries to pretend that it is possible to stand outside of history and look down on it from a position that is all-seeing and objective, and thereby capture everything that matters. On closer examination, however, conventional history tends to be told from the standpoint of groups at or near the top of the hierarchies in Canadian society — those with power rather than those who are oppressed. Some conventional sources of history these days, like the Heritage

Minutes broadcast on CBC or the citizenship guide the government gave to my mother, include some token stories about the groups that were absent in my high school history lessons, but they still do not talk about power and oppression, or about many of the things central to shaping the experiences of those on the receiving end of oppression. There are Heritage Minutes that talk about the origins of the Iroquois Confederacy and Nellie McClung and the Underground Railroad. But there are none that reflect the 500-year cultural genocide against indigenous peoples; none about the ongoing history of women being abused and murdered by their male partners; none about hardworking Canadians kept poor while other people get rich off their blood and sweat. The citizenship guide may claim to emphasize the importance of knowing our history, but in its celebration of how wonderful and accepting Canada supposedly is, it forgets to talk about things like the existence of slavery and the various measures the government took over the years to keep people of colour out. When examined a little more closely, the guide's exhortation to learn history seems more about encouraging newcomers to buy into the dominant set of myths and stories about Canada in order to be "real Canadians" than about actual critical learning. This is perhaps a hint that another way of understanding what I am calling "conventional history" is as nationalist history written from the (hidden) standpoint of those with power within the nation.

This book and its companion, in contrast, emphasize not only that standpoint exists and is unavoidable, but that there is a political and moral imperative to enter history from the standpoints of those who are oppressed.

That leads into the final difference between conventional history and history as it is understood here. Conventional ways of presenting history treat it as something that only happens *to* ordinary people through the actions of "great men" (and rarely women) and the actions of mysterious "social forces." Yet no leader would have an ounce of power without ordinary people doing their bidding, and when you examine what "social forces" really are, you find nothing more than the socially organized doing of many ordinary people. That is, ordinary people like you, like me, like the people you see around you every day are not just *done to* by history but have the capacity to *do*, to help shape tomorrow's history. Our actions are already what make the social world; our efforts, therefore, can change it to be more just and liberatory.

Such efforts, whether community-based struggles or social movements, are a key piece of what gets excluded by conventional history. And we cannot truly understand the present without them. They are an absolutely necessary piece for me to be able to understand how it is that I came to benefit from socialized medicine or from a family of origin supported by unionized jobs. It is also necessary for me, as someone who is white and who is not indigenous to this land, to understand my complicity in what indigenous peoples in northern Turtle Island[13] continue to struggle against. And I could name many other aspects of my life that are how they are because of social movements and community struggles. Though we are taught not to see it, every life has been shaped by such struggle, and every life will continue to be shaped by the struggles ongoing in the present.

It should be clear by this point that what are excluded from conventional history are not just abstract ideas and random facts with no concrete importance: Conventional history fails to name injustice, and fails to educate us about what ordinary people have done and can do about it. This erasure of the past in turn affects the present. By obscuring the centrality of injustice in years gone by, the message to the learner today ends up being, "Everything is as it should be." Learning history this way encourages people to remain oblivious to the existence of oppression, and to their own privilege. Those who are on the receiving end of injustice in the present have their realities denied and their marginalization reinforced in yet another area. This book talks about history in a way that recognizes the existence of oppression and imbalances in power, and tries to take the standpoints of those who seek justice, particularly those who have attempted to seek justice in collective and public ways. This approach can be described as "history from below."[14]

Doing History Differently

There are places where you can find history done in ways that take seriously things like power and justice. If you look, there are journals and seldom-aired documentary films and books (see the References section for a few). These things are not always the most accessible resources in the world, but they are out there. A small number of people are able to take university courses that teach history from below. In many history departments, however, such material is far from the norm. Disciplines like women's studies, labour studies, peace studies, and indigenous studies more reliably feature such history, but relatively few of the people fortunate enough to have access to a university education study these areas. A few unions also offer worker education programs that include some material of this sort.

Some readers will have had their attention drawn to the realities of oppression and resistance that lie at the core of Canada's history from an early age, particularly if they come from communities for whom seeing those hierarchies and navigating their impact is just part of the everyday struggle for survival. Other readers will have made choices later in life that lead to their presence in the middle of such struggles, and therefore to learning some of this history, as in the anecdote with which I began this introduction. In all of these cases, though reading and watching are important, a crucial source of learning is the spoken words of elders who have come before. Age is no guarantee of wisdom and no basis, by itself, for claiming leadership that others should feel obliged to follow, but it *is* an indicator of experience, and by paying attention to that experience those of us who are younger can learn about the world. Again, however, this is a kind of learning in which not everyone is well placed to engage.

The particular approach I have chosen for exploring Canada's history goes back to my reaction in the story with which I started: Beyond just providing a new source of information about Canada's history from below, at the heart of what I want to accomplish with these books is a desire to share that sense of powerful connection that I felt on the bus to St. Catherine's and that I have been lucky enough to feel on many occasions over the course of this project. My choices in realizing this goal are steps toward figuring out how those of us in movements and communities might recover our histories as an ongoing part of how we act in the world — and, I have realized more recently, also serve as an implicit contribution to conversations happening in a few corners of academic history as well.[15]

The core building blocks of these books are oral history interviews done with long-time activists. Over four years I conducted forty-seven interviews with a total of fifty people, in eight cities, in six provinces and one territory. In this book I share in a detailed way the stories of nine of those people: Doreen Spence, Donna MacPhee, Madeleine Parent, Lee Lakeman, Shree Mulay, Sadeqa Siddiqui, Chris Vogel, Richard North, and Shelley Finson. (A few links to short audio clips from most of these nine interviews can be found on the project's website, www.talkingradical.ca; see the endnotes in each chapter for the addresses.[16]) The stories of another eight interview participants can be found in the companion book, *Resisting the State: Canadian History Through the Stories of Activists*. The factor all participants have in common is that they are "long distance runners"[17] in the struggle for social change: All have been active for at least twenty years, with at least some of that time in Canada. Beyond that, though, it is a very diverse group. They have been active in a wide range of physical locations, in several different eras, and in quite a number of different movements. Though all perspectives from within social movements seeking justice and liberation tend to be distorted, ignored, and marginalized, that is particularly true of indigenous women and men, women and men of colour, white women, and gay, lesbian, bisexual, and transgender people of all racial backgrounds. Both in terms of the interviews done and in terms of those I chose to include in this book and its companion, this project has tried to recognize the existence of that exclusion and work against it.

In understanding how each interview is presented, it is useful to think of the clichéd but still apt metaphor of history as a huge, rich tapestry with a complex weave of many different threads. Each human life is a thread that comes into the tapestry in a particular place and whose general location and course is shaped by the patterns in the tapestry, but that can also weave around unpredictably and chaotically. Conventional history tells you it is possible to stand far above the tapestry and sketch out some of the more important features without losing any important information, but as discussed above this almost invariably results in the features important to those with power and privilege defining what we understand as "history" and produces a very simplistic picture.

Instead, in this book each chapter is built around the idea of entering history by following one or two specific threads to learn about the particular features of the little bit of the tapestry through which they run. Of course, as mentioned above, the threads that have been chosen are those that represent people normally excluded from conventional history, and particularly those that have participated in collective, public efforts to create social change.

At the same time, the picture obtained solely from following a single thread will inevitably be a narrow one — if you hear a single person's story with no context, it might be engaging and moving and wonderful, but if you do not know anything about the place or era or identity or movement that the person is talking about, there is a good chance you will miss a lot of what is important in their words. Therefore, in this book I enter history through the threads represented by the interview participants, but I also take care to talk about the designs that preceded that thread's entry into the tapestry, and the other threads and patterns through which it passes. This means that along with the words of the interview participants in each chapter, there is an effort to present ideas that might challenge the reader to think about history and society in new ways and important pieces of historical context that come before and happen alongside the specific experiences of the participant. And in the spirit of using the potential for connection between people to mediate understanding and learning, when I talk about new ideas I try to avoid talking about them in any more abstract and academic a way than I have to. Rather, I try to connect you to them through my own journey of discovery, reflection, and analysis.

Gender and Sexuality

Understanding a complicated world can be simplified by grouping things together, and any book must have a finite number of pages, which necessitates making decisions about what to include and what to leave out. Therefore, this book focuses on a subset of struggles — those in which gender, sexuality, or both are central.

However, it is important to approach those categories carefully. There is a long history of classifying and labelling struggles in politically troubling ways. Borders are created and patrolled that dictate that *this* is a "real" workers' struggle but not *that*, or one thing is genuinely a struggle for women's liberation but not another, often reflecting actual practices of exclusion within movements. This kind of dynamic is captured by the title of an important work by Black feminists in the United States called *All the Women Are White, All the Blacks Are Men, but Some of Us Are Brave* (Hull, Bell Scott, and Smith 1982). That is, simple ways of categorizing (and common ways of organizing) struggles often lead to people who are marginalized on multiple axes being further marginalized.

Common understandings of phrases like "women's struggles" or "gender struggles," both in mainstream spaces and in some feminist spaces, would include important things like winning the right to vote for women, protecting rights to reproductive choice, opposing violence against women, and seeking equal pay for work of equal value. Yet things like struggles by indigenous women against colonization or struggles by women workers against exploitative employers are sometimes not seen as being significantly about gender, which can lead to them being ignored, or at least seen as peripheral, when questions of gender are being considered. Those who wage such struggles, in such circumstances, are being partially or wholly evicted — functionally if not formally — from the resulting homogenized, simplistic understanding of "woman." Yet colonization happened in important ways through attacks on indigenous ways of organizing gender and sexuality, and on indigenous women themselves, and the struggle against it has been forced into the everyday lives of indigenous women on Turtle Island for the last five centuries (Stevenson 1999; A. Smith 2005). Indigenous feminist Andrea Smith (2006: 16) has argued, "If we were to recognize the agency of indigenous women in an account of feminist history, we might begin with 1492 when Native women collectively resisted colonization." Oppression in capitalist contexts and the other oppressive facets of capitalist social relations have always happened in and through each other, so resistance by groups of waged workers who are women are also very much gender struggles.

Refusing to see these realities not only reinforces the oppressions of the more deeply oppressed; it can allow those whose struggles *do* let them fit comfortably in the resulting homogenized and simplistic categories to have very partial and limited analyses of their own situations. For example, when struggles by women workers get treated as peripheral to "real" workers' struggles and to "real" women's struggles, it helps to obscure the fact that all experiences of workers (including men) are socially organized by gender, and all experiences of women (including relatively privileged women) are organized by capitalism — and, in fact, by all of the elements of social relations listed earlier in this introduction. Perhaps most harmful of all, categorizing struggles in simplistic and rigid ways means that much of the time, we fail to see that apparently disparate struggles are actually connected in important ways.

To try and respond to this, this book takes up the idea of gender and sexuality struggles in a deliberately expansive way. The first chapter focuses on the efforts of two indigenous women in Calgary, Doreen Spence and Donna MacPhee, to work against colonization through their efforts to build and support the first indigenous-controlled, indigenous-focused school in an urban centre in Canada. Chapter 2 talks about Madeleine Parent, a fixture for decades in the labour and women's movements of Quebec and Canada, and her leading role in a pivotal 1946 strike waged mainly by women and children against the Dominion Textile Company. Chapters 3 and 4 talk about differently experienced and differently conducted struggles against violence against women, and also touch on questions of difference itself and when it matters politically. Lee Lakeman's experiences in Woodstock, Ontario, and in Vancouver are the focus of Chapter 3, while Sadeqa Siddiqui and Shree Mulay talk about their experiences in Montreal in Chapter 4. Chapter 5 is based on an interview with Chris Vogel and Richard North about their decades of experience in gay struggles in Winnipeg. Chapter 6 looks at the experiences of Shelley Finson at the centre of feminist struggles and more peripherally in queer struggles inside the United Church of Canada.

The companion book, *Resisting the State*, which is centred on struggles related to the Canadian state, embraces a similarly expansive understanding of its mission. As such, avoiding a too-simplistic understanding of the categories around which these books are built requires one further step: recognizing that many of the chapters could have been placed in either book. A core element of Lakeman's involvement has been challenging state practices that are hostile to women's liberation, the Quebec state was a central player in efforts to suppress the Dominion Textile Strike, and many important elements of queer struggle in the last few decades in Canada have involved efforts to challenge heterosexism within state relations, just to cite three examples. And in the other book, Kathy Mallett's organizing with other indigenous women in Winnipeg against colonial attacks on their community by the Children's Aid Society is without a doubt about gender, for instance, and it would be hard to see Josephine Grey's struggles for human rights as a woman of colour living in poverty as not being about gender in important ways. Similarly, other ways of grouping at least some of the twelve chapters in these two books could also be found — at least half are anti-racist struggles, for instance, and depending on how you understand the terms, several or many are about challenging the ways in which capitalism organizes suffering and violence into our lives.

Introduction – 19

Connection and Action

The voices and struggles published here are only a beginning at painting a full picture of social and political struggle through Canadian history; many could not be included at all, and none are explored in a way that comes close to being exhaustive. I am sure most readers will think of other voices they would like to hear and other struggles they would like to hear about, as well as other tools for understanding the organization of social relations that have produced those experiences.[18] But beyond the practical limitations of a finite word count and number of pages, this book and its companion are explicitly and intentionally incomplete because history itself is incomplete, both in the sense that there are always more stories of small and large scale resistance to oppression and we should never presume that we know all that is to be known, and also because history itself is a work in progress that flesh and blood human beings continue to make. This, in fact, is part of the point: Let whatever connection you feel to the voices in this book inspire you to seek other sources of history from below. Read. Surf the web. Speak to elders-in-struggle that you know in your workplace or community. Treat this book as a jumping-off point for further critical exploration.

I also hope this book contributes, in some small way, to something more. That hope makes me think back to some words spoken in one of the earlier interviews in the project by participant Lee Lakeman, a Vancouver feminist long active in the movement against male violence whose story is in Chapter 3. She is very clear in defining her organization not as a service giving women charity but as part of a movement for social change. One outcome of this is that the abused woman who comes to Vancouver Rape Relief "understands herself as being aided by the movement, not by some great, genius counsellor — not by some Joan of Arc, but by an ordinary feminist whom she could be."

By sharing the stories of ordinary women and men whose actions have helped shape history, and doing so in a way that sparks some hint of the connection to the past I have felt talking to them, I hope this book encourages people to get active themselves and supports people who already live the struggle every day. I hope that it inspires a sense of connection to the making of history in the present, that it shows that the people in these pages are not saints or terrorists, not super humans or fools, but ordinary activists whom *you* could be.

Notes

1. Much of this introduction is the same as in *Resisting the State: Canadian History Through the Stories of Activists*, but some material toward the end is specific to this book.
2. The Days of Action was a series of mass demonstrations, often accompanied

by mass strikes, co-organized by coalitions of labour and community groups in cities across Ontario in the late 1990s after the election of the Conservative provincial government of Premier Mike Harris. See Camfield 2000 for one account of those struggles. The Multilateral Agreement on Investment (MAI) was an attempt in the 1990s by many governments to secretly negotiate a treaty organized around empowering investors and corporations. For a discussion of the MAI that uses a left nationalist approach written by two of the Canadian activists central to the successful efforts to block the treaty, see Clarke and Barlow 1997. Though it does not deal specifically with the MAI, see Chapter 6 of *Resisting the State* for some of my own somewhat different understanding of neoliberalism, the political agenda of which the MAI was a part. Since the MAI was defeated, governments have continued to try to implement many of the measures that would have been contained in it in a piecemeal fashion in other venues and through other agreements.
3. For a fascinating look at the struggle in Spain itself that focuses on women's participation, see Acklesberg 2004.
4. The ideas about how the social world is put together that I briefly sketch under the heading "Social Thinking" are adapted from others, though not necessarily in ways of which they would approve. One important source is Canadian feminist sociologist Dorothy Smith — she has published many books, but I have mainly learned from D. Smith 1999 and D. Smith 2005 — and less direct absorptions from writers that take up her ideas and use them in other ways, such as Kinsman 1996, Bannerji 2000, and Frampton et al. 2006, as well as writers that take up the idea of "moral regulation," such as Valverde 1991, Little 1998, and, though I don't think he uses the term, Warner 1999. Also, please note that the terms that are initially presented in italics in this section and those that follow are ones that I think are particularly relevant to understanding how I think about things.
5. For a much more sophisticated and detailed elaboration of power-to and power-over and an analysis of the implications of power understood in this way see Holloway 2005.
6. Though indigenous authors have pointed out some politically crucial distinctions that can be made between the underlying meanings of "indigenous" and "Aboriginal" (e.g., Alfred 2005: 126–136), I will largely use these two interchangeably where referring to a specific nation does not make sense. As well, any descriptors of identity in quoted material have been left as originally spoken even if I do not otherwise use the term. "Settler" is the flip side of "indigenous;" it refers to those who settle on land to which they are not indigenous, the descendents of those people, and the institutions they create.
7. Some readers will likely be critical that this book does not begin from a more fully elaborated analysis of capitalism and a more explicitly stated anti-capitalist position. While I agree that anti-oppression politics that neglect a critical analysis of relations of production have serious limits (as do the many strands of anti-capitalist politics that neglect or downplay other aspects of social relations), the choice to begin from a fairly sparse framework that provides tools for incorporating new stories and unfamiliar aspects of social relations into a larger picture rather than a more elaborate framework claiming to have all of the answers is a deliberate political and pedagogical choice. It is my understanding that an

approach based on listening to stories told from different social locations and puzzling out the ways in which those disparate experiences are produced by common forms of extra-local organization, especially when that puzzling is informed by diverse radical political traditions, will lead to a critical understanding of capital, albeit perhaps not one that looks like the anti-capitalism advanced by traditional Marxists. More ideas related to relations of production are presented elsewhere in the books, especially Chapter 2 in this book and Chapters 4 and 6 in its companion.

8. For more on the use of the term "queer" see Chapter 5.
9. "Cisgender" is an adjective that refers to people whose biological sex assigned at birth matches their gender identity. It is the antonym of "transgender."
10. People who identify as "genderqueer" tend to blur gender norms. They may also identify as male, female, both, neither, or reject gender altogether.
11. For a more extended discussion of power and difference, and when and how it matters, see Chapter 4.
12. Different writers have talked about standpoint in different ways. Some (e.g., Harding 1988) emphasize that people who have experienced a particular oppression have privileged access to the truth of that oppression, and should be given priority when relating or theorizing about that experience. Others (e.g., D. Smith 2005: 7–26; Frampton et al. 2006: 7, 38) treat a given standpoint as a place to begin investigating the world, with an emphasis on using the experiences that shape that standpoint as a source of direction for investigating the social organization that creates those experiences. The approach to history in this book is influenced by both of these, in that it tries to prioritize the words of participants themselves *and* it uses their experiences as a basis for selecting and presenting context.
13. "Turtle Island" is a term used commonly by indigenous people of different nations to refer to the North American continent.
14. This phrase is often associated with English historian E.P. Thompson, who produced such classic works as *The Making of the English Working Class* (1966). The idea that ordinary people have the capacity to make history is central to his work, though he does not generally give much attention to relations of power and oppression other than class.
15. In decades past, most conventional historians had little interest in experience or memory, though for people doing history-from-below and various forms of oral history, experiences of oppressed peoples, often as accessed through reminiscence, were seen as a way of accessing historical truth that could be counterposed to dominant histories in a fairly straightforward way. By the 1990s, the application of post-structuralist insights to history resulted not only in serious fundamental questions about the reliability of memory and experience, but about the very notion of historical truth. For some, particularly at that time, basing work on memory and experience came to seem inappropriate if not outright impossible. Others, however, have argued that a more nuanced understanding of what memory and experience have to offer can still lead to valuable avenues for producing historical knowledge. If memory is understood not as some clear window into truth but as an active process in the present of producing meaning about the past, it still bears the imprint of the social relations we wish to under-

stand. Remembering will have its own holes and confusions as we make such meaning, but careful and sensitive attention to knowledge production as an active, material process can still allow us to identify distortions in dominant histories as well as lives and struggles that often get erased, and to produce knowledge to counter those things. It is no longer a simple matter of one dominant lie and a single, subordinated truth, but a much more complicated, multiplicitous contest that is still, nonetheless, all about the ways that power-over shapes dominant knowledge and about intervening to support struggles for justice and liberation. For more on these conversations, see Hodgkin and Radstone 2003. For examples of academic histories that try to practically work through such questions, see Furniss 1999 and High and Lewis 2007.

16. Please note that after the recordings were transcribed, each participant had a chance to edit and approve the transcript, and some chose to make lots of changes. That approved transcript is the basis for the material quoted in print in this book. Even that has been further edited by me, usually by cutting out some material or by changing the ordering of larger chunks of material in ways that are sensitive to the spirit of what the participant was trying to communicate but that improve the flow. For these reasons, what you hear in the sample clips may not correspond exactly to what is quoted in the text.

17. I take the expression "long distance runners" as it applies to activists from the work of long-time U.S.-based radical Staughton Lynd (1997: 63–64).

18. In the course of writing these books, I have reached my own conclusions about things that are missing, some of which I knew all along would be the case and others that caught me by surprise. This is only a partial list, but I am particularly conscious of the absence of any indigenous struggles that were land-based or focused in reserve communities; efforts by Palestinian Canadians against the colonization of their homeland; struggles by people with disabilities; struggles by trans people, and by people with broadly queer sexual practices that cannot be understood simply as "gay" and "lesbian"; struggles against police violence and prisons, particularly based in African Canadian and indigenous spaces; many other sorts of initiatives in and around workplaces; struggles by French-speaking people in Quebec and Canada; struggles against borders and other aspects of so-called "national security"; voices that explicitly proclaim the revolutionary character of their politics; and environmental struggles. I was surprised that Christianity, particularly Protestant Christianity, became so present in the work, though in retrospect that should not be a shock given its dominance in most of Canada since settlement began. While I think it is important to examine the role of associated institutions in organizing oppressions and of people mobilizing faith-related resources in struggles for justice and liberation, and I am glad to have done some of that, I regret not doing more to contest Christian hegemony in Canada by focusing on the roles of other spiritual traditions in both social organization and resistance.

Chapter 1

Decolonize Your Mind

Doreen Spence and Donna MacPhee on the Plains Indian Cultural Survival School

It was a relief when Doreen Spence came to the door and welcomed me into her home. I was getting around mostly on foot and Calgary is both a very spread out city and rather a chilly one in November. Not only that, the stories of the activists I had already interviewed and the vibe I had felt from the city in my walking confirmed its reputation as rather a cold place overall for people who want to change the world. But Spence's home felt warm — the tea I was offered, the easy chit-chat before we got down to business, her frequent laugh, the cosiness of her art-filled living room. When I spoke to Donna MacPhee the next day — that interview happened in the kitchen of the friend's house where she was crashing while she looked for a place — I felt a similar welcome. I valued the brief haven in a cold city at the time; I think I've come to appreciate it much more in the years since.

Most of the art in Spence's living room had been gifts of one sort or another, mostly from other indigenous people. There was an inukshuk that she got during a few weeks spent in Greenland, a didgeridoo from some Australian Aborigine youth she had worked with, a painting from a Mexican friend. I suppose she has many opportunities to be given such beautiful things, given her long history of work with two prominent international indigenous groups, the International Circle of Elders (which meets in New Zealand) and the United Nations Working Group on Indigenous Populations. Yet in talking about the pieces, she seemed to have a special place in her heart for those that were gifts from youth she had supported over the years.

It's not the sort of support she had much access to herself when she was young, outside of the grandparents who raised her. From standing up for herself in an otherwise all-white grade school in the Alberta of the 1940s to risking her new nursing career to stop the involuntary sterilization of a young indigenous girl, she had to find a lot of strength inside herself from a very young age in the face of a hostile, often overtly racist, always colonial environment. Perhaps these experiences help explain why supporting young indigenous people has always been such a priority for her, particularly when it comes to education and to knowledge. She supported her own children's early forays into the settler education system decades ago, and at the time of our interview was devoting a good part of her energy to mentoring young indigenous women. In between those two, Spence spent seventeen years doing anything and everything to support the students and the organization of the Plains Indian Cultural Survival School, or PICSS — the first school in an urban setting in Canada to be run for and controlled by indigenous people.

Donna MacPhee had no art to show me — the home she was staying in was lovely but not hers. She grew up in Alberta's Drumheller Valley and has lived much of her life in Calgary, but the only time she has really felt at home anywhere was during the months she participated in the indigenous occupation of West Bragg Creek Provincial Park: "I was standing on my piece of the earth, and I've never had that feeling before." Yet, like Spence, she has had no choice but to make herself at home in the middle of struggle since she was a child, from dealing with the everyday racism of friends and schoolmates and her own white Canadian grandfather — "the biggest bigot I met in my life" — to her forays into collective struggle as an adult, first multi-issue anti-racism and solidarity with indigenous struggles around the country, later anti-globalization, and at the time of the interview anti-poverty activism in Calgary. Yet for her as well, knowledge and education have been core commitments. She became an adult student at PICSS not because she lacked a diploma but to reconnect with the culture that had been stolen from her, and spent years as a member of its board and a volunteer supporting younger students in their learning and their everyday battles with racism, sexism, and colonialism.

Knowledge and Difference

I talked initially to both Spence and MacPhee on the phone; I asked each for a few hours of her time and was told yes after only a brief conversation. I did not appreciate the historical significance of it then, but I realize now I was also asking for something more than just time. At that point, I had a little bit of experience in the role of white ally in anti-racism work, which translates into at least some opportunity to get familiar with how much ignorance of the world white privilege[1] allows us to get away with. In terms of what I knew about the five centuries of struggle by indigenous peoples on Turtle Island, though, I really wasn't much beyond what conventional history had given me plus a vague conviction that colonialism, empires, and genocide were all bad things even if I didn't really know too much about them. I certainly did not get the full historical implications of a white guy — that is, a person who wouldn't live the relatively privileged life he lives if someone hadn't taken someone else's land some years back — sitting down with indigenous people and asking for access to their knowledge so that he (I) might produce a book. Nor did I fully appreciate the favour done me when the answer wasn't no.

What I failed to appreciate at the time was the intimate relationship between colonialism (and the struggle against it) and knowledge. What little I had learned about how northern Turtle Island went from a network of indigenous nations to what we call "Canada" today focused more on land than anything else, but land in a very simplistic sense — they had it, we took it. I didn't learn much about the deception, dirty tricks, and brutal violence of how that happened, but even in a high school history class it is hard to avoid the fact that, somehow, it did happen. And the land part of it *is* important. It was the land and the resources attached to it that the European empires really wanted, and the theft of it has been devastating to indigenous peoples. But I only saw the material part, the wealth and potential wealth forced from one set of hands to another. I did not see past my assumption that there was only one way to think about land: as property that could be owned, bought, sold, and stolen. But that is a very European (and a very capitalist) way of thinking about land; the traditional relationship between indigenous peoples and the land is much different. In order to take the land and do what they wanted with it, the institutions that came to be because of European conquest and settlement (including "Canada") not only had to take what was not ours, but they had to insist on (and enforce through violence and the threat of violence) the right to define what land is and how people should think about it and relate to it. It was a matter of redefining land *as* property and making sure that definition came to reign supreme in northern Turtle Island.

In other words, the conquest and settlement of this continent — colonialism — was not just about guns, not just about what happened on battlefields. Colonialism is also about language, definitions, ideas, ways of seeing the world. It is about what happens in people's heads. It is about knowledge.

Those of us in the dominant culture rarely think of ourselves as having "a way" of knowing and being and doing — we have the privilege of being able to just go about our business and know and be and do. But even for us it isn't too much of a stretch to appreciate that our ways of knowing and being and doing are not the only ones that are possible and that others exist. What can be trickier to wrap our heads around is what such difference really means. The indigenous nations of North America and the European nations before contact, for example, had very significant differences in these areas — the former from the latter and to a smaller but still important extent the former among themselves. As with the difference around the conception of the land, this wasn't as simple as different words for the same ideas or different technologies for doing similar things. Rather, there were differences in very basic ideas about the nature of time and history, about gender, about the relationship between individuals and society, and about many other central ways of thinking about the world. These differences between the two groups in terms of ideas and language and ways of understanding things — their *knowledge* — were pretty profound.

I stumbled across one concrete example that helped me to appreciate the depth of the differences: the concept of "justice." Justice is a central idea in a lot of discussions of this thing we call "Canada." The dominant institutions and groups brag that Canada is already just, or at least as just as you can reasonably expect. The majority of people in social movements and communities forced into struggle may have different ideas from those in charge about what exactly "justice" should mean and would point out that we do not have it, but some expanded version of justice is still often a goal. Yet Patricia Monture-Angus (1995: 238–9), a woman of the Mohawk Nation and a legal scholar, asked elders from a number of different indigenous nations in North America what the word for "justice" was in their language and she found that most indigenous languages have no such word. In fact, a number of the elders she talked to found the question funny.

It is important, however, for white Canadians to avoid the trap we tend to fall into of seeing "different" as "inferior." All of these systems of knowledge were fully functional and not lacking in any respect, notwithstanding a few differences in technological capacity for inflicting violence. The absence of a word that corresponds to "justice" does not mean that pre-contact indigenous societies were unjust. In fact, the evidence points toward them being far more just than contemporary Canada. But in terms of how they thought about personal conduct and social organization, a quite different framework was used.

As well, the minute you talk about difference, you get lots of people justifying conflict or even domination of one group by another purely on the basis that they are not the same. Yet you can imagine a long process of talking and listening and making an effort to respect the other side, and developing a shared vocabulary and shared knowledge that would help the groups be and do without interfering with one another. From what I have read about the treaty processes on Turtle Island, the indigenous nations appear to have believed, particularly early on, that this was exactly the sort of process that they could engage in with the European nations — not mass surrender but dialogue toward respectful, peaceful coexistence and sharing.

This idea is embodied, for instance, in the treaty and traditional Mohawk teaching of the Two Row Wampum. The Mohawk understanding of their initial treaties with Europeans was that they had

> negotiated an original and lasting peace based on coexistence of power in a context of respect for the autonomy and distinctive nature of each partner. The metaphor for this relationship — two vessels, each possessing its own integrity, travelling the river of time together — was conveyed visually on a wampum belt of two parallel purple lines (representing power) on a background of white beads (representing peace). In this respectful (co-equal) friendship and alliance, any interference with the other partner's autonomy, freedom,

or powers was expressly forbidden. So long as these principles were respected, the relationship would be peaceful, harmonious, and just. (Alfred 1999: 52)

Of course the European empires, the colonies they created, and the states that evolved from those colonies have had rather different practices in dealing with these divergent ways of knowing and being and doing. With control of land and resources as the prize, knowledge became just another site and tool of conquest. But it has also been central to resistance, too.

Knowledge and Conquest

What does that mean, exactly, for knowledge to be a site and tool of conquest? Given that I am a settler who is dabbling in the production of knowledge related to indigenous peoples — and knowledge production across other forms of difference elsewhere in this book and its companion — it is pretty important that I have at least some idea so I can avoid contributing to the process.

The general pattern is that European settlers and their descendents have developed many different kinds of knowledge *about* and *from* indigenous peoples in ways that justify and support colonial domination, that appropriate indigenous knowledges, and that treat indigenous peoples as objects rather than subjects — that is, complete human beings capable of defining their own existence and deserving of dignity (L. Smith 1999).

This has included knowledge about indigenous resources, strengths, and weaknesses used in direct repression, to allow settler institutions to break acts of indigenous resistance without having to deal with any of the underlying injustice. It has also included an entire spectrum of supposed knowledge about indigenous cultures that justifies colonial domination through infusing the dominant white settler imagination with racist narratives and imagery that portray indigenous peoples as inferior or defective. Over the centuries, this kind of colonial knowledge has helped settlers preserve a self-understanding as "good people" even as many have killed, violated, and oppressed indigenous peoples, broken solemn treaties with them, and ignored the persistence of patent injustice. The present-day versions include myths about the "lazy Indian" or the "drunken Indian," and old favourites like "savage" continue to lurk in the white settler imagination. Specific variants target indigenous women, as an integral part of the ongoing violence and other attacks they face from settler individuals and institutions (Stevenson 1999: 55–63).

Colonial knowledge production has also always involved appropriating indigenous knowledges for the benefit of settlers and settler institutions. This has included taking indigenous knowledges of territories, plants, and animals and labelling them "discoveries" made and owned by the Europeans who stole them. It has included corporations and governments patenting the genes of indigenous peoples or of crops they have developed over millennia. It has included sacred objects from living faith traditions stolen for museums and private collections, and elements of indigenous spiritualities appropriated by affluent white people seeking to purchase some meaning for their lives. It has included researchers, including those who see themselves as "helping," producing knowledge about the problems faced by indigenous communities in ways that build careers for said professionals but that fail to fundamentally challenge the colonial domination at the root of most of those problems.

Obviously, for what it's worth, I do not intend to contribute to any of these things. Spence's and MacPhee's stories are told from and in their own words as much as possible, and the material that I am using to put them in context is largely from authors who also write from indigenous standpoints. I reveal nothing — indeed, I know nothing — that could be of material use to institutions that oppose indigenous struggles. And though the fact that you are holding this book is evidence that I have gained personally at least a little bit, I hope that something of a reciprocal relationship exists, and that what I produce also gives back by in some way supporting struggles that are ongoing in the present. But I am well aware that even with my best efforts to base the work on the voices of the people I have talked to and enter history from their standpoints, "the research product is ultimately that of the researcher, however modified or influenced by informants ... [and the resulting document] is a written document structured primarily by a researcher's purposes, offering a researcher's interpretations, registered in a researcher's voice" (Stacey 1988: 23). It is up to others to judge whether my intent matches up with my practice.

Knowledge, Gender, and Assimilation

Knowledge was not only at the heart of my interactions with Spence and MacPhee, but also central to a lot of what they talked about in their own lives. This is related to another way in which struggles over knowledge have been central to colonialism and anti-colonial resistance. European empires and the institutions they spawned in North America have struggled for centuries to undermine and overrule and replace indigenous ways of knowing (and associated ways of being and doing) with their own ways. This has included a wide range of tactics over the years, with religious missionaries, government officials, and paternalistic settlers bullying, bribing, and forcing people to give up their traditional knowledge, and thereby to adopt settler ways of being — that is, to assimilate.

From the standpoint of the conquerors, assimilation is the only logical end point for conquest other than physical extermination. A group of people that are bound together in some way is always going to be able to put up more of a fight than a bunch of individuals who are isolated from one another. Indigenous nations provide that kind of stick-togetherness, and it is their ways of knowing and being and doing that are the glue. Functioning, cohesive nations by their very existence challenge conquest much more powerfully than individuals starting from complete separation. The empires, colonies, and settler states have put a great deal of effort into getting rid of that glue, with the end goal of dissolving the nations so that the conquest can be complete, but the resistance to this process continues in communities across Turtle Island to this day.

Attacks on indigenous women and on indigenous ways of understanding and doing gender[2] have always been central to this process, and women have always been central to resisting these attacks (Stevenson 1999; A. Smith 2005; Olsen Harper 2006). There was certainly variation between nations, but by and large, compared to the elite white women who embodied the dominant European ideal in that era, indigenous women in the years before colonization had significantly more power within the family, larger roles in public life, greater political power within their nations, central involvement in work and roles that Europeans associated with men, and much greater autonomy with respect to their sexual lives and relationships. According to Cherokee activist and scholar Andrea Smith (2005: 23), "In order to colonize a people whose society was not hierarchical, colonizers must first naturalize hierarchy through instituting patriarchy." This imposition of knowledge — of oppressive ways of understanding and doing gender — happened in a number of ways. Sexual violence by settlers was an integral part of the larger process of dehumanizing indigenous women in the dominant settler imagination. Settlers, particularly Christian missionaries, put tremendous effort into cajoling, bribing, and forcing indigenous people to reorganize their gender, family, and sexual practices along European Christian patriarchal lines. This included in at least some cases considerable effort to compel or bribe some of the more vulnerable men within some nations to take up practices of violence and abuse against the women and children in their lives until they accepted the new ways of doing things (Stevenson 1999: 61).

Such measures were necessary because, from the very beginning, indigenous women resisted this imposition of colonial and patriarchal knowledge and related practices. Though there was plenty of variation in choices and tactics, as staunch and resolute as resistance to colonization was among indigenous peoples as a whole, generally it seems to have been even more so among indigenous women precisely because they had more to lose (ibid.: 60). Cree scholar Winona Stevenson (ibid.: 63) quotes M. Annette Jaimes and Theresa Halsey as writing, "it was women who have formed the very core of indigenous resistance to colonization since the first moment of conflict between Indians and invaders." Both because of their pre-colonization autonomy and equality in many nations and their unrelenting resistance to colonial and gender oppression since contact, Smith (2005: 24) has argued, "The historical record suggests ... that the real roots of feminism should be found in Native societies." She points out that the attacks and demonization of the relatively powerful and autonomous indigenous women were not only part of colonization, but were also in part a strategy by white European men to maintain their power over women in their own families, communities, and nations.

This history of colonially imposed gender oppression and sexual violence continues today. Indigenous women earn significantly less money, face more barriers to education, services, and jobs, and have their children taken from them by state authorities in vastly disproportionate numbers[3] (Olsen Harper 2006: 35). Tireless effort by indigenous women activists and their allies in recent years have begun to bring mainstream attention to the huge numbers of indigenous women who have gone missing and been murdered in Canada over the last few decades, mostly with very little mainstream notice or action by authorities (Razack 2002; Olsen Harper 2006). Noted human rights organization Amnesty International investigated the issue and found that police and other Canadian settler state authorities have consistently failed to protect indigenous women or to respond usefully when violence against indigenous women is reported (Amnesty International [Canada] 2004).

Schools

From the early 1600s — the early years of settlement in New France — European efforts to colonize Turtle Island used schools as a site for the settler assault on indigenous ways of knowing, being, and doing, related to gender and otherwise (Miller 1996). The hierarchical educational approaches of the Europeans were starkly different from the traditional indigenous educational practices, which were largely based on respect for autonomy, not imposing one's will on the learner, and learning from examples, from stories, and from "purposeful play" (ibid.: 20). Without the scope to truly coerce the students, the earliest attempts at residential schools foundered on the unwillingness of the students to relate to them with the subservience that the missionaries who ran the schools had hoped and on the resistance of their families and communities to participating. In response, the colonizers "recruited children by preying on families in desperate straits and by making generous presents to those who surrendered their children" (ibid.: 43). However, these efforts in New France by and large failed: indigenous people were mostly not interested, missionaries decided there were other tactics they could use to implant Christian and European ways of knowing and doing that did not require boarding schools, and for the moment the European merchants and the military authorities were not terribly interested in an aggressive campaign of assimilation.

Still, the impulse to push settler knowledge on colonized peoples continued. In 1744, in declining a proposal from colonial leaders in Virginia that they begin to take responsibility for schooling young Iroquois men, Chief Red Jacket said, "You, who are wise, must know that different Nations have different Conceptions of things and therefore you will not take it amiss if our ideas of this kind of Education happen not to be the same as yours" (Brant Castellano et al. 2000: xii).

To press the point home, Red Jacket added,

> We are ... not the less oblig'd by your kind Offer, tho' we decline accepting it; and to show our grateful Sense of it, if the Gentlemen of Virginia will send us a Dozen of their Sons, we will take Care of their Education, instruct them in all we know, and make Men of them. (ibid.)

It is always dangerous to project such things back into history, of course, but I can imagine that second bit being delivered in a tone of grim humour.

After the War of 1812, indigenous peoples in eastern Turtle Island became much less important as military allies to the British, and significant settlement began across more of what would later be known as "Canada." Indigenous people were no longer seen as a tool to be used but as an obstacle to settlement. Experiments with residential schooling had never entirely ceased but were now pursued with renewed vigour by imperial authorities and British Protestant churches. In 1830, Sir George Murray, the British Secretary of State for War and the Colonies, bluntly put it that in dealing with the obstacle that indigenous people represented for settlement-based colonization, there was now a "settled purpose of gradually reclaiming them from a state of barbarism, and of introducing amongst them the industrious and peaceful habits of civilized life" (Miller 1996: 74). When decoded a bit from Murray's blatant racism, what he is talking about is replacing indigenous knowledges, indigenous ways of being and doing, with settler knowledges and settler ways of being and doing. By the 1840s, schooling with assimilative intent was becoming more systematic in the colonies of British North America. As one study put it, "Thus the interests of church and state merged in a marriage of convenience that was to endure more than a century: the churches could harvest souls at government-funded schools while meeting the shared mandate to eradicate all that was Indian in the children" (Fournier and Crey 1998: 53–54).

This systematization accelerated after the unification of many of the colonies into the Dominion of Canada in 1867 and thereafter. Federal legislation first mandated school attendance for those indigenous people it designated as "status Indians" in 1894. The burgeoning "Indian affairs" bureaucracy, with its "Indian agents" who exerted significant power over indigenous families living on reserves, often used their power to threaten families if they did not send their kids to residential schools. By 1896 there were forty-five church-run schools. On the prairies, a combination of growing famine and pressure from the Mounties helped the school populations grow. Complaints from indigenous parents at the harsh physical punishments their children received in the schools were recorded as early as 1889. There are many records of escape attempts by students, and in the first decades of the twentieth century estimates are that 40–50 percent of the students who were forced to attend died because of it (Fournier and Crey 1998: 49, 61; Henry et al. 2000: 125). The peak usage of residential schools was in 1931: there were around eighty schools and it is estimated that almost 75 percent of indigenous youth aged seven to fifteen were in the system (Fournier and Crey 1998: 61; Fleras and Elliot 1999: 181). The last federally run residential school was not closed until the 1980s.

The purpose of these schools was quite explicitly to hasten assimilation and the dissolution of indigenous nations. A Department of Indian Affairs annual report in 1889 said,

> The boarding-school dissociated the Indian child from the deleterious home influence to which he would otherwise be subjected. It reclaims him from the uncivilized state in which he has been brought up. It brings him into contact from day to day with all that tends to effect a change in his views and habits. (Fleras and Elliot 1999: 181)

Researchers have described the schools as "an all-encompassing environment of resocialization," and as tools of "coercive assimilation, supported by the government agencies and churches that ran the schools" in which "Aboriginal children were forbidden to speak their language, to practice their traditions and customs, and to learn about their history" (Henry et al. 2000: 125). Many indigenous people who attended residential schools also speak of experiencing physical and sexual abuse there, and the schools "are largely responsible for the epidemic rates of sexual violence in Native communities today" (A. Smith 2005: 3, 35–54).

George Manuel, a leader in the Shushwap Nation in British Columbia and first head of the National Indian Brotherhood (later reorganized as the Assembly of First Nations), attended a residential school in his youth until health problems allowed him to get out. He described such schools as "the laboratory and the production line of the colonial system" (McFarlane 1993: 30). He said that after years spent "learning to see and hear only what the priests and brothers wanted you to see and hear, even the people we loved came to look ugly" (ibid.: 31).

Spence

Doreen Spence was born in 1937, when residential schools were near their peak, but she managed to avoid that particular ordeal. She said,

> I was raised in northern Alberta near the Good Fish Lake Reserve. I spent more time on the reserve when I was little, until I was probably about seven or eight years of age, just around the time the children were being scooped for residential schools. My grandparents moved off, then. We were nomadic for awhile.

In a step unusual for that era, her grandparents sent her to a mostly white school in a rural area for grades seven through nine. She remembers that "it was all Ukrainians, basically; all of them newcomers to our land." Being in spaces defined by and for white Canadians was not an easy thing for Spence: "There was very, very blatant systemic discrimination. You never felt safe. You never felt you were part of society."

In such an environment, just surviving is an important act of resistance, but Spence remembers standing up for herself in some more overt ways too. She was not allowed to play on the school baseball team because she was a girl. This made her mad, and one day she finally told her teacher that she was not coming back to school unless she was allowed to play. She told her teacher, "I can run faster than them. I can bat harder. I can make home runs. *They* say I'm one of the best players on the team!" The teacher was taken aback but did not give a flat no. "They had to sit down with everybody in that community and through that they decided that, yes, I could play on the team with the boys. I was the only girl that would travel with these boys in the wagon."

Spence learned from that. Over time, she says, "I became so I knew that I could make change that way, just by deciding what my values are and really keeping in harmony with those values.... That was a very big part of my initial pushing forward for social change."

Her grandparents wanted her to have the best education she could get. They could not afford to send her but she won a scholarship to attend Breehan Bible College in Calgary. It was a difficult transition. Even the journey south to Calgary was "overwhelming" and as they moved form the forested north of the province to the prairies she "could feel the loneliness already.... I was going through a grieving process as I came." At seventeen years old, she was one of the youngest people at the college and she was the only indigenous person. She remembers, "It was very alien and very lonely and scary. I had to build, within my environment, some sort of safety.... Basically I just threw myself into the books. I forgot about the rest of the world."

But Spence also had no choice but to make those three years about a lot more than the books, too.

> I used to get up at five o'clock in the morning and do gratis work for the whole college. I'd do the laundry for the college, both the girls' and the boys' dorms, the sheets and stuff like that. That would be about five to six in the morning. Then from seven to eight we had to go to chapel. Then breakfast, and after breakfast we would go to class. After class I would come home, I'd drop my books, I'd change, and I'd go down to the Teakettle Inn or the Carolina Restaurant, just off of Centre Street. I'd waitress for a few hours. I had to make money. Then I'd get on the bus by — I think it was eight o'clock, because I had to be in bed by nine.... I did that for three solid years.

Being in such an educational institution was a trade-off for Spence, the kind of trade-off that most white Canadians (particularly those who are not recent non-French, non-British immigrants) do not have to even imagine making. On the one hand, being there was necessary to find a way to make a living in the settler society. On the other, it was an environment that was actively hostile to her culture. Spence was raised in traditional ways, and by the time she had been in college for awhile, "they had all had a shot at [converting] me, because I was condemned to Hell by the time I was eight years of age, or something." She paused and added with a laugh, "I knew I wasn't going to be alone when I went down there."

There was no active urban Aboriginal community in Calgary at the time, so the only indigenous people Spence saw were the Morley people in the nearby Stoney Indian Reserve. Youth from the college would go out there on Sundays to preach Christianity to them, and eventually, somehow, Spence was able to convince them to take her along.

> Of course, being traditional, I realized that I couldn't go and tell these people how to live.... [When] I ended up in Morley, the first thing I did was say to the people, "If you would just let me go, I need to find an old man. There's an old man here that I need to talk to." I remember walking up this big hill and finding this old man. I walked into this little log cabin. He was lying on a cot. It was very cold in there, no heat or anything.
>
> I said to him, "Grandpa, I'm Cree. I'm from northern Alberta. These people have sent me over here to evangelize and Christianize you people. But I'm just a young kid. Who am I to be coming and telling an old man how to live and what to think and how to believe?" Of course I would've been dismissed had the college known that, but now I can tell my secrets. *[laugh]*
>
> He said to me, "You are very wise for your age. You're very wise. We've had people come and Christianize us since they came. But they keep taking and taking and taking, and there's nothing

left anymore. Even our culture, our language, our traditions, and everything is disappearing very fast."

I asked him what he would suggest that I do … so that I don't get thrown out of the course, so that I make it through, but that I come out being who I am rather than selling out.

Spence said he told her,

> "Always listen very well. You don't have to get into debates with anybody. You don't have to sell out to them. You don't have to defend yourself, because you know who you are and what you're here for."
>
> So I played a very silent role all throughout my three years there. I didn't have that many friends, as such, because I knew I wasn't there to socialize. My only aim was to get through this, get good marks, and get out. *[laugh]*

During this time Spence decided that she wanted to be a nurse. Being Aboriginal, she was not able to enter nursing in Alberta at the time, and instead went to a college in Montana, which was yet another exercise in enduring harsh racism in a mainstream educational institution. She survived, however, and in 1959 finished her time as a student. She graduated as a practical nurse and went to work in Alberta, a career she followed (with a brief stint in Toronto) for thirty-seven years. Throughout it was, in her words, "a very cold environment" for her as an indigenous woman. "I was pretty proud of myself for hanging in."

Her career was almost derailed early on when she was confronted with an instance of involuntary sterilization of an indigenous woman,[4] a common practice in Canada for many years (A. Smith 2005: 79–108). Forced sterilization was legal in Alberta from 1928 to 1972 (Sawyer 1981).

> One of my first jobs I was asked to do would be to go up north to [a hospital] in northern Alberta. It was run by Catholics. The minute I walked into that hospital I was told what I could do and couldn't do, what areas were off-limits to me, and so forth. But yet I was put in charge of this unit, and it was a very busy, active surgical unit.
>
> One day, maybe three months into my job up there, along came this list of my [operating room] slate. In that slate there was a thirteen-year-old Native girl that was going for sterilization. There was no consent form on the sheet. She didn't know what she was going for. There was no pre-op teaching to the parents or her. I, of course, couldn't question that with the Sisters or they would have run me out of town. I couldn't ask the doctors because of the same thing — they were the gods.… I tried pushing her back further and

further on the slate, and I didn't know what to do.

They had a telegraph office at the Hudson Bay Company downtown, so I took my lunch hour and ran down there. I telegraphed the attorney general's office in Alberta. Now, the Catholics insisted on their "spiritual beliefs" — you had to honour their spiritual beliefs, their religion. When I wrote the attorney general I used their words, that it was against my spiritual beliefs to go ahead and do this sterilization without the parents' permission and knowledge, or the young girl's.

I sat back and I knew something was going to hit the fan, and it did. Of course I got hauled in and got accused of everything else.

Spence was not fired, but was subjected to extended verbal abuse. After that, in the course of her work, she

> really had to pay for it in other ways. I had to get out of there as quickly as I could and come back to Edmonton. It wasn't like a failure to me, though. I put my life on the line for other people, because I couldn't not do it. I couldn't sell my values.

Still, her act of defiance worked, because in the end "the girl didn't go for sterilization. She ended up going home."

Even through her years working as a nurse, however, Spence's attention returned to education. It did so initially through her own children. She remembers taking her eldest daughter to kindergarten for the first time in the late 1960s, and

> everything that I had gone through in school — all the racism, the hurts, everything — it hit me like a ton of bricks. Here I was, taking a part of me to a system that doesn't understand Aboriginal people. Systemic discrimination is ingrained in the history, in the schools — that's where it begins ... I remember just bawling. I sat on the steps and I just bawled. But after I had a good cry, I thought, "There has got to be something that can be done." I went back and I knocked on the door, and I talked to this teacher.

The first approach to taking action for Spence was sitting on the Parent Teacher Association. It was a period filled with "frustration," but she persevered and pushed small changes however she could and "got to the point where I knew their system better than they did." She was also very involved in organizing a women's group and youth activities on the military base where her husband was stationed.

A different way to be active in education came for her in the late 1970s in the form of the Plains Indian Cultural Survival School, or PICSS. Earlier in that decade, because of local activism in communities around the country and because of leadership from the National Indian Brotherhood under George Manuel, the slogan "Indian control of Indian education" became visible as a central demand of indigenous peoples in Canada. The first school to be controlled directly by indigenous people was in Blue Quills, Alberta, in 1970. The Department of Indian Affairs (DIA) originally ran the school and had decided to close it and sell the building, so people from the reserve occupied it until the DIA agreed to turn it over to the local band council to run. Since then, community control of schools on reserves has grown, though it has been a slow and difficult process because of underfunding, foot-dragging by the government, and a number of other barriers.

In urban areas, the struggle has been different but just as difficult.[5] Most schools are run by provincial governments, generally via local school boards, and in urban areas indigenous peoples have had little choice but to go to these schools even though, historically, indigenous students and students of colour have found provincial schools to be a hostile environment to a greater or lesser degree.[6] In Calgary in the 1970s, the degree was definitely greater: According to statistics published in 1979, 94 percent of Aboriginal students who started junior high school in Calgary did not graduate, and 83 percent of Aboriginal students had dropped out by grade nine — or, as some writers have characterized non-completion of mainstream schooling by people forced to deal with racism and colonization, they had been pushed out (Pratt 1979: B1; Antrop-González 2008). Spence's own experiences should give a flavour of what indigenous youth had to endure in settler-dominated schools. They faced racism, blatant and subtle, from fellow students and from school employees, and the curriculum was based exclusively on colonial knowledge — something that even the extremely conservative Alberta provincial government was forced to acknowledge during the 1980s, which led to a process of making at least some modest changes in its content.[7]

A few indigenous people in Calgary saw the desperate need and decided to do something different. Community members, a principal/teacher, and a handful of students began a do-it-yourself school in a basement — a school that was explicitly controlled by and run for indigenous people, and firmly grounded in indigenous cultures. This grew and moved and eventually became PICSS, the first school controlled by indigenous people in an urban area in Canada.[8] The project was in its early stages when Spence was called to become involved. Initially, she was hesitant.

> I was kind of afraid because I'm Cree, I'm not from this area. We're in Blackfoot Confederacy territory here. I went to see elders on a local reserve, Frank and Mary Onespot. They told me that I should do this — that, first of all, I had the right spirit, that I wasn't in it

for the honour and the glory of it; and that I also had the love, the passion, the dedication, and the education to do it. I thought about it for awhile and eventually got involved.

Spence became the president of the school's board, which involved helping guide the school's path, fundraising, counselling, conflict mediation, constant struggles with the public school board and other government bodies, and teaching the occasional Cree language class. She was still raising a family and working full-time, but, she said, "I gave it my blood, sweat, and tears. Every ounce that I had.... I was chief cook and bottle washer!" She played this role from 1978 until 1995.

MacPhee

Donna MacPhee's role in PICSS was somewhat different. As with Spence, she identified the experience of being an indigenous woman in Canada as enough to leave no choice but to learn how to speak out and resist. She described anti-racist struggle as being an unavoidable feature "all [her] life." In particular, because she had never had the opportunity to be part of a reserve community, it was encountering a local group called the Committee Against Racism (CAR) that shaped how she expressed that need to struggle. For many years MacPhee was involved in all kinds of collective anti-racism work in Calgary through CAR, which included supporting the struggles around land claims of the Lubicon Nation of northern Alberta and of the Mohawk Nation during the standoff at Kanehsatake (also known as Oka) Quebec.[9] Through her involvement in CAR she also became connected to PICSS, as both an adult student and as a member of the board of directors. She explained, "I had my grade twelve. I just went for the culture."

The "culture" that MacPhee went for was not just a little add-on at the end of the day, as such a thing might be treated in a mainstream school, but was integral to how PICSS worked. It was vital to Spence that the school's approach be "holistic," which in indigenous teachings is often linked to balance among spiritual, mental, physical, and emotional factors. It meant creating a physical environment that was welcoming to indigenous students, that had their own people's artwork on the walls and books by indigenous authors in the library. Spence said, "It means having elders involved, and that you really listen to those elders. To have those young people realize that they have a uniqueness and a richness to their culture, to empower them." This also meant creating a space in which indigenous cultures were not only not overtly denigrated, but were also not shown as being strange, exotic, and part of a dead past; instead they were presented as a living, vibrant part of how indigenous peoples live today. Crucially, it was about welcoming everyone who came, from thirteen-year-olds to adult learners wanting to complete their grade twelve or just wanting to learn a culture that colonial institutions had so far denied them.

Spence emphasized that it was crucial to create "a safe environment" for indigenous learners so that they would "be able to see that they're wanted, they're loved, and they're cared for. That's something that I never felt through my whole career of education … so alone, so alien, so cold."

As much as possible, particularly in history and the social sciences, PICSS refused to teach the parts of the mainstream curriculum that ignored, marginalized, and just plain lied about the history of northern Turtle Island. Spence said that students learned about the realities of colonization, about the realities of the treaties — "That we never relinquished our lands. We were never conquered. We were to live in peace and harmony, and share the wealth of the land to the depth of the ploughshare, nothing further." Students read many indigenous authors.[10]

A crucial feature of the school was that it was open to whoever needed it. It was designed to feel like a community, a coming together of young people and older people to work toward a common goal and support each other on the journey. Spence gave this example of an adult but still youngish learner called Isaac:

> I remember he always used to be outside smoking when he was supposed to be in class. One day I walked up and I said to him, "I think one of these days I'm not going to tell you to go to class anymore. Something's going to happen here one of these days if you don't go to class." I walked on.
>
> All of a sudden, one day, I walked up to the school. Here he was. He was standing out there smoking. I didn't say hi to him. I just grabbed him by the back of his collar. I opened the door and took him in. I knew he was supposed to be in social so I took him over, opened the door of the classroom. There was a little thirteen-year-old guy that was always in school. He was a really diligent student, quiet, never bothered anyone, really bright little Native guy. I asked one of the buddies to move over. Took Isaac and sat him down. The teacher was teaching.
>
> "See," I said to this little thirteen-year-old, "This is your big brother. He has a hard time with smoking. He's always outside instead of being in class. You have the responsibility to tell him, hey big brother, you can't do that, you have to be in class, you have to study. You're always here, you do this best, so you know what to do. You look after your big brother." I walked out.
>
> [Isaac] never said a word. And that guy, he came about!

For MacPhee, an important part of her role as an older student and as a mentor was to help the younger students deal with the challenges of the everyday racism and sexism they faced in their lives. Inevitably, incidents happened when students were out at events in the broader community. MacPhee described a few, including this one:

> A group of us were going downtown [on the bus] and I was sitting by myself on this seat and there was four kids sitting over there by themselves. I can't remember where we were going — some Native event. I was sitting there and this old guy came and sat with me and put his arm around me and I said, "Don't touch me!" and he put his arm away. He ended up grabbing my boob and I ended up knocking him off the seat. I was just totally embarrassed, him doing that in front of all the little kids across there. They're looking at me and I'm just — *[laugh]* I threw him off the seat and I wanted to throttle him. He dove off and got off the bus.
>
> A kid said, "I really don't feel like going to this event today." We went and had coffee and we talked about it. We talked about different ways I could have handled it.
>
> So that's being a mentor, just using what happens as an example. Even though it's hard, and hard to stomach, you have to say, well, yes, it happens sometimes. Okay, if it happened to you, what would you do?
>
> You had to be truthful. That was part of it. If something happened, you handled it and then you debated how you handled it after. Say, "Okay, anybody else have any ideas how the situation could have been handled?" That way it was a learning experience for all of us. It's hard sharing when you're oppressed and you don't have any power over that situation. But then when you stop [and think], you do have power — you [just] don't have much, because of the oppression.

It was not only the students that had to deal with a hostile environment, however. One of the features of colonialism is that colonized people and their organizations are often not allowed to do things in their traditional ways but are forced to adapt to the ways in which the dominant people and institutions do things. This harsh reality was ever-present in shaping what the volunteers and staff at PICSS had to do to keep it up and running. On a basic, everyday level there was the need to function in environments defined by people and institutions with authority that had ways of work that were very different from traditional indigenous ways of work and to appease those people and institutions. Spence shook her head as she recalled: "Meetings and meetings, and nothing productive. And paperwork and paperwork, but no change. That is the way the bureaucracy runs. You just spin out the paperwork, and no changes."

In 1978, after many meetings and much paperwork, the school board in Calgary agreed to fund the school for the academic portion of its work. Negotiations with the school board were not easy, however. Spence described this incident as a detailed example of what they had to go through:

> I remember, one day, I had been trying to get the school named to Plains Indians Cultural Survival School. We had meeting after meeting after meeting with the school board people. They would meet and they would go. They would come with their briefcases and sit for ten minutes, and then they would be gone. They would tell us what was good for us and they would be gone.
>
> [On one particular day,] I was going to tell them that this was my last meeting with them, and that I was going to let the media know if they didn't make a decision.… I came home from work, I took off my uniform, got dressed in a suit, got in my car and drove over there. I could see them. I sat in the parking lot, watching them. By this time I had studied very well how they behaved toward us. They would get out of the car and they would go into the school. Finally, the grand poobah, the Great White God there — the superintendent — he got out of his car and they walked into the school. I waited about ten minutes.
>
> Once I figured they were all settled in, I got out of my car and took my time. I took my briefcase. I walked in there. I knew they were all in that room, in the principal's office. So I kind of knocked and walked in at the same time.
>
> I said, "Well, I'm glad you're all here for this meeting." Blah blah blah, like they would say. "I've got my briefcase here. Here's all the paperwork that you need. This is all the updated dialogue that we have had on this same issue for X number of years. This is my last meeting with you, so I just want you to know that I'm too busy. I can't waste my precious time any longer. I've got too much to do." Or something like that, like they always told us, that they've got this busy agenda. So then I put this briefcase on the table and I said, "You each have a copy. Let me know what your decision is." And I walked out.
>
> They said, "Well how can we meet when she's not here?" They told the principal, "Is she coming back?"
>
> He said, "I don't think so. She's not coming back." And I didn't.
>
> A couple of days later we got the letter in the mail that said we could change the school name from Melville Scott to Plains Indians Cultural Survival School.
>
> So, yes, there were a few incidents. *[laugh]*

Though the school board provided consistent funding for the academic portion of PICSS's work for many years, they would not fund the cultural component. Despite frequent and persistent lobbying, and a treaty obligation under the traditional indigenous understanding of the treaties, the federal Department of Indian Affairs refused to provide the necessary funding. Supporters of the school had to invest immense effort in fundraising every year. But, somehow, they managed to do it — school board funding for academics, private fundraising, the occasional foundation grant, and in later years some provincial money to cover the cultural component. And for many years, PICSS survived.

In the early 1990s, the provincial government of Alberta cut the amount of money going to school boards in the province, forcing the boards to cut their budgets in turn.[11] One of the ways that the Calgary board decided to save money was to stop funding academics for students over the age of nineteen. This accounted for somewhere between half and three-quarters of the PICSS student body, so the loss of that money was potentially devastating, particularly given how important it was to the school's way of doing things — that learners of all ages be present together. The board gave the school a year's extension on the deadline, and some emergency funding from Human Resources Development Canada, a federal government department, helped extend things another year or two, but the constant uncertainty and the need to devote huge amounts of effort to acquiring the money to keep the doors open put a great deal of strain on the organization. The Department of Indian Affairs continued in its refusal to provide significant funding. In 1995, Spence decided to retire. That year, amid bitter community controversy about certain aspects of the school and its funding, PICSS was significantly restructured, and years later it was closed completely. In MacPhee's pithy summary: "The [school] board chopped that program to shit."

Though her involvement in it came to an end, in reflecting on what PICSS did for the urban Aboriginal community in Calgary, Spence said, "I think it had a tremendous impact on us." She still works regularly with younger people who had been students at PICSS.

> I am very encouraged by their ability to be able to speak those truths, and to be able to say, "Okay, that was our history." It helps them deal with that anger that they have had, down there.... When you deal with reality that way, you get a healthier person because you are speaking the truth, you are talking the truth, you are working with the truth. When you speak with those values and work around those values of truth, honesty, respect — those values, you cannot go wrong with.

MacPhee saw many good things come from it as well. She said,

> A student would come in so abused they wouldn't even talk to us. They'd shun us. They wouldn't speak. And then after about a week, they'd have their chair so they're looking at us. Pretty soon they're in the conversation. It was so nice to see such a change in so little time. That school brought up hope. There's so many Aboriginal workers out there right now and they all come from PICSS.... All the top players in town now [in the Aboriginal community] are from PICSS. It did make such a difference when everyone was together, the adults in with the kids.

She believed that having an indigenous-controlled space was crucial to this success. She said,

> Where do you go that there's just Aboriginal community, where you see your image mirrored? There's nowhere unless you go on the rez, and if you aren't part of the rez system then there's nothing, so PICSS was a real haven for a lot of people.

Referring to many of the students, she concluded,

> They were in a mess but didn't know how they got there and then you showed them the real true history of Canada and what happened to the Nations. Then they start getting a little spark and that spark grows and pretty soon they're activists and not taking abuse on the buses any more and standing up for who they are. It's a wonderful feeling and it's lasting.

Notes

1. Tim Wise (2005: ix) writes: "I am not claiming, nor do I believe, that all whites are well-off, or even particularly powerful. We live not only in a racialized society, but also a class system, a patriarchal system, and one in which other forms of advantage and disadvantage exist. These other forms of privilege mediate, but never fully eradicate, something like white privilege. ... But despite the fact that white privilege plays out differently for different folks, depending on these other identities, the fact remains that when all other factors are equal, whiteness matters and carries with it great advantage." One aspect of white privilege is that we can easily go our whole lives without understanding the ways in which white supremacy and colonialism have shaped our history, or even acknowledging that they have. Other useful works that touch on white privilege in one way or another include Foster 1996, Razack 1998, Bishop 2002, Kivel 2002, Jensen 2005, Muscio 2005, and Thobani 2007.
2. Talking about gender as something that is *done* builds on the recognition by many writers in the last few decades that masculinity and femininity are not biological essences but rather describe ways of enacting ourselves constrained by and

produced in the context of the social relations in which we find ourselves. In different times and places, social relations of gender have not necessarily been limited to just two possibilities, and those possibilities have not necessarily looked anything like the dominant forms of "masculinity" and "femininity" in twenty-first-century North America. For more on this way of understanding gender, see, for example, Butler 1990, Connell 2005, and other works by Judith Butler and R.W. Connell. As this paragraph and those that follow it briefly discuss, forcibly changing indigenous social relations of gender and attacking indigenous women was crucial to the European colonization of Turtle Island. For more on gender systems among indigenous peoples on Turtle Island, see Roscoe 1988 and Roscoe 2000 as well as the other references in the body of the text.

3. See Kathy Mallett's story in Chapter 3 of the companion book, *Resisting the State: Canadian History Through the Stories of Activists*, for an account of one struggle by indigenous people, mostly women, in Winnipeg against local child welfare authorities.

4. To hear some of Spence's memories of this incident, go to www.talkingradical.ca/audio/spence_sterilization.mp3.

5. Chapter 3 in *Resisting the State: Canadian History Through the Stories of Activists* examines other aspects of the struggles of indigenous peoples in urban centres in Canada.

6. For an excellent account of struggles around equity issues in Toronto school boards from the 1970s until 2001, see Tim McCaskell's *Race to Equity* (2005). The book covers struggles around a number of different equity issues, but its primary focus is on anti-racism, though with surprisingly little content that is specific to indigenous peoples.

7. A study published in 2005 looking at the experiences of African Canadian students in Edmonton confirmed that curriculum continues to exclude non-white students, and that "Canadian curriculum does not merely teach Western ideas and culture, it teaches the *superiority* of Western ideas and culture; it equates Western ways and thought with *Civilization* itself" (Codjoe 2005: 66; emphasis in original).

8. To hear Spence talk about PICSS, go to www.talkingradical.ca/audio/spence_picss.mp3.

9. For an introduction to the struggles of the Lubicon Cree, see Kulchyski 2007: 124–127. For a moving documentary film about the struggles by the Mohawk Nation at Kanehsatake, see Obomsawin 1993; see also Simpson and Ladner 2010. To hear MacPhee talk about some of her memories of supporting the Lubicon, see www.talkingradical.ca/audio/macphee_lubicon.mp3.

10. Something I never did once in a mainstream high school in southern Ontario.

11. This was one of many expressions across the country in the 1990s of shifts that included public sector cutbacks and privatization, which were part of a larger agenda that many authors have called "neoliberalism." For more on this trend in general see Chapter 6 of *Resisting the State: Canadian History Through the Stories of Activists*.

Chapter 2

Against Company, Church, and State
Madeleine Parent and the Dominion Textile Strike of 1946

I never had the chance to see Madeleine Parent[1] in the thick of battle — on a picket line, in a court room where the judge was in the pocket of her enemies, or in the blistering heat of debate at a labour or women's movement gathering, for example. But I can imagine. She may have looked "like a nun disguised in civilian clothing," as feminist Shree Mulay[2] (2005: 113) has fondly written, and she may have laughed frequently, but her carefully chosen words reflected her cutting political insight, and she often delivered them with an unmistakeable passion and firmness.

Parent grew up in a middle-class white Francophone family in Montreal. Living through the Great Depression and seeing the right-wing provincial government of Maurice Duplessis elected in 1936 might be enough to prime anyone to start thinking critically about the world, but Parent also happened to be at McGill University as Canada's first student movement was taking shape there. Student activism drew her in and by the time she graduated in the first year of the Second World War, she knew she wanted to remain active. She turned to the labour movement. The year 1946 saw a wave of strikes across numerous industries in Canada; Parent was a leader in one of the most important of the struggles to happen in Quebec that year, a strike waged mostly by women workers against the Dominion Textile Company. That struggle is the focus of this chapter.

Parent's decades of activity far exceed what a single chapter can cover.[3] She continued for many years as an organizer and leader in workers' organizations, and played important roles not only in countless strikes and other efforts against employers but also in struggles with more conservative elements of the labour movement itself. Parent also became very involved in the women's movement. She played a key role in the grassroots takeover of an early federally-funded conference on women's issues that resulted in the founding of the National Action Committee on the Status of Women (NAC),[4] which was Canada's largest national coalition of women's groups for many years (Rebick 2005: 29–30). She played a role in brokering the changes in both NAC and in Quebec's main feminist organization, the Fédération des femmes du Québec (FFQ), that opened these two groups to more substantive participation by immigrant women and women of colour. When I interviewed her, she was still involved in movement activity.

People, Not Things

Behind *things* you will always find *people*.

Take the chapter you are reading, for example. You've already met two of the people behind it — the author, me, and the person whose stories form its core, Parent. We are far from the only people whose doings lie behind this particular thing, however. Editors helped shape these words, both those paid to do so by the publisher as well as friends and allies who have offered me input over the long writing process. Printers ensured the words were transferred to paper. Other people cut, pulped, and processed the trees. It has also been shaped by the work of other writers — both those I have referenced directly and others I might have read in earlier years that influenced my thinking in more general ways — and by many political conversations whose details I have long forgotten. Similarly, the many doings that shaped this chapter will hopefully shape in turn the doings of others — other writers who take these ideas farther, students writing essays, readers having conversations, activists trying to change the world.

It is not just about one chapter of one book, of course — much of what shapes our lives prioritizes things and erases what really should matter, the makings and doings of human beings. Some people would argue that this substitution of things for people is a key characteristic of the particular way we organize human doing in the world today.[5]

People make things and do things in every human society. By this making and doing, food is provided, shelter constructed, the young and the old cared for. And since we need roses as well as bread, as the old labour anthem says, such making and doing goes beyond basic physical needs to include providing information, spiritual nourishment, beauty, entertainment, and lots of other things.

There are many different ways to socially organize all of this activity. Human beings have tried different approaches at various points in history, but many other potential forms of social organization have not been tried and await their turn. For each approach to organizing human beings in our making and doing, it is possible to ask certain questions: What, exactly, gets made and done? Who does what? What determines who does what? Who benefits from the making and doing, and how does that benefit get apportioned? What technology gets used? Who gets access to the goods and services that are created, and how is access to them controlled? How does that access relate to what people actually need? How is unpleasant or dangerous work handled? How equal and fair is all of this? Where does the power lie to make changes in all of these things — where at the global level, within each nation, in each community, in each workplace, in each individual's daily life?

It is beyond the scope of this book — far, far beyond — to try and answer these questions for the Canada of today or of decades past in any kind of comprehensive way.[6] But it is important to outline a few of the basic features of how making and doing have been organized. The biggest part of any answer to these questions — and of how we get sewn into the web of relationships that must be described by any answer — is that it all has rather a lot to do with money.

When I was a baby, a toddler, a child I had no money, but my life depended on food and shelter bought with money acquired by my parents. As a middle-class late-twentieth-century white Canadian teenager — for other people, other times, other places it can happen much sooner and much more insistently — I did things like wash dishes and enter data into computers to begin the transition to selling my own time and labour to get money, the generally expected method for acquiring it. And that is mostly how it has been ever since — doing laboratory research, pushing paper in a government office, marking essays, pumping gas, washing more dishes, writing freelance articles, compiling reports on homelessness and other social issues, teaching. Writing this book is unpaid so far and I haven't earned a wage for being a stay-at-home dad, but I depend on my partner's salary. At times I have done things that made me need money a little less — grown a backyard garden, for instance, or even engaged in that quaint practice called neighbourly sharing — but you can't get away from money.

Besides waged work, some adults get money from scholarships or welfare, and others, disproportionately women, are put in positions of depending on money brought in by a (usually male) partner or spouse. Though all of these sources often get dismissed as being "free money," all have work associated with them, and many have reduced status and power compared to working for a wage. Not everyone is expected to work to acquire money, of course. A few people are able to get enough money to live (and often much, much more) not by working but by owning. "Owning" boils down to being in a position to take some of what other people make and do because the state enforces the right of a select few to control the things that everybody else needs in order to make and do — the buildings, the machines, the vehicles, the intellectual property.

Let me say it again: having access to money is not an option in our society, and for most of us, selling our time and sweat to others is the only way we have to get money. The number of jobs that are pleasant, empowering, creative, self-directed, flexible, interesting, and well-paid is very small compared to the number of people who need to have jobs to live. In other words, the ways in which relations among people are currently organized depend on lots and lots of people having no choice — no matter how hard they work, no matter how devotedly they do the things that we are all told are necessary for success — but to do work (directly waged or not) that is unpleasant, dangerous, poorly paid, monotonous, difficult, only minimally under their own organization if at all, lacking in any opportunity for empowerment or the realization of their desires as whole and integrated human beings, or some combination thereof. Indigenous women and men, women and men of colour, white women, and people with disabilities all face various additional barriers to trading their time and sweat for the means to live, tend to be disproportionately pushed into worse jobs, and have more trouble finding any employment at all (Armstrong et al. 2004; Galabuzi 2006).

Entire libraries have been written on how things came to be this way and what might be done about it. A key point is that while individual effort may allow a few to escape to better circumstances, changing the landscape that makes such labour the lot of the majority cannot happen by individual effort. Acting together, though, ordinary people who work for a wage have significantly more power and a better chance of changing things.

What this "acting together" actually looks like can vary considerably. Sometimes it is a product of years of deliberate effort, but it can also happen completely spontaneously. Sometimes the "togetherness" remains informal, while at other times creating an enduring organization of some sort is part of the point. People have also come together on many different bases. They might share a skill or trade. They may have the same employer or work in the same industry. They might share some sort of community outside of the narrow confines of paid work, whether that is living in the same area or sharing an identity or something else in common. In some times and places, the mere fact of being a worker, any worker at all, has been enough to bring people together.

The actions taken by these collectives of working people have varied a great deal as well. It might involve things that are not very visible, like negotiating with employers or providing mutual aid and personal support to fellow members. Or it might look more like the stereotypical example we often think of, the refusal to sell labour to employers until demands are met — that is, going on strike, as the workers at Dominion Textile did in 1946. It can involve other sorts of actions, too, like organizing a boycott of an employer's products, holding demonstrations, seeking some sort of action from government, or attempting to elect workers themselves to office. In certain times and places it has extended to include things like rioting, seizing control of workplaces so that workers might run them without owners or managers, and sometimes society-wide confrontation with owners and the institutions that owners control with the aim of creating new ways of doing things on a broad scale.

Much of what workers have tried to accomplish through working together in these ways can be understood as attempts to increase the social priority given to people relative to things. On a superficial level, worker struggles are often about what happens to the money generated by the results of their making and doing: how much of what workers produce are they actually able to benefit from, and how much is taken by owners. It can also be about how the work happens — how workers get supervised, managed, regulated, sped up, restricted, disciplined, spied upon — and the desire of owners to have work processes that produce the most for the least; meanwhile workers are interested in work not being too unsafe or too unpleasant. These are all different facets of the underlying tension that comes from a few people having power over many, in part because *things* are treated as more important than *people*. A few workers in every age, and many in some, have dreamed outright of a radical transformation of making and doing to reverse that.

Origins

Except it has never been that simple.

Our current way of organizing making and doing had its origins in Europe. The previous way of organizing things there had its oppressive aspects too, of course, and was the focus of much struggle, but the vigour with which many peasants resisted the new way of doing things — the nascent capitalist way — is telling (Federici 2004). Violence and the threat of violence were used by elites to force many ordinary people into different relationships to making and doing, to the benefit of the elites. Peasants were forced off collectively held land, cut off from previously held collective rights and ways of making and doing that were partly for their own direct benefit, and pushed into the kind of compulsory work for money that continues today. Karl Marx and other nineteenth-century writers described this use of violence to accumulate wealth and to change social relations as "primitive accumulation," with the idea that violence was necessary to get capitalist social relations started. More recent writers have recognized that such violence continues to this day, whether it involves forcing Latin American peasants off their land, using police and courts to attack indigenous people who are asserting their rights to territories in what we call "Canada," or the various and sundry less spectacular but no less destructive versions of taking social commons of various sorts and putting control of them in into private, elite hands (McNally 2006: 83–136).

The experience and impact of the violence that forced the transition to capitalism, and of the social reorganization itself, were different for different groups of people.[7]

Chapter 1 touched on some of the ways that this violence specifically impacted non-European peoples — the conquest and genocide in the Americas to provide European access to land and land-based resources. This violence also included the brutal abduction and enslavement of Africans so they could be brought to the Americas and used to produce cheap commodities for European consumption. Later, many Asian populations were subjected to indentured labour and other forms of colonial subjugation. Both during the initial transition and in later centuries, the wealth generated through this ongoing violence and oppression directed at non-white peoples has been crucial to the growth of capitalist social relations. Also as touched on in Chapter 1, these attacks were often focused on non-European women and the imposition of European ways of doing gender (and patriarchy) (Stevenson 1999; Federici 2004; A. Smith 2005). So while in-group and out-group dynamics were frequently a feature of human collectives in earlier eras, it was during the period of transition to capitalism that a European and Christian sense of innate superiority was translated into enduring colonial social relations that ultimately organized some people into experiences of whiteness and privilege and others into racialization[8] and oppression.[9] At the same time, all manner of rationales emerged, obscuring the ways in which racialization and racial oppression were results of socially organized human activity and making them seem to be supposedly unavoidable results of religion, biology, or culture.

The violence of the transition to capitalism and the shape of the resulting relations also impacted European women in a way that was distinct from European men (Federici 2004). For one thing, the loss of access to common lands and resources had a heavier impact on poor women, who had fewer other options than poor men for meeting their needs. As well, though European societies had been marked by gender oppression for millennia, the transition to capitalism involved a marked increase in the intensity of this oppression as elite men, generally with the complicity of non-elite men, imposed new hardships and boundaries on women. Greater limitations were placed on the presence of women in public spaces. Popular and learned literature began to be filled with increasingly degrading portrayals of women, particularly targeting strong, autonomous women who refused to be subservient. There was an active campaign, lead by elites and by the men in craft guilds, to exclude women from much paid work to which they had previously had access, even from a few areas where they had previously been a majority. Law reforms reduced the legal rights of women. With the (much sharper) separation of work into waged work done outside the home and unwaged work done inside the home, the latter was often not defined as "real" work and came to be seen as "women's work," which also played a part in creating barriers to women doing any sort of work for pay. More and more poor women were pushed into prostitution, but at the same time prostitutes faced increasing levels of violence from both men and the state. All of this served to enhance the dependency of individual women on individual men, and in a sense forced women increasingly into the role of a resource from which men could benefit.

A central element of this kind of attack was the witch-hunt, in which many thousands of European women, mostly poor women, were killed in the course of about two hundred years. European peasants had a long history of uprisings against their feudal rulers; women were significant participants in — and in some cases leaders of — such struggles, and this record of rebellion was associated with long traditions of active and defiant ways of doing "womanness" among ordinary women in Europe. The violence and terror of the witch-hunt that largely targeted poor women with these rebellious ways of moving through the world helped to push women into more passive expressions of femininity while at the same time seriously weakening the capacity of peasant communities to resist the attacks that were forcing the transition to capitalism. Fear, superstition, and violence were actively mobilized to divide peasant men from peasant women, to the extent that across two centuries there is only one recorded example of a male-dominated organization in Europe actively resisting the persecution of women as witches.[10] The witch-hunt also involved extensive focus on supposed reproductive and sexual crimes by women; this focus combined with the law reforms and campaigns in the popular culture to undermine the relatively greater degree of control that peasant women had had over their own bodies during the Middle Ages in Europe and to increase state and male control of women's sexuality and reproduction. Italian feminist Silvia Federici (2004: 103) has observed, "The witch-hunt destroyed a whole world of female practices, collective relations, and systems of knowledge that had been the foundation of women's power in pre-capitalist Europe, and the condition for their resistance in the struggle against feudalism."

These histories have echoed down the years to the present day in many different ways, not least in the organization and experience of making and doing in racialized and gendered ways globally and in Canada (Das Gupta 1996; Armstrong et al. 2004; McNally 2006; Galabuzi 2006; Sharma 2006; Thobani 2007). These relations also shape the field upon which resistance can occur. Some have observed that capitalist social relations seem to foster the proliferation of new axes for organizing humanity into groupings that experience differential privilege and oppression — groupings associated with static (one might say thing-like) identities rather than with ways of moving through the world that are fluid and responsive to desire and circumstance (Holloway 2005; Sharma 2006). Quoting Federici (2004: 115) again, "Thus primitive accumulation has been above all an accumulation of difference, inequalities, hierarchies, divisions, which have alienated workers from each other and even from themselves."

The Labour Movement in Canada

Making and doing coordinated primarily through money were unknown on Turtle Island before colonization; making and doing among the pre-contact network of indigenous nations were organized very differently.[11]

Early resource extraction activities by European visitors and settlers were also organized rather differently; mass dependence on making and doing coordinated primarily through money only came to predominate later in the nineteenth century, though pockets of wage labour existed much earlier. Gradually, local owners sought ways to invest in local production, and the concentrated ownership of colonized but not yet settled land forced more and more people to survive by earning money.

In earlier years, indigenous people were excluded from the wage-earning working class in some places at some times and included in subordinated ways in others. There have been wage workers of African heritage in this part of the world since at least the mid eighteenth century (alongside African and indigenous slaves from the early seventeenth to the early nineteenth centuries) as well as Asian Canadian wage workers since at least the nineteenth century (Winks 1997: 27). Still, deliberate policy implemented by the Canadian state to prevent or at least minimize immigration by racialized people — as well as significant barriers to those who were already present obtaining paid employment beyond certain narrow possibilities — meant that until the second half of the twentieth century, people in Canada who worked for a wage (or depended on those who did) were overwhelmingly white. Middle-class white women tended to be excluded almost completely from waged work, while working-class women, white and racialized, often had little choice but to find ways to earn money, though their options for doing so were very constrained compared to working-class men.

As relations of production changed and increasing numbers of people came to depend on wages, workers' organizations also grew. Skilled workers in Halifax's building trades and shipyards organized themselves as early as 1798. The first large-scale employment of unskilled labourers in Canada was for the building of the Welland Canal in 1842, which employed mostly Irish immigrants. In response to horrific conditions, strikes and riots by canal workers were common in the 1840s. Between 1850 and the late 1940s, the labour movement had its own rhythm of rise and fall, militancy and retreat, growth and erosion, and its form and tactics adapted to the needs of each era. An early high crest in organizing and resistance came in the form of the Noble and Holy Order of the Knights of Labor, an organization originally founded in the United States that expanded into Canada.[12] After the Knights of Labor began to fade in the late 1880s, Canada's organized workers' movement mostly involved skilled tradespeople affiliated with U.S.-based unions in the American Federation of Labor (with the significant exception of the Industrial Workers of the World, which existed primarily in Western Canada and in the years before the First World War).

Though there was plenty of ebb and flow in the meantime, the next great upsurge of working people followed the First World War, with particular radicalism in Western Canada. In light of the recent revolution in Russia, this labour unrest — which took forms like the Winnipeg General Strike of 1919 and the effort to create One Big Union to bring all workers together in a single organization — was taken seriously by Canadian elites and was soon crushed (McKay 2008; Francis 2010). Aside from ongoing bitter labour conflict in Canada's coal fields, the rest of the 1920s was a time of retreat for labour. Communist-lead organizing in the early 1930s provided some sparks, but it wasn't until later in that decade that the movement truly rose again (Abella 1973). The slightly earlier growth of the labour movement in the United States inspired Canadian workers to better their own conditions, and a climactic strike in an auto plant in Oshawa, Ontario, in 1937 finally ushered in the era of widespread and enduring industrial unionism — an approach in which all workers in a plant, skilled and unskilled, are in the same organization rather than the skilled workers belonging to separate unions based on their craft or trade and the unskilled workers being excluded (Abella 1974). During the Second World War, unions continued to expand and managed to wring some concessions from government in terms of recognition of their legitimacy and of the rights of workers to organize.

While there were occasions of solidarity between white workers and workers of colour, there were many more of white exclusion of and opposition to their sisters and brothers of colour, including at some points labour support for immigration policies that excluded on the basis of race. As well, up to the beginning of the First World War, it was official labour movement policy to seek the elimination of waged work by women, though even before that — sometimes with some form of support from the official labour movement, but often enough on their own — women also engaged in labour struggles and a few became prominent writers, speakers, or leaders (Kealey 1998: 18 and *passim*). Women workers tended to be seen by the mainstream of the labour movement as unreliable, "unskilled," difficult to organize, and as low-wage competition for jobs that should go to men, and despite numerous instances, militancy by women workers tended to come as a surprise to union men each time it happened. The struggles for inclusion by women and men of colour and white women in the labour movement have tended to parallel these struggles in the broader society.

Trade unions were not formally legal across the country until Sir John A. Macdonald's Conservatives passed legislation in 1872, though by that point older legal mechanisms like conspiracy charges were rarely used against unions. The new legislation actually granted workers little in the way of new rights and served to dictate in much greater detail what they could and could not do in the pursuit of better wages and conditions. In the early twentieth century, governments very gradually took on a greater role in regulating some aspects of workplaces and occasionally got involved in labour disputes as a mediator. However, labour was also at times subjected to naked state repression — it was not unusual for militia to be called in to suppress major strikes, for example, and the Royal Canadian Mounted Police was created partly in response to the Winnipeg General Strike of 1919 and more generally to worker radicalism after the First World War. It wasn't until the Second World War and its aftermath that the current system of legal structures governing workplaces and unions began to take recognizable shape.

Parent

Madeleine Parent's commitment to social change did not begin in the labour movement, however. Her family of origin was middle-class and she had the opportunity to attend university — McGill University, where instruction was primarily in English, which she said she attended "because there were exceedingly few women in the French universities at the time." Parent said,

> It was at McGill that I began to be involved in social matters, partly as a woman and also simply as a person who found a cause. That was the Canadian Student Assembly, which had only one plank to its platform, and that was to demand of the federal government subsidies for young people who were from underprivileged families and could not afford the university fees. It was very clear that this was to be for both men and women, which was not always clear in the 1930s and forties.... The campaign started in 1937.

Quebec in the period surrounding the Second World War was a particularly hostile place for struggles against oppression and exploitation. Most of the powerful owners in Quebec at the time were English Canadian, and they were quite happy to have the Francophone population tightly controlled by a conservative and powerful Catholic Church; progressive voices did exist within the Church, and even within its hierarchy, but they were usually kept under tight control. And then there was Premier Maurice Duplessis. Originally elected to the Quebec Legislature in 1927, he became Conservative party leader in 1933. In the 1935 Quebec election, he joined forces with a group of dissident Liberals, mostly reformers and nationalists, to form a new party, the Union Nationale. Any trace of a populist agenda disappeared quickly from the party, however, and deeply right-wing politics and tight personal control marked his rule over Quebec from 1936 to 1939 and again from 1944 until his death in 1959. His most notorious piece of legislation was the Padlock Law, which allowed the government to lock up any property suspected of being used for the spreading of "communist" ideas and to imprison those involved. The law required no presumption of innocence, denied free speech, and was so vague that it could be applied very broadly against activists whether they had anything to do with the Communist Party or not. It was not struck down by the Supreme Court until 1957. Duplessis also served as Attorney General while he was premier and was notorious for his tight hold on the provincial courts.[13]

In that political context, especially given the corporate and mostly Anglophone character of McGill's governing board, Parent said,

> We activists were tolerated, not liked. The campaign spread to other campuses across Canada, but as soon as war was declared [in 1939], they clamped down on us. The last year was exceedingly difficult. Some of us, including myself, graduated in 1940, in the first year of the war. Since a number of us were graduating or close to our final period at McGill, the movement fell during the war. But it was not lost, because for the first time in our history, after the war, veterans were offered an education free with allowances in the universities. That tended to break the spell of the fraternities and of the privileged classes from the board of governors on down, at colleges and universities in Canada.

Parent's politicization was not limited to the struggle for bursaries. In her final year, Parent became president of the campus French club for women, even though the head of the quite conservative French faculty "did not tolerate French Canadians' prominence in the French Club." She did things like invite progressive speakers to club meetings. These included Thérèse Casgrain, a prominent activist to get women's suffrage in Quebec, who spoke at Parent's invitation in 1939, six months before Quebec women got the vote. To Parent, her student organizing in all of its aspects

> was a big training ground. I just about gave my everything to it. I felt I'd found what I wanted to do, though of course I wouldn't be a student all of my life and I would have to continue my activity in one way or the other.

Parent was also involved in efforts to secure civil liberties in Quebec, and after attending a conference on the subject she was invited by a fellow student to meet Lea Roback, a labour organizer in the garment industry. Much of the earliest strike activity involving women in Canada was in the textile and garment manufacturing industries. This is not surprising, since those industries employed large numbers of women when many others did not, though often in areas of work that were or were seen to be lower status and less skilled. Montreal and Valleyfield, Quebec, were sites of textile manufacturing as early as the 1860s and had a long history of strike activity. Nonetheless, by the end of the Second World War, most of that history involved a series of defeats or, at best, transient victories that brought with them no stable union recognition. One of the largest strikes by women had been only a few years before, and Roback had been a prominent organizer in the effort. Parent said,

> I was interested in knowing how the Ladies Garment Workers strike had gone in 1937 — what was required, what happened, and so on. She was very generous with sharing her experiences and information, and it was later on, when I was still trying to figure out what I wanted to do in life, that I decided I wanted to be a union organizer.

It was not clear to Parent exactly how to manage this. She

> already had a name because of the civil liberties activities and the Canadian Student Assembly activities, at a period when Quebec was involved in a witch hunt of considerable proportions. It didn't make it easy for me if I wanted to get a job in a factory, for example.

Parent instead set her sights on a staff job with a labour organization. At the time, the major labour organizations in North America were an alphabet soup of acronyms, a few of which are important here. The Congress of Industrial Organizations (CIO) was a collection of industrial unions that started in the United States, spread to English Canada by the late 1930s, but still had little presence in Quebec in the late 1940s, and so was not an option for Parent. There was a collection of unions that existed only in Quebec called the Confederation of Catholic Unions (CCU) that were conservative worker organizations controlled by the Church. A little after the story in this chapter, progressive forces within both the CCU and the Catholic Church helped their transition to the progressive nationalist Confederation of National Unions, or CSN in French, but at the time they were not an appealing alternative for Parent either. That left unions affiliated with the American Federation of Labor (AFL), a much older central comprised mainly of unions based on skilled trades, again originally U.S. American but with a strong presence in Canada and Quebec.

The Second World War was a very fertile time for organizing unions. Workers faced rising prices, despite government claims to be limiting increases in the cost of living, but often still worked for Depression-era wages. As well, the war effort required massive production of arms, airplanes, and other supplies, so there were many new industrial workers to organize. For most of the duration of the war, the federal government took from the provinces the power of regulating labour issues. In this period, rules governing workplaces and unions underwent major changes. In earlier years, usually the only way to achieve official recognition of the union as a legitimate representative of the workers was through a strike forcing the company to do so. In this period, unions won the right to official certification by the government if a majority of workers in a plant became members.

The AFL divided its organizing efforts between industries which would likely cease to exist once the war was over, through the War Labor Organizing Committee, and all other industries through a General Organizing Committee. Parent began with a position with the former, officially as a secretary but, as she said, "it was a period where, if you were a secretary, you were an organizer as well." Not long after, she was switched over to the General Organizing Committee, which was not necessarily an ideal environment for someone of Parent's enthusiasm. It "had more of the business unionists" — an approach that emphasizes collaboration with management, suppression of rank-and-file militancy and democracy, and relative political conservatism — "though you had a couple who were serious about organizing."

For the General Organizing Committee at the time, Parent recalled, this meant that

> when you proposed an additional organizer, "Well, let him organize war industries."… The business unionists in the AFL were not that active in organizing new people. They clung to what they had. They knew how to control that, whereas if you got all kinds of new people into your union, you weren't sure where they were going, especially if they refused demands from the bosses. They assumed that this kind of war industry would close down after the war, and they would continue with their leadership, their business union leadership.

Nonetheless, "Workers would come into the union office after work — at all hours, really — with their desire to know more about unions, to decide whether they were going to organize or not, and to tell us about their problems." They received interest from "brewery workers, there was a glimmer of interest from textile workers — just beginning — and an unfortunate strike of the Belding Cortiselli workers, who made parachutes, that was lost. And there were others — the steel mill workers, and others."

It was in this period that Kent Rowley — he would later become Parent's long-time co-organizer as well as her husband — applied for a job as an organizer with the General Organizing Committee of the AFL in Quebec, and Parent "got him to a meeting." Given the long history of valiant but never fully successful struggle in the industry, Rowley, according to Parent, "had thought about it before coming and he decided that this could be a propitious time to organize cotton mill workers."

However, she said,

> there was, except for one of the leading tradesmen on the committee,

> a general refusal — "It is a bunch of women and children. They are not equipped to organize and to keep a secret. You know what the experience was, they always lost."

Rowley had a counter-proposal: He would go to Valleyfield, Quebec. It was home to a plant that manufactured explosives, and organizing this factory would be his formal assignment. However, he asked, "You have no objection if I do what I want in my free time?" They said, "Oh no, do what you want." Valleyfield also happened to be home to the largest cotton mill in Canada. Soon enough, Rowley had the majority of workers in the mill signed up, and Parent managed the process of applying to an AFL textile union for affiliation; it was granted, Rowley was hired by that union, and certification by the federal government soon followed. However, according to Parent, this

> did nothing with the Dominion Textile Company. They said, "No!" and "No!" and "No!" It was obvious that we had to organize some of their other mills, and at that time, since I was involved in the organization of the cotton mill workers from the organizing committee, I was asked to take on the job of organizing the workers in the Montreal cotton mills.

The process of organizing sounds deceptively simple in retrospect — sign members up and try to encourage a spirit of working together, of solidarity — but it could be gruelling and dangerous work.[14] It began simply enough, however, with visits to people's homes, to hear about their concerns and offer them information about the union. One of the features of the workforce at the cotton mills was that, unlike many factories, many of the workers were women and children, while the men tended to be concentrated in particular trades and in the mills' machine shop. Even at this early stage, Parent ran into ways in which the division of power and status between men and women might serve the interest of the owners by keeping workers divided, and she had to tackle it head on. Near the start of her effort,

> The mechanics responded, and there was an appeal by a minority amongst the mechanics that this be only a men's union. I explained that this is not a trade union but an industrial union, and we will *not* organize unless the women and children come in as well. And in fact, we wouldn't be recognized because we couldn't collect a majority from just the tradesmen. Then some of the better mechanics opened up. To even get *them* to open up, I had to ask them, "Where were the women in the strike of 1937?" Some remembered that they were very good on the picket line, and that they went after the women scabs,[15] that the men could not have handled them. It

was only six years later, less than six years later. "Where were they now?" "Oh, they were still there, in the plant." "Really?" So I got a number of names.

It was interesting when I went to visit those women strikers of '37. They were glad to be visited. It was showing them respect, because it was obvious that we weren't advanced.... They were quite proud to be approached, and joined in and recruited other people.

The workforce was not just adult women and men, however, but also children. The legal age to work in Quebec at that time was fourteen, which was young enough to be working full time in a cotton mill, but many were actually younger than this. Parent said,

When you consider that cotton mill workers were badly paid, poor, and — with the Church's influence — there were quite a lot of children in these families, they needed another salary. They would come in with the baptism certificate of an older sister or brother. It was easy for their bosses to find out whether they were as old as the paper said or not, but they didn't find out. They were quite willing to take them.

Parent remembered once when visiting workers outside a plant on their midnight meal break, she "met a little girl of ten on the night shift. She said, 'Yes, but I'm a big girl.' *[laugh]*" Another time, she met a group of young boys that hadn't gone back into the plant after the meal break at midnight. A boss had beaten one of the boys up and he did not want to go back in, but he also did not want to go home and face questions, so the others were keeping him company.

So I brought them to the police station and said, 'One of these children was beaten up.' Of course, that was none of their business. *[laugh]* They wouldn't go to the mill and find out who was responsible. But I said, 'Just let them sleep on the benches until six o'clock in the morning, so they can go home in the daylight.' Well, that was okay, and they looked after them.

In terms of children being a part of the union, Parent said,

Some of the traditional organizers said you couldn't organize children, but our experience was that in the cotton mills, the women workers protected the children, either from being molested by a foreman or by warning them about accidents in the plant where they might lose an arm or a leg or an eye. So when the women joined the union, the children gladly followed them. They joined and they followed the women in all of the meetings and all of the union activities.

After putting together a solid and committed group of members through easily hidden activities like home visits, it was time to turn to more visible tactics.

> That was only when we had a strong enough core of members in the mills, because we didn't want to get the company alerted, which meant they would start searching who would be the activists in the union as much possible. But once we had a fair core of people, then we would put out leaflets.

Under most circumstances, leafletting in Canada today is a pretty low-risk activity, but this was not the case in the Quebec of the 1940s.

> You had to figure out the time when the largest number [of workers] went into the mill, say, at entry, at the start of work at seven a.m. One must understand that in Montreal it was illegal to distribute any leaflets. It was under the anti-littering legislation. If you were there from twenty to seven until ten to seven, you'd probably beat the police, because by then the company guards had called the police and the police were after you. I was saved a couple of times when one militant young worker took to her heels as soon as the police came down the street. They said, "That's the one!" It wasn't at all, it was me. *[laugh]* I just moved in with the workers who were around the fence and they didn't recognize me. They went on a wild goose chase. If I would just move in amongst the workers and read one leaflet, having a bag or something — they all had a lunch pail or something — nobody would ever denounce me.

The journey from leaflets to a signed contract was neither short nor smooth. Parent became involved in the organizing in 1943. The Dominion Textile Company had three large cotton mills, a finishing plant, and a machine shop in Montreal, and the union won government certification in one after the other. But over the course of the organizing, the landscape of struggle changed in important ways: the province recovered its powers around labour issues from the federal government and, in 1944, "the government was changed and Maurice Duplessis, the notorious anti-labour government head, was back in power, and was working hand-in-hand with all the big corporations — including the Dominion Textile Company, of course."

The legislation that had evolved over the course of the war compelled employers to negotiate "in good faith" with certified unions in theory, but left a great deal of leeway about what that actually meant in practice. In addition, before workers could strike it was mandatory to go before a conciliation board or arbitration board, consisting of members appointed by the company, the union, and the government; these committees had no power to impose a settlement, just to convene the parties (Baillargeon 2005: 61). According to Parent, the legislation notwithstanding, "the company just wouldn't negotiate in any practical way."

According to another brief published account of this strike:

> The company had flatly refused to recognize the duly accredited union as a bargaining unit; neither did it agree to negotiate with it or its agents. The company systematically blocked the creation of the conciliation and arbitration committees by delaying the naming of their representatives until the very last minute, postponing the sessions under various pretexts (the company lawyer was often sick or travelling) and presenting dissident minority reports each time it disagreed with either of the committees.... Procrastination and repeated delays — even though the committees' decisions were not binding — were used to discourage the workers. Only unflinching energy and an intense organizing campaign could maintain solidarity and cohesion for so long among the pickers, the carders, the spinners, the winders, the slashers, the dyers, the weavers and the many others involved in cotton production. (ibid.: 61–62)

One of the outcomes of these aggressive tactics to delay and obstruct was that the arbitration boards for each plant were on widely different schedules. This meant that the ability to strike would be legal for each group of workers at different times. If, indeed, each plant struck at different times, production would never be completely shut down, and possibly the company could shift production to the other plants in turn and crush each strike separately. It was autumn of 1945, and Parent and the other leaders knew they must take action to address this potential weakness.

> So our rabbit punch — and of course the workers were exasperated — was to call a quick strike just on a Saturday morning in Montreal, at the three main Montreal mills and the general machine shop.... I had arranged in advance for an appointment with a Deputy Minister of Labour. Kent went into Quebec City while I was helping to keep the strike organized. By one p.m. or so he had a promise from the government. It ran this way: it was all negotiated with the Deputy Minister of Labour, who would get the agreement from the Minister of Labour ... that all of the proceedings toward getting a contract would come under the single so-called arbitration board, which at that time — and that was the only one — had a good judge. When

I say "good judge," he was independent of Duplessis. That's what it meant. Because many of them were just his agents.

So we were able to unite the proceedings, which would bring us to a legal strike date later on. When this was announced to the members, they understood immediately what it meant, of course. And they endorsed the decision and went back to work on the Sunday night and Monday morning.

The strike began on June 1, 1946. Parent and the union faced not just the company, but the provincial government and the Catholic Church as well. Early in the strike, for example, "Duplessis falsely declared the strike illegal [in Valleyfield but not in Montreal] since the workers had not gone through the different steps of conciliation and arbitration" (Baillargeon 2005: 62). And in July, according to Parent,

> the company applied to the courts to have an injunction against the strike. I remember the judge called me *"une pétroleuse,"* which recalls the women bearing petrol in the early time of the revolution in France,[16] and that the judge fell asleep when the company witness was testifying. The judge refused to give a decision. When he was put on the spot by the company, he said if he were forced to do so he would have no choice but to rule for the union. Refusing to render a decision was really the bravest thing a judge could do, because if he ruled against the company he would likely have been sent up to the north country by Duplessis.

Though the company applied its obstructive tactics to negotiations during the early part of the strike, by the end of July a settlement had been negotiated. Unfortunately, due to what Parent termed "a technicality," it was offered only to the workers at the Montreal locations.

> We got the Valleyfield workers to agree, in meeting, to allow the workers in Montreal to accept that contract. When [the president of Dominion Textile] Blair Gordon got the news, he didn't want to sign any more, but of course in those days, even when a businessman gave his solemn word, if he went back on it — it wasn't like it is with George Bush today — he'd lose face completely. So he was persuaded to sign anyway, in Montreal. But then all of the attack was on the Valleyfield workers.

It was in Valleyfield that the Church was most active in trying to undermine the union. In fact, as Parent described, their efforts to do so began years before the strike itself.

Valleyfield had a cathedral and a bishop and auxiliary bishop, who was the pastor of the cathedral. Altogether there were four parishes in Valleyfield. The auxiliary bishop was Monsignor Paul-Émile Léger, who subsequently was appointed by [Pope] Pious XII as Cardinal over Quebec, and a pro-company man if you ever found one. He would preach regularly against the strike and the union, and against us personally. He just put everything into his campaign. We had some Catholic youth organizations in those days which were — first of all, they thought there were nationalists, but they were right-wing Catholic youth, completely misled by Léger.

Léger had organized one riot against us, in '44 I think it was, where they surrounded us. We were at a meeting. They sacked our union hall and they surrounded the city hall where we were meeting in. This carried on for hours, until after midnight. Somebody had called the provincial police. They came, but they stayed out of town until the riot died out. Bishop Léger came on the streets at twelve o'clock, congratulated them on their patriotism and their faith, and turned around and went home. After twelve o'clock, some of the parents of these youths were roaming the streets looking for their sons. They found them surrounding our building. *[laugh]* Many of these parents were members of a union, and others were maybe not in the mill but they knew what the mill was all about. They just grabbed the kids and brought them home. So, it was difficult. But we survived and rebuilt, because we had a core that were good, and with them we rebuilt.

During the strike of '46, it was on August 13 — just less than two weeks after the settlement in Montreal — that the Church had been building up and building up a group of scabs whom they invited to go to Mass every morning. There was a leaflet that said — in each of the four parishes — "When we will be numerous enough, one of our priests will lead each group toward the mill, where the police will take charge and bring you through." So this was the third day, when scabs were being led in that way, and people decided, no, this has got to stop. At our meetings the wives and mothers of strikers attended, too. Nearly everybody had worked in the mill at one time or another, and most of these wives and mothers had worked there. So the women got working. In those days the iceman delivered, the milkman delivered, the baker delivered, and they put them all to work telling everybody where they went, "We meet at eleven o'clock at the factory gates." Because the scabs had to come at twelve and go in as one and go to work. So by the time just before noon hour came around, there were 5,000[17] people around the mill gates — women, boys of fourteen or over, not little girls, and the strikers, of course.

> And friends. The police fired tear gas on the strikers and the strikers responded by throwing rocks, but never threw a rock except after a tear gas volley. At least one striker grabbed a tear gas canister with his bare hands and threw it back into the building the police were firing from, forcing them to relocate upstairs. And so we broke the back of the Church and scab movement at that point. And also, you see, one of the features of the Valleyfield strike was that they never got any scabs in the mill for those two months.

Soon after that, Rowley was arrested and held in a Montreal jail, where he remained until the strike was over, but Parent and the leaders among the workers continued on. Finally, in late September, the company had no choice but to make a serious offer to the Valleyfield workers.

But the union was still concerned because of the powerful, coordinated opposition from the company, the provincial government, and a newly proposed "company union" — a technique sometimes used by companies to undermine militant unions, in which a nominally independent organization is created that is actually controlled in some way by the company. This was of concern because

> one of the conditions was that we had to submit to a vote against the company union, a secret ballot vote. We thought we were strong enough to do it, and our strike committee had met for a whole night long, discussing the offer, in writing, of the Minister of Labour.... Well, our troubles weren't over because the government sent the election chair with his crew of twelve men to Valleyfield the day before the vote, to negotiate. Of course the negotiations didn't come out as we wanted, because, if you look at it, at each poll the company had the government vote supervisor, the company representative, and the scab union representative. We had only one person, and the voting lasted over twelve hours, so no person could stand there [to prevent the ballot boxes from being stuffed] without even going to the washroom. So that had to be negotiated.
>
> Then there was a warrant out for me that day. I went into hiding while the union lawyers were negotiating. The police were looking for me in different houses. I was in one of the workers' houses, which they didn't come to; we figured they'd miss that one. They negotiated in Montreal for $500 bail if I showed up. So I got from Valleyfield to Montreal and over the bridge without the police catching me. I was released on $500 bail and I got back to Valleyfield during the mass meeting, just before the vote. I announced that we wouldn't let them get away with stealing our vote. People were then more convinced that Duplessis planned to steal the vote. If I

hadn't been arrested, that would have been different. Some would still have suspected him, but then, just about everyone knew that he was trying to steal the vote.

I got back to the union office with people following, of course, and phoned the election chair. I said, "I want to see you."

"Oh. I have withdrawn for the night."

I said, "I'm sorry, but you better get down into the lobby because I'm going over with one of our committee men, and we want to negotiate the way in which the balloting will be held."

So I go down there. He's got his twelve men behind him, lined up, and he's adamant that he's not changing, and I'm explaining. Then suddenly I start hearing some singing in the street. It was the union women marching toward the hotel. They had these big windows, you know. They serenaded us until he agreed. *[laugh]* So we had two scrutineers instead of one.

When the balloting was finished, the ballot boxes very carefully were brought over to the courthouse, where they were counted. I had people all around — the union office was opposite the city hall, and the marketplace was there — waiting for the results. And I got a phone call from the mayor of Valleyfield.

"What's the problem?"

"Well," he said, "the government, the chair of the elections, has a problem."

"What is it?" I said.

He said, "There's 1,500 cyclists around the courthouse." *[laugh]* "He can't go home."

He intended to run off and not let us know the results. And of course our scrutineers would've known individually the results from their poll, but Duplessis would have fixed it even then. So I said, "After what's happened, you can understand there is a problem."

He said, "Yes."

I said, "Look, if you can give me, on your word of honour, the results, when you get them, phone me." (I said all of this in a loud enough voice for the people around me to know exactly what was going on.) "Phone me, and we will see what we can do."

So he phoned me later on, gave me the results. We had won. I repeated the results out loud so everybody would hear. A couple of people went and told the people around the courthouse to come down to the marketplace and union hall, we had results. You didn't have to tell them much. They understood. It took another couple of months to negotiate the contracts, but they were stuck. They had to sign. At that stage the government had to let it happen.

After 100 days on the picket line for the workers in Valleyfield, they had won. It was an historic victory. The workers made gains and the union was officially recognized by the company. Moreover, though attention more often focuses on the strike of miners in Asbestos, Quebec, in 1949,[18] the Dominion Textile strike of 1946 was also an important early contribution to the processes that led to the seismic shifts in Quebec society that have been called the Quiet Revolution. It did not reach the level of government until 1960, with the election of Jean Lesage's Liberals, but already ordinary people in Quebec, as well as liberal intellectuals and progressives within the Church, were straining against the triple repressions of English-Canadian capital, a conservative social structure dominated by conservatives within the Church, and the repression of Maurice Duplessis.

Parent's union went on to another major strike in 1947, this one at the Ayers Woollen Mill in Lachute, Quebec, which got Parent arrested multiple times and eventually charged with seditious conspiracy — a charge that corrupt courts dominated by Duplessis were able to keep alive for eight years before they were finally dismissed (Scher 1992: 136–141).

Unfortunately, the most immediate gains from the Dominion Textile strike of 1946 were short-lived. The union was forced into a strike in 1952 and then crushed by the company and the government with the added antiworker momentum provided by the Cold War and right-wing forces within the U.S.-dominated labour movement. Parent and Rowley were expelled from their union. However, they continued their significant involvement in worker struggles by founding the Confederation (later Council) of Canadian Unions, which became a small but vibrant coalition that waged a number of ideologically important struggles in later years and was a persistent spur in the side of the larger unions and labour centrals in the country to become more accountable to their Canadian members and more progressive in their orientation. As mentioned at the start of the chapter, Parent also became very involved with the women's movements in Canada and Quebec.

Perhaps one key to Parent's skilful navigation of conflict, to her decades of weathering defeats like 1952 as well as victories like 1946, has been the same impulse that has driven her decades of involvement in struggle — the impulse to prioritize people over things. Kent Rowley liked to quote U.S. socialist leader Eugene Debs, who famously said, "No strike is ever lost" — a comment about how even a strike that does not win its demands can still teach ordinary people about our power to act collectively in the face of those who try to exert power over us (Salutin 1980: 14–15).

Parent observed,

> I found that members in Quebec and elsewhere were very responsive to the call to organize and willing to tell the story of their exploita-

tion. In many cases I found that after joining the union, no matter how difficult the struggles, active workers, and especially women, would become aware they had rights but they had to go out and fight for those rights. They saw things in a different light. In a very sad meeting at a difficult time, one woman spoke up and said, "There's something they can never take away from me now: I used to go to work in fear but now I know that I'm a person with rights, and nobody can take that away from me."

Notes

1. Parent passed away on March 12, 2012.
2. Mulay was also one of the interview participants in this project — see Chapter 4.
3. Parent's life has been documented more than most of the activists I interviewed. See for example Hogue 1986, Scher 1992: 136–141, Parent 2000, and Lévesque 2005.
4. To hear some of Parent's memories of this meeting, go to www.talkingradical.ca/audio/parent_nac.mp3.
5. See the works of Karl Marx, of course, but many others as well. See Holloway 2005 for a more recent version of this thesis. Holloway also uses (much more lyrically than I) the example of his book as a thing that stands in for and obscures a social flow of doing.
6. Given the interconnectedness of apparently disparate aspects of social relations, I would argue that almost every book listed in the References section that focuses on critical analysis of different aspects of Canada's past and present could play a role in developing a complete answer to these questions, even books that do not necessarily take them up directly.
7. The material in the following paragraphs which talks about the role of the violence of primitive accumulation in creating or enhancing other oppressive relations that persist (in shifting forms) to today is drawn most directly from Federici 2004, unless otherwise noted. For more on the changes and intensification in patriarchal relations that have come along with capitalism, see also Mies 1998, and for one take on the intertwined character of relations of reproduction and relations of production in the Canadian context, see Ursel 1992. For a sample of some of the ways the co-evolution of capitalist relations of production and relations of white supremacy have been written about — some of which also pay significant attention to gender while others do not, and some of which deal with the transition to capitalism but many of which focus on more recent eras — see also Sakai 1989, Roediger 1991, Das Gupta 1996, McNally 2006, Galabuzi 2006, Thobani 2007, and Goldberg 2009.
8. Note that this is not arguing that racism or any other oppressive social relation can be reduced to mere expressions of capitalism, as some on the left have argued in the past. That position (and the analogous positions that reduce everything else to patriarchy or everything else to white supremacy) leads to all sorts of political problems and oppressive practices. Rather, all of these relations inter-

sect and interact with each other, and in significant ways happen through each other, but they are not the same. Even when the historical origins of particular relations are deeply enmeshed, such as with capitalist relations of production and relations of white supremacy, the ways they shape our lives and the ways they are socially organized make it quite clear that one cannot be reduced to the other.

9. Mass trials of women were happening in the Basque region. Fishermen were absent for an extended period during cod season, but they cut their annual trip short when they heard rumours of the persecution of their wives, daughters, and mothers. They returned home and liberated a convoy of "witches" being taken to the place where the burnings happened. This act of resistance had the effect of ending the series of mass trials in the region (Federici 2004: 189).

10. Grace-Edward Galabuzi writes that in expressions such as "racialized groups," the language of racialization "denotes that process of imposition" in which "minority status" gets imposed on racially marked populations through "the social construction of the [racial] category, and the attendant experience of oppression" that results (2006: xvi n. 1). To say that some aspect of social relations is racialized is to point out that it reflects and reproduces such socially constructed categories and attendant oppressions.

11. Much of the otherwise unreferenced material in this section is drawn from Palmer 1992. For an important source on struggles by radical workers in Canada in the early twentieth century, see McKay 2008.

12. The Knights of Labor were an early example of a trade union that tried to unite all workers, both skilled and unskilled; it also had elements of a political reform society, a religious brotherhood, and a service club.

13. For a conventional lay history of the Depression that includes discussion of Duplessis and the Padlock Law, see Berton 2001. For a more detailed study of the struggle against the Padlock Law, albeit one that is not particularly sympathetic to the desire for radical social change, see Lambertson 2005: 16–67. For a conventional history that includes plenty of material on Duplessis and the Union Nationale see Quinn 1979.

14. To hear Parent talk about some of her memories of this organizing work, go to www.talkingradical.ca/audio/parent_organizing.mp3.

15. Slang for workers used to replace other workers who are on strike.

16. *Les pétroleuses* were supposedly working-class women who supported the revolutionary Paris Commune of 1871 and who used gasoline to burn down many buildings as government troops retook the city. However, research has shown this appears to be a myth started after the fact by elite politicians to discredit the Communards. In the aftermath of the defeat of the Commune, no women were convicted of arson, and most of the major instances of the destruction of buildings by fire have been explained in other ways. For more about the struggle around the Paris Commune see, for example, Gullickson 1996 and Tombs 2008.

17. Estimates vary, of course. Baillargeon (2005: 64) reports 2,000.

18. For an account of the pivotal Asbestos struggle, see Isbester 1974.

Chapter 3

Women Against Violence (Part I)
Lee Lakeman on Feminist Anti-Violence Activism in Woodstock and Vancouver

As I biked from my sister's apartment on Commercial Drive toward the area of Vancouver where Lee Lakeman lived, I did three things: I stopped frequently to check my map, because I am perennially on the verge of getting lost even in my own city let alone when I am someplace new; I enjoyed the bright summer sun in the absence of the oppressive heat and humidity that often accompany it in southern Ontario, where I lived at the time; and I worried about the interview. I worried because Lakeman's was the first interview I was to do after making the move from vaguely defined interest to concrete, committed project — I had already done a few back in Ontario without knowing how I would use them, but this was the first irrevocable step by a very little-feeling me on a very big-seeming journey.

Lakeman's neighbourhood was full of small, older homes. I remember the streets being quiet, almost empty, and the gardens seeming very green. I locked up the bike I had borrowed from my sister's partner and knocked on Lakeman's door. She welcomed me in, made some tea, and we sat down to talk.

Lakeman's social movement involvement began in the early 1970s, as feminists across many nations began to talk about violence against women and to act by equipping their movements to respond in organized ways to this violence through shelters and hotlines and efforts to force patriarchal institutions to change their practices. Lakeman was involved in founding a shelter for battered women in the small city of Woodstock, Ontario, and was one of the women whose energy pushed it from its beginnings as an urgent conversation over lunch, through to a phone line in one woman's living room, and on to a functioning organization that had an impact on the political life of the community. In 1978, she moved to Vancouver and soon became involved with the Vancouver Rape Relief collective, which she has been a part of ever since. In Vancouver's vibrant feminist scene, she was a part of Take Back The Night actions, direct actions to confront abusers, and long, hard struggles to respond to right-wing provincial governments. She has also been vigorous in her work as part of the anti-rape movement at the national level, with the Canadian Association of Sexual Assault Centres.

Tea, Embodiedness, and Violence

My first jolt of recognition that I would have to read and think about the stories I heard from the activists I interviewed with some reference to my own experience of the world, even though it was years before it occurred to me that it would make sense to write about them in this way too, might well have been over the tea during my meeting with Lakeman. Like I said, Lakeman made some for us. She put on a kettle, got us each a mug, and when the water had boiled she set a pot to steeping. After a suitable interval, she poured herself some, slowly drank it as the interview progressed, and then poured herself some more. It was only at this point that I realized that my mug remained dry. Partly this late realization was because my interest in tea was superficial at best, as part of the informal ritual of welcome and hospitality but only peripherally for the tea per se. But upon later reflection, I realized that it was also because I had, on some level, assumed that she would pour the tea for me. It's what I do when I make tea for visitors, and it is part of how that little bit of human theatre usually plays out, in my experience.

Of course I have no idea why she chose not to do so. Perhaps it was because she had no way to know how strong I like my tea and I'm a grown-up so I could pour my own when it had steeped enough for my taste, end of story. But it also occurred to me later that this might have been an act with deliberate politics to it.

Unwaged service to others, including the work of hospitality, tends to fall mostly on women. The assumptions that underlie this are probably much older, but it is certainly related to the reorganization of women's lives and work that was touched on in the last chapter and the production of distinct public and private spheres in European and Euro-American societies. Women were largely pushed out of the former and confined in the latter. This confinement of women's activities to the private sphere was never complete, particularly for the many white and racialized working-class women who had no choice but to earn money, but the pressure in that direction served as a powerful norm that organized dominant ways of judging and regulating women. This meant that unwaged work of direct benefit to other people in their immediate environment shifted from something that was organized in gendered ways but was integral to the lives of ordinary people of all genders into something that was decisively "women's work," with associated social consequences for women who could not or would not take up this work to patriarchal satisfaction. Meeting the everyday needs of men and higher status women was, and often still is, a core expectation for women, including much of the labour and ritual of hospitality. Some men of younger generations do take on more of this work than their fathers or grandfathers, but the gendered expectation and burden persists. Understood in this context, Lakeman's choices could be seen as embodying a way to still demonstrate welcome and courtesy — and I want to emphasize that I did not experience this as being at all unwelcoming or discourteous — but to do so in ways that break with historical patterns of enforced domestic servility and deference by women.

Even if my speculations on this point are somewhere close to the truth of things, I'm not foolish enough to think that it was intended as an act of communication — that is, an act that was in some way for my benefit — rather than someone making choices so as to be true to herself and her politics. Nonetheless, noticing compelled me to seek potential political meaning, which had the effect of drawing me — the embodied me who moves through the world as a man, among other experiences of social relations that have led to much unearned privilege and a particular vantage from which to see the world — into the orbit of the stories and ideas being discussed in a very real way. The politics of our conversation became for me not just something "out there" but also, just as much, something "right here."

I belabour this point because I think it is very relevant to the ways in which most of us (particularly men but lots of women as well, in my experience) respond to the phenomenon of violence against women. It is not shrouded in silence and invisibility to the extent that it once was — thanks in large part to the decades of work by the movement of which Lakeman has been a part — and many more people now than four decades ago see that it exists and see it is an issue that requires political intervention rather than being a purely personal cross to bear.

And yet.

And yet there is a disconnect almost everywhere, almost all of the time — a refusal to see or a refusal to understand or resistance grounded in privilege and ideology. This violence surrounds us, shapes us, but we refuse to see it. Which is true of many issues raised in this book, I suppose, but this one is particularly galling to me because regardless of our individual experiences of gender or violence or gendered violence, every single one of us already has people in our lives whose experiences in this area might shock us into feeling the horror it deserves if only the experiences could be safely shared, if only they were heard, if only they were understood politically rather than just as individual misfortune or pathology. And yet they are often not safe to share even with loved ones. All too often, gendered violence is treated as shameful — it will not be heard, it will not be believed, it will be dismissed as a rare exception, the victim/survivor will be blamed. Even many pro-feminist men, even some self-identified feminists, even some women for whom this is an everyday/everynight experience can remain disconnected from the social magnitude of the horror of it. For some this is a tactic to be able to keep on functioning in the face of it, but all of us are subjected to the ways this violence is constantly downplayed, reframed, undermined, and suppressed in public discourse even if it is no longer as easy to completely deny its existence.[1]

Denying Violence Against Women

Outright denial manages to remain a common way in which disconnection from the magnitude and political significance of violence against women manifests. Some people say it is not a problem, or not a real problem, or not a big problem. They quibble about methodology or semantics to draw attention from forest to trees, or they refuse to admit even the possibility that social relations of power might have some bearing on the issue of violence against women.

Yet at this point, outright denial is little more than blatant self-deception. The best national-level data collection on violence against women in Canada was done in 1993 by Statistics Canada. It found that 51 percent of Canadian women had experienced at least one incident of physical or sexual violence since the age of sixteen, and of those women at least 60 percent had experienced more than one such incident (Federal-Provincial-Territorial Ministers Responsible for the Status of Women 2002: 10). The number of these women who had experienced violence at the hands of men known to them was more than twice the number who had experienced violence at the hands of a stranger (ibid.). More recent evidence collected by Statistics Canada via less specialized (and potentially less sensitive) instruments indicates that the prevalence of violence against women may have decreased very slightly since that time, but it is not at all clear that this reflects a real change rather than a shift in methodology, and when seen in light of the increasing demand for emergency shelter spaces by women fleeing male violence over that same period it is hardly a cause for optimism (ibid.: 13).

Almost 60 percent of victims of sexual assaults that were reported to the police in 1998 were younger than eighteen years of age (Tremblay 1998: 6). More than half of girls under sixteen in Canada have reported unwanted sexual attention, including 24 percent who have experienced sexual assault and 17 percent who have experienced incest (Holmes and Silverman 1992). Researchers have estimated that 83 percent of women with disabilities will be sexually assaulted in their lifetimes and that 92 percent of women experiencing absolute homelessness have experienced severe physical or sexual violence at some point in their lives (Stimpson and Best 1991; Josephson 2005: 83). There are many different specificities to the ways in which women who are differently placed within social relations experience violence, including particular barriers faced by racialized women, immigrant women, indigenous women, and queer women, and a disproportionate targeting of indigenous and other racialized women by both men and by the state (Amnesty International [Canada] 2004; A. Smith 2005; Sokoloff and Pratt 2005; Incite! Women of Color Against Violence 2006).

A frequent tactic from those who practice blatant denial is to try and obscure the realities of the gendered ways that sexual assault and violence function in the real world. Those who use this tactic often look to particular strands of academic research and even to the more recent Statistics Canada surveys on the subject that reduce complex real-world relations to decontextualized numbers that claim to show some level of parity across genders in terms of the experience of violence. A close examination of these numbers shows that to be a gross distortion (e.g., DeKeseredy and MacLeod 1997: 63; Jiwani 2000; Sev'er 2002: 37–39). Analysis of the Statistics Canada findings, for example, shows that its methodology excludes a number of the most vulnerable groups of women and that it does not include the full spectrum of violence and abuse experienced by women. Most importantly, it collects and analyzes data in ways that distort the context in which violence happens: Use of violence by women is most often in self-defence, and women tend to experience violence that is more frequent and more severe, that more often results in physical injury, and that has more severe psychological and emotional impacts that work in concert with other forms of social marginalization of women to keep them under the control of the men and institutions that abuse them (Jiwani 2000).

Researcher Yasmin Jiwani (ibid.), in refuting these attempts to obscure gender relations in the experience of violence, points out that Canada is

> a country where 3.4 wives are murdered for every one husband killed (Locke 2000), and where previous statistics reveal that 98% of sexual assaults and 86% of violent crimes are committed by men (Johnson 1996); where women constitute 98% of spousal violence victims of sexual assault, kidnapping or hostage taking (Fitzgerald 1999); and where 80% of victims of criminal harassment are women while 90% of the accused are men (Kong 1996).

For me, however, the strongest evidence of how completely deluded are those who outright deny the existence or severity or gendered character of violence against women is what I have heard from women in my own life. *Almost every woman with whom I am close enough to know this sort of thing has experienced some form of physical violence or sexual violence from a man.* The relatively smaller proportion of men I know who have experienced violence have mostly experienced it in much different contexts — in particular, the contexts tend to be much less intimate and the violence much less likely to be sexualized, especially for violence experienced by men as adults — and still those committing the violence have mostly been other men.[2]

In most spaces that I hang around, though, blatant denial is pretty rare. For me personally, for whatever reason, it has never been something I've bought into — perhaps a by-product of previously witnessing some troubling gendered exertions of power and knowing I didn't much like it even if I lacked analysis of it at the time. What has been much more common for myself and for many other people I have observed in broadly defined progressive spaces might be thought of as the "Oh, yes, it definitely happens. Yes, it's a very bad thing. What's for lunch?" approach. In other words, we admit the existence of gendered violence and declare our opposition to it in an abstract sense, but never quite get around to engaging with it personally or politically.

There are very few spaces that I have been a part of — including social movements where most people would understand themselves to be feminist or pro-feminist — where gendered violence is an issue that gets talked about, where information and analysis about it coming from people who have focused their political work around it is available and treated as central to understanding the world, and where people regularly and explicitly ask themselves and each other, "What does this mean for what we do?" With a few rare exceptions, I have never been in a social space with all men or with mixed genders where the topic of the violence experienced by women was discussed thoroughly, respectfully, and with political insight. Generally speaking, men do not speak about it at all or it comes up in ways that are, to put it mildly, unhelpful. My sense is that beyond a particular subset that are explicitly feminist, there are also plenty of barriers to a thorough engagement with the topic in many spaces that are constituted by all or mostly women. I suspect that one of those barriers is the way in which relations of power and oppression inevitably organize limits to the safety within any group that supposed sameness can create, at least for the more marginalized individuals and groups within that group.

I think another important barrier that keeps a lot of us from really wrestling with politicized understandings of the violence experienced by women (and with other facets of gendered relations of power) is the way they cut right through the middle of the most intimate settings in most of our lives — family (conventional or self-made) and sexuality and desire — in ways that other relations of power are less likely to do for most of us. Those intimate spaces are still shaped by all of the axes of privilege and oppression, but since our social networks are often quite segregated by things like race and class, embodied differences along those axes in intimate spaces are a lot less common (though still important where they occur) than differences in gendered power. And, obviously, settings of kinship and partnership are of utmost importance to us. They can be important spaces of relative safety in a white supremacist world for people who experience racism, and they can be a central institution for people who are able to do so to access certain aspects of privilege. And they are crucial sites in which we discover, define, and see ourselves reflected. All of which means that, for most of us, engaging seriously with gendered relations of power, including violence against women, means opening up for critical appraisal, questioning, and challenge the interpersonal spaces and relationships that are at the heart of who we are. There is obviously a powerful incentive to avoid this opening up, even in many cases for people who experience gender oppression.[3]

For men, a particular consequence flowing from this technique of avoiding the issue — acknowledgement with no or superficial engagement — is that it makes it easier for us to avoid asking hard questions about how we ourselves benefit from and participate in the oppression of women. Even many men who identify as "activist" and/or "pro-feminist" have engaged in behaviours that should be understood as contributing to the violence and sexual violation experienced by women. Leaving aside for a moment the more spectacular violations, all of us need to be asking ourselves how we might be engaging in behaviours that are not violent themselves but that are more mundane, everyday instances of the same social dynamics — from talking over women in meetings to depending on women for caretaking that allows us to avoid really dealing with our own (socially produced) emotional baggage to falling into the infamous objectifying gaze. The problem of supposedly progressive men avoiding engagement with these issues is not just an individualized problem to be seen in moralistic terms, but a fundamental barrier to building movements that will change the world; it is the relationships that are in part shaped by these behaviours that will or will not build the groups that will or will not build the movements that will or will not result in radical social change.

A final way that some people develop only partial engagement with the issue is through paying attention *only* to gender. More and more people in North America — particularly some radical indigenous women and women of colour who, in their political work, prioritize violence experienced by women — have been advancing politics that draw attention to the ways in which gendered violence works as a component of other relations of oppression, on the one hand, and how violence against women who are oppressed along axes other than gender cannot be understood or dealt with adequately in a political way by talking and organizing only around gender (Razack 1998; Bannerji 1999; Sokoloff and Pratt 2005; A. Smith 2005; Incite! Women of Color Against Violence 2006). Responding to the violence in the lives of indigenous women and women of colour requires challenging not only the violence done by individual men against individual women, but challenging as an integral part of the work the ongoing gendered violence of colonization and the attacks on indigenous and other racialized communities by the settler state through police, the courts, the education system, and so on. This is in contrast with certain more mainstream ways of thinking about gendered violence that focus only on the interpersonal dimension or on the interpersonal plus certain institutional aspects that are most narrowly about gender and that see little problem with responding to gendered violence by empowering the settler state.

Women Resurgent

We've already seen that resistance to gender oppression on Turtle Island began not within the settler society but against it. Additionally, some indigenous women have pointed out that the relatively autonomous and powerful roles women played in many indigenous nations served as a source and an inspiration for the early challenges by settler women against patriarchal social relations in their own societies. Within the settler society itself, perhaps the most clearly remembered facet of the early stages of women organizing against gender oppression was the effort by women to win the right to vote in the late nineteenth and early twentieth centuries. The first organization focused on women's suffrage in Canada was formed in Toronto in 1876. By 1922, women had the vote at the federal level and in every province except Quebec (Adamson, Briskin, and McPhail 1988: 30-37; Griffin Cohen 1993). Many of the women active in this struggle were middle-class white women, at least some of whom understood their involvement in social change activity in terms of the social gospel movement[4] that was prominent in some branches of Protestant Christianity in the early twentieth century. They may have been active as well in issues such as temperance, the promotion of peace, and others, which many also understood as tightly intertwined with their feminism. For some, however, this coexisted with clear support for empire and racism (Valverde 1991).

African Canadian women and working-class white women were also politically active in this era and organized in the context of Canada's Black communities and white working-class, and consequently grounded their pro-women politics in ways different from the more visible pro-suffrage activists. Black women in Canada had been organizing to meet the needs of their communities in practical and political ways and against slavery and racism for as long as there have been Black women in this part of the world. Labour struggles and socialist organizing by women persisted in the face of indifference or even hostility by the mainstream of the labour and (sometimes) socialist movements. And many of these women were active in suffrage activities as well, either individually or collectively (Adamson, Briskin, and McPhail 1988: 30-37; Bristow et al. 1994; Kealey 1998).

The so-called "first wave" of the feminist movement is commonly understood to have ended with the victory of the franchise for most (white) women in Canada in 1922, or perhaps with the decision by the British Privy Council in 1929 that (white) women could be legally admitted to the category of "person." There is then presumed to have been a great void until the upsurge of the women's liberation movement in the late 1960s. This is not accurate, however. A number of important organizations that had their roots in early organizing by women such as the Canadian Federation of University Women and the YWCA continued their work through the intervening years.

Quebec women won the vote in 1941 and the first laws around equal pay were instituted in the 1950s (Griffin Cohen 1993: 3). As we saw in Chapter 2, struggles by women in the context of waged work were happening through those years as well. In 1960, women from across the country, initially impelled by the threat of nuclear war, came together to form an organization called Voice of Women, which went on to play a crucial role in both the peace movement and the women's movement (Rebick 2005: 3–5). And in the early 1960s, under editor Doris Anderson, the mass-market magazine *Chateleine* was regularly printing feminist content (Griffin Cohen 1993: 4; Rebick 2005: 5–6). The first organization explicitly by and for immigrant women of colour formed in Toronto in 1958, but as the next chapter shall explore more fully, it is only much more recently that such organizations have decided that strategic engagement with the mainstream of the women's movement was a useful focus for their energy.

There is no doubt that the late 1960s and early 1970s saw a massive resurgence of feminist organizing in Canada. The 1960s were a decade of popular uprisings of all sorts around the world, from national liberation struggles in many countries that had been colonized by European powers, to renewed labour militancy and struggles against war and racial oppression (Dubinsky et al. 2009). In many ways, at least until around 1968, Canada did not experience as much visible upheaval as many other places (Kostash 1980; Palmer 2009). However, there were at least three strands of activity that fed into creating a visible, national women's liberation movement.

One was the ongoing evolution of the Voice of Women, which had always placed an emphasis on the role of women in changing the world but which became more explicit in advancing clearly feminist politics. A second strand was the increased activity from the older institutional expressions of earlier feminisms in seeking women's rights as the sixties progressed. In particular, these older groups were key in pressuring for a Royal Commission on the Status of Women, which was appointed in early 1967 after extensive lobbying. The Royal Commission served as a focus for organizing by feminists across the country and across the movement's political spectrum, which helped to create a sense of national feminist momentum. In 1970 the Commission delivered its report with a set of recommendations that, while inevitably incomplete and partial, served to galvanize much more organizing across Canada in the following years.

Perhaps the most crucial element in creating a new sense of energy and radicalism was the wave of grassroots organizing by young women. Many of these women, at least at first, had already been politicized in other social movement spaces. In those groups, organizations, and movements they faced sexism no less relentless than in society at large, and an unwillingness by the supposedly radical men that dominated those spaces to take women's issues seriously (Kostash 1980: 166–187; Rebick 2005: 7–13). This was true in the student movement, the peace movement, the movement for Quebec sovereignty, movements against racism, socialist organizations, and many more. Different women made different decisions about how to act on this new consciousness; some fought for changes in how these groups operated, some for women's spaces or collectives within these other groups from which to more effectively pressure for feminist change, and others left these other movements completely and devoted themselves entirely to women's liberation. Some did all three. This created a resonance with many other young women who had never been active in other social movements before but felt that fateful "Click!" and decided that now was the time to take up the struggle for their own liberation in collective ways.

A final key element that shaped how the women's movement re-emerged in the 1960s and 1970s was the response by the Canadian state to the social movements of that era, including the women's liberation movement. The details varied but a general pattern of the early part of Prime Minister Pierre Trudeau's reign was a willingness to grant certain kinds of reforms demanded by movements and to provide funding for certain kinds of activities. This flexibility created an opening for the women's movement and other movements to make certain kinds of gains and to acquire resources that could be put toward struggle for other gains. However, the relationship between social movements and the state was always uneasy, and working in partnership with the state and accepting funding from it always carried the spectre of co-option and subtle (or not-so-subtle) shaping of the movement's agenda by the state (Kostash 1980; Ng 1990; Schreader 1990).

Lakeman

Lakeman grew up in a working-class white family in Hamilton, Ontario. There were members of Lakeman's family with a background in radical politics — a grandfather who was a prominent member of the Communist Party of Canada at one time and an uncle who had been involved in the anarchist-inspired Catholic organization known as the Catholic Worker Movement.[5] However, she knew neither of these men directly as a child and in her family context their politics were not treated with much respect. In addition, from what she learned growing up and since, neither of these men showed any particular consciousness of gender oppression. Rather, as has been so crucial in the context of the women's movement, Lakeman identifies the source of her politicization much more in her own personal experience.

> At twenty-one when I was a student at Ryerson [Polytechnical Institute in Toronto] in journalism, I got pregnant. I had been dating an African foreign student, and suddenly found myself pregnant

with a Black baby-to-come with a lover who was about to go back to Africa, and I had no way of supporting myself or this baby. Certainly nobody imagined a single parent being a journalist, which is what the plan had been up until then. I knew no woman who had kept a child who wasn't married. I didn't even know *of* a woman who had kept a child, at that point. Never mind crossing the race barrier, and this was in the era of the movie *Guess Who's Coming to Dinner*— a little before that, and several classes below that. So it was a very politicizing experience.

I learned quickly on the streets of Toronto what people thought of a white woman being with a Black man. And I learned very quickly what little social support there was for women who wanted to keep the child, or for a child who needed support. I quickly became one of the young women who said to her history professor, "Yes, I'd love to come to the study group, and yes, I'd love to be part of your Marxist configuration, but I don't have child care."… And very quickly I found myself out of school and at home with a small baby. And that meant in the slums and on welfare. So that was one part of the lesson.

Another element of that lesson occurred after Lakeman's social worker told her that she would be "stealing from the poorest people in the country" if she worked under the table and didn't declare the extra income in order to save. Lakeman agreed that it "wasn't ethical" and decided she wouldn't do it.

Until that worker disappeared. When I asked where she was, I discovered that she had been able to get a student loan, and so she had taken her earnings from the welfare department and she went to Europe to spend her pay before she would start living on the interest-free student loan and bursary that came from the same tax dollars. At that point I learned a very, very big lesson about social workers, about class, about savings, about honesty, and about political struggle. And I never looked back, really. I decided never to be a social worker, never to be part of anything like it, not to lie to people who were poor, to understand peoples' individual adaptations to the horrible situations they were in, and I learned to fight, seriously fight. And devil take the hindmost.

Lakeman ended up attending teacher's college, though toward the end of that experience seeing a film by Ivan Illich called *Deschooling Society* made her realize she could not work for the long term in the compulsory schooling system. She moved to Woodstock, Ontario, and did some supply teaching, but ended up getting removed from the supply list for refusing in a health and sex education class to endorse the use of feminine hygiene spray by young women. This helped catapult her into involvement with feminists in Woodstock. Lakeman encountered an ad in the local newspaper about some women who were forming a consciousness raising group. Women across North America were participating in such groups in the early seventies and they were a key form of feminist organizing in that era. Small groups of women would get together to talk about their lives. In the process of doing so, they would discover the many ways in which their experiences were shared by other women and come to political and collective understandings of their oppression. Though later reflection has revealed that this approach was more accessible and more liberatory for some women than others, for many of those who participated it was a key step in their politicization (Griffin Cohen 1993: 7–8; Agnew 1996: 76–82). Lakeman answered the ad and they invited her to join.

In response to a question about why she would want to get involved in the movement, Lakeman says that her friends remember her saying, "Because it is what's going on, and someday I'll have a granddaughter, and when she asks me, what did you do in this struggle, I want to have something to answer." She continued,

> It was easy, in those days, to see yourself as wanting to be in on it, because feminist politics were in the air. You more had to explain why you weren't connected than why you were. It was just like breathing. An insurrectionary attitude was kind of normal. You were a bit of a dud if you weren't in on it somewhere.

A Conference and a Lunch

Lakeman remembers two key events that shaped both her consciousness and the course of women's liberation in Woodstock over the next several years: a conference and a lunch (though she could not remember which happened first).

The conference[6] was called "The Changing Role of Women" and it was funded by a grant from the federal government. As Lakeman noted, "This happened in every community in those few years." The funder asked the conference organizing committee about the absence of poor women in their organization. "I was the one [poor woman] they knew, so they invited me into the organizing committee." Lakeman ended up chairing both the organizing committee and the conference itself, which was attended by "a hundred ordinary women from Oxford County.... There weren't a lot of desperately poor women, but there were a lot of ordinary working women and ordinary housewives."

Lakeman remembered that the conference "was a little preview of five thousand struggles I would later live out in full," from anger by some participants at a presentation that mocked marriage, to bitter conflict about having lesbianism as a topic of discussion, to all of the other divisions you might find in a politically diverse group of women at the dawn of women's liberation. She said,

> It was amazing how suddenly serious all of these things were. Things that were unspeakable became items on an agenda. Choices and possibilities suddenly had weight and substance. For me it was an example of what popular education really means, and all of a sudden oppressed people have discourse, and have language, and have a way of communicating their experience to each other. And then there's just power everywhere in the room. It's a wonderful, wonderful experience.

This conference helped lay the groundwork for a women's centre in Woodstock, something that Lakeman was not very involved with. It also helped to move forward the idea of an organization responding to the needs of battered women, an idea that originated in a casual lunch that happened at around the same time.

> We were at lunch — Julie, Janet, and I. Janet was working at the YWCA. Julie worked for Information Oxford, which was a job creation program. We were having lunch, and Julie said she'd had a call from a woman who was in hospital, who had been badly beaten and had nowhere to go. And didn't even have the money to get to a lawyer, and hadn't yet collected her kids, and wasn't sure how she was going to escape this guy. I said to Julie, "You know my friends are going out west and I'm going to have the house. Why don't you send her to me?"
>
> Julie's response was, "Well she's not the only one, you know. I've had these calls before." And somehow by the end of that lunch, Julie had committed a hundred dollars a month, and then Janet committed a hundred dollars a month, and that between us we could keep the space open in my house. Within a month, somehow, we were full. Not long after that we were trying to figure out how to turn this into a legitimate organization. We went on from there.
>
> We were open and functional for six months before we knew anyone else did this. Barbara Yakachuk brought us a clipping from the *Globe & Mail* about the Women's Aid Project in London, England, and suddenly we knew we were part of what [British Columbia feminist] Jillian Riddington has called a "spontaneous combustion" across the industrialized West.

In short order, the group had to make decisions about how the organization would be structured. In looking back from decades later, Lakeman described their decisions in this area as "the worst."

> We immediately set up being a charitable corporate structure, so we had a board and I was seen as the executive director. There were no other people to work there in the beginning. Some of the women on the board volunteered some hours. There was even a man on the board then. So I would say all the mistakes that you could make in that situation, I made. I would say you should never have a man on your board. I would say mostly you shouldn't have a board. I would say that if you have a board, it should be collective, and the collective should include the women who work in the organization, and nobody should be allowed on the board who doesn't work in the organization. So I've corrected all of that in my next life, but I made all of the usual mistakes at that point. I even went around town asking people in all other institutions like the Children's Aid, and various places, if they'd like to come and be on the board. Thank God they didn't.

The State

The main focus of their activities was, of course, supporting women who were fleeing abuse by providing them with a refuge. They also put quite a bit of energy into public education around the issue of violence against women. However, by necessity, one of the key focuses of the group's work was a constant, complicated struggle around their relationship with the state. On the one hand, there was recognition that the state was the only place to get the sort of funding that would be necessary to support the sort of activities needed by women on an ongoing basis. Lakeman said,

> In our mind the government had an obligation to support the needy, which was how we saw women in transition houses. I now see it quite differently. I do see it as supporting the needy, but I more see it as supporting women's attempts to establish equality. So it's even more important. In my mind it has gone from a charitable act to a political commitment to the whole concept.

At the time, the path to funding led straight through a shelter's local community, which had to support the organization in order for it to be eligible for any money from the higher levels of government.

> I think it was very important that it involved the local community, and you had to win over the local community. So we actually had to

go to the houses of the tobacco farmers sitting on county council, or the dairy farmers sitting on county council, and convince these guys that it was a good idea to support a transition house, and what one was.

They did support it in the end. We won them over. Mostly they didn't think that women should be left to rot in terrible situations. And they all had stories. They all knew of women, they all knew people whose families had been horrible to live in. So in the end, we won their agreement and got the provincial and federal money. And we got some of the very early women's programs money from the federal government, too, which supported it.

There's some pretty outstanding stories. One husband in particular came with us to county council to fight for the money, for which I've always been pretty impressed. He was a jerk, a real jerk, to his wife, but it wasn't that in cooler moments he didn't know that, and it wasn't that in cooler moments he wasn't enormously glad that there was someone to help her escape and to protect his children. A few months after she had escaped him, he was joining us at county council to fight for the existence of the house. And there were neighbours right next door who were Dutch Reform people, who absolutely, totally did not approve of women leaving men, did not approve of abortion and knew we did, did not approve of anything that was going on there, who stood up at county council — they just happened to be there on another matter entirely, and saw that we were in this struggle for approval — and they stood up for us as good neighbours and useful members of the community, and absolutely helped us get the by-law changed that we needed to be able to keep functioning in that house.

On the other hand, organizations like the police, which are an integral part of the state, and regulated professions such as those associated with the medical and legal fields, which have some autonomy but are organized through state practices, play an important role in responding to the violence experienced by women and in organizing the experiences of women in a larger sense as well. Feminists quickly became highly critical of the relationship between these groups and the oppression of women. In terms of the police, for example, Lakeman said

> I don't have a deep and abiding respect for these kind of authorities. I think it's very important to realize that we have a relationship with the state that's not friendly, and we have a relationship with professions that's not friendly. In fact, neither the police nor any — any, any, any — profession is committed to establishing women's equality.

You kind of have to go from there. They are agents of the status quo, and so we are in a pitched battle.

Feminist organizing around the criminal justice system's ways of responding to violence against women has been ongoing since the early seventies, though Lakeman is quite clear that the police and the courts are not the only or even the primary site of struggle for ending violence against women. The issues confronted have ranged from sexist behaviour by individual officers to an entire spectrum of policies and procedures that organize policing and that result in women who go to the police after experiencing violence — a population that has always been a small proportion of the total number who have such experiences, precisely because of these problems — having unpleasant, unproductive, and even traumatic experiences at the hands of the criminal justice system itself while only a tiny proportion of men who abuse women actually end up facing any kind of state sanction.

Despite these decades of effort and some important victories to show for it, a book published by Lakeman in 2005 based on research done in sexual assault centres across the country about the experiences of women who choose to report their assault to the police shows a shamefully inadequate response by the justice system in a consistent way and on multiple levels.[7] She wrote about the movement's "frustration" with the intense apathy and institutional resistance by police and lawmakers to feminist efforts

> to make fair law, to make police come when they are called, to make them protect us, to make the detectives do an adequate legal investigation, to make the prosecutors effectively put the facts before the courts, and to make judges and jailers and probation and immigration officers hold the abusers humanely in community or if need be, in state custody, until all women and children are safe from them and until society imagines, and successfully executes, plans to change the conditions of women and to change men.... Why is it so hard, so rare, for Canadian women who tell on their abusers, who ask for help, to get an effective conviction against the men who commit violence against women? (Lakeman 2005: vii–viii, xi)

In the interview, she concluded that

> one of the biggest problems in Canada still is lack of accountability by the police and lack of ways for us to complain about the police. Especially to complain about policy and procedures of police, not the individual cop. Over the years I've spent a lot of time training medical people, criminal justice system people. I find most of it a big waste of time. I think it's much more important to realize that

> these are hierarchies, and what you have to do is affect the top and make the top affect the rest of the hierarchy. You're not going to have much impact by training the troops.

Because of this ongoing hostility from the state to women's liberation, to be active in the service of supporting women in their escape from and struggle against abuse is to regularly break the law.

> This is probably true of almost every transition house, even the most conservative transition houses: all the workers break the law. It's almost a requirement of transition house work that you are into civil disobedience. You may not even have the term, but you will be hiding prostitutes, illegal immigrants, mothers who are in contempt — and rightfully so — of the courts, because the children have been incested. We all do the same thing. We shut up. We take the women into the houses. We take up collections between ourselves as workers, and buy women airline tickets. We just forget women's names, and use other names. We fail to report what the government would like us to report. To do anything less than that is to be less than a transition house. It's just a requirement of the job. The state does not support women's liberation. No state, anywhere, supports women's liberation, yet. We have to pressure them, publically, and we do, but we don't sacrifice the individual women or their babies.

In her early years in Woodstock, Lakeman also came face-to-face with the tensions between supporting women in their direct, collective confrontations with the state while receiving funding from that very same state.

> There was a strike of public health nurses. I considered public health nurses one of the key professionals for battered women. For one thing, they couldn't lock you up, they couldn't take your kids — they didn't have the power to do so — but they could be enormously helpful in getting your kids out of Children's Aid or getting you some material aid, and they were the key link to a lot of rural women. So when they went on strike, I went to join them on the picket line. The women from the house sort of naturally followed me. We sat around making picket signs and then we went over to support the strike. Little did we know that our board didn't think that was too cool. It never crossed my mind, really, and I was utterly shocked to be scolded for this. I now think I shouldn't have taken the scolding. I sort of took it at the time. I think there's a very key interrelationship there, and we were smart to support the public health nurses. What our board was mad about was our funding came from the

same place, of course, and we were threatening the funding. But you have to speak out or there's no point in existing.

Vancouver

After attending a conference on violence against women in Vancouver, Lakeman decided in 1978 to move there. "I thought that I'd become a big fish in a small pond, and there were feminists who knew more, and more of them, in Vancouver, and I could get here and learn a bunch of things from other women." She was hired from a newspaper ad by Vancouver Rape Relief, where she became one of five paid staff as a part of a collective of about thirty or thirty-five women. At the time, Rape Relief was part of a provincial network of five rape crisis centres, all organized as collectives.

Though Lakeman saw many similarities between working against male violence in Woodstock and in the much larger city of Vancouver, the political environment she entered in 1978 had a distinct sort of momentum and energy that was far beyond what was possible in Woodstock.

> There's kind of swirl in my mind from about 1979 through until '83. There was a whirlwind of activity. An unbelievable amount of activity. International Women's Day was a big day. Pretty fast there was a new event called "Take Back The Night," which developed locally, and we turned it into a national event. There were Pride marches and the campaign against — what was her name, in Florida, with the right-wing, anti-gay stuff. Anita Bryant. There was a need to raise money because we decided to buy a transition house.... We learned to confront [abusive] men from the women in Santa Cruz, to do what were called "confrontations." There were posters put up all over town threatening guys and telling guys we were watching them. There were millions of things going on. We would pull demonstrations very quickly against pornography — individual events and Red Hot Video moving into town. Stupid fashion shows, actions against bride fairs. Very dramatic cases, legal cases. There were big debates about reform and revolution, about tactics.... There was just tons of stuff going on. It was a very exciting time to be alive.

Looking at two of these things in more detail can give a sense of what the feminist environment was like in Vancouver in that era. A lasting and visible contribution from that context to the national scene is Take Back The Night, an event now held annually in cities across Canada.[8] Lakeman remembers that at the time, Vancouver Rape Relief was renting a building in the city that it shared with other groups. One of the other groups

> organized a demonstration in town pretty much modelled on the anti-pornography conference that had just happened in San Francisco, where Andrea Dworkin[9] had taken women to the street.... [It was] an anti-porn demonstration and march in the West End which ended with burning a man in effigy on English Bay. When the police were swirling around them they stickered the cop car and did other various and sundry saucy and delightful things.

By the following year, that group

> was either weaker or on to other things, I'm not sure which, but we took over the action, and started to call it Take Back The Night.[10]
> Now, this is important, because most people get this wrong — Take Back The Night is a direct action, it is not a demonstration. Take Back The Night gathers women in the street to say, with our bodies, collectively we're strong enough to take the street. We don't ask permission of police. We don't ask permission of men. We don't invite men to be with us, because it muddies the water. We, individually and collectively, take the street, and prove to ourselves that it's possible to act as free women. So we've done it every year since in Vancouver. By 1981, I think, we'd proposed it as a national action to an association of sexual assault centres, and it happened all across Canada for ten or fifteen years. Lots of Canadians think it happens all over the world. It doesn't, of course. It's more developed here than it is anywhere. There were similar kinds of actions in London and San Francisco, but it's quite developed here.
> It still goes on. In some cities it has been watered down into a nice, polite demonstration in which the police give security, but mostly it still is an occasion in which women feel some sense of collective power, and in which women talk about street violence and public violence and display both outrage and some of the *joie de vivre* that's possible when you're not at risk.

Another important example from this period of women exerting power for themselves was the tactic Lakeman called "confrontations."

> A confrontation is a tactic of getting the story from a woman of what a man has done to her, and then working with her friends, neighbours, co-workers, and some of us to decide how to really lay it on him. We pick either going to his house or to his workplace or his sports arena or whatever, and publically say, "We know what you've done." We work out a script between us. It's a very tight action. Maybe fifteen or twenty women will show up. Five of them

will have a script worked out. The victim speaks first, and then four or five other people will speak behind her. A sentence or two, not a big speech. And then split. It's a way of holding him accountable without using the criminal justice system. Either because the criminal justice system won't stand up for it — there's no appropriate charge, or there's not enough evidence to make a charge stick. Or women might decide not to go [to] the criminal justice system. One situation would be if he is a man of colour, and she doesn't really want him jailed. But the more likely is that there's no evidence, or not enough to convict.

Even among some other feminists, this was a controversial tactic, and it was also "scary to do," according to Lakeman. However, she added, "It's very effective." In planning such an action there are a number of key things that the women had to think about:

Whether or not he's violent ... in the sense of immediately dangerous to us. How to make him hear the whole the thing. Whether or not he is living with a woman, and if there's any risk to her, and if so, how to get her out of there. How to make sure she is not present — that is, not stuck with his immediate response — without revealing to him that we are in communication with her. How to be in communication with her without her telling him. Those are tricky, though we've managed it. How to keep the group together.

If you have ten women at a man's door, you swing the door open and you say these things to him, he's likely to believe there were 150 women at the door. It's just that, you know, their eyes grow as big as saucers, and the misogyny goes from a rage at women to a fear of women in mere seconds. So that's kind of interesting. We've had men shut the door but then they can't stand it. They have to open the door again, because they can't stand not knowing what's going on. We've had men immediately call the contacts that we left them, desperately hoping for some information and wanting out of this situation.

One of the harder things is trying to find a resource to which to refer him. You don't want to leave him without resources. You want to be able to say, "If you want to talk more about this, or if you want to learn about this, here's a man to go and see." Or, "Here's an agency to go and see." There are pitifully few places where you can tell a man, "This man will tell you the truth about violence against women. This man will not blame us, will be responsible, will be of value to you when your intentions are good." It's hard to get the women not to take care of him. We're willing to confront him, but then we want to pick up the pieces and put him back together, and that's not a good thing to do.

Those are the considerations, mostly. How not to get nailed by some authorities is another one. *[laugh]*

It's wonderfully human. It's very straightforward. It's not dangerous. It's not violent. For me, it's not a problem believing a woman and just saying what her version of truth is in this situation, because so what if somebody was wrong? Big deal. It's not like you jailed him. I do believe that little shock to the system means a few men will hesitate to do whatever they were doing before. It's particularly useful in situations, I think, where men have just crossed the line. They may not have thought women would be that mad about it, or may not have — they knew they weren't in the realm of the criminal. They knew they were just being obnoxious.

Take Back The Night and actions like confrontations raise questions about the relationship between feminist political practice and both men and the state. In different times and places, different feminists have answered these questions in different ways. This became a particularly acute source of conflict when Vancouver Rape Relief decided to work with men under very specific circumstances to raise money to open a transition house that would be independent of government funding (which was itself controversial among some other feminists, who thought it was a mistake to set up social services not funded by the state). The pages of Vancouver feminist newspaper *Kinesis* sizzled with heated debate on the topic. Lakeman relates some of the conclusions they reached within the Rape Relief collective:

> What's difficult about this question is keeping yourself in radical relation to the question. So I'll just give you a range of things we've decided. We've decided no men in our organization, ever. It's a women only organization, and that's the way it's going to be.[11] We've decided we will work with men in mixed coalitions, but that will be explicit and selective — we'll know why we're doing it, for how long we're doing it, and on what terms we're doing it. We do accept support from men, in the form of cash, but also we have what's called the house funding committee, or Friends of Rape Relief Committee. That group raises money for us, but it's on the understanding that they will have no say in the use of that money. We don't give them financial statements, even. We account for the money we collect, to them, but not how we spend it. If they are willing to accept those terms, then we're willing to play.
>
> What we do is chair that committee, and we — in our minds, we're starting out with the assumption that it's not our obligation

to teach men about women's liberation. But, to the extent that men are willing to put up support that we can use — you know, privilege in various forms, on that committee, that we can use — we are willing to teach, in the form of constructive criticism. So we will spend a fair amount of time teaching men how to work with each other, teaching men what books are worth reading if you really want to understand women's liberation, or working in a respectful manner that is productive to both of us. We consider that generosity. So that's what we do.

There are other levels to working and not working with men. Like, we don't let any social worker or any other kind of authority into our transition house without the permission of the woman who is involved. And if it's a male professional, we'll probably — we'll tolerate it, but we're not crazy about it. So it's a fine line. We try to favour women politically, and at the same time we know, for instance, that not all women are in the same economic position, so when there was a farm workers' picket line, we walked the farm workers' picket line as an organization. That was both to support the women in the fields who were trying to raise kids in difficult circumstances, but also because compared to those men in those fields on economic issues, we were the privileged. We considered we had things that we owed in that situation. In terms of gender, they are the privileged. So in terms of violence against women, we set the terms.

The Resurgent Right

The question of relating to the state, which had appeared initially in Lakeman's work in Woodstock, reared its head again in Vancouver, with much more dramatic consequences. In part, this was because of increasingly well organized resistance to feminist gains by the early 1980s. Across the industrialized world starting in the late 1970s, business and right-wing groups began to mobilize against the gains that had been made by the constellation of social movements that rose to prominence in the 1960s and 1970s, including the women's movement. Perhaps the most globally visible signs of this retrenchment of elite power were the election of Margaret Thatcher in Britain in 1979 and Ronald Reagan in the United States in 1980, both staunchly conservative figures.

In British Columbia, electoral change was a less obvious indicator of this shift. The conservative Social Credit Party, or SoCreds, ruled the province almost without a break from 1952 until 1991, except for three years of rule by the NDP beginning 1972. It was toward the end of the period of NDP rule that the B.C. Coalition of Rape Crisis Centres first received government money. The SoCreds had their origins in right-wing populism, but when they returned to power in 1975 they began to distance themselves from that history and instead relied more on an alliance between Christian conservatives and business elites. The SoCreds, according to Lakeman, "had no soft spot for feminists or women's issues," but for a number of years the funding of Vancouver Rape Relief and its sister collectives in other parts of the province remained untouched.

This changed in 1982. Lakeman said,

> They decided to wipe out the B.C. Coalition of Rape Crisis Centres. They didn't like us because the police didn't like us, which is a badge of honour, if you ask me. They didn't like us because we didn't see ourselves as fitting into government structure or social service structure. We saw ourselves as a necessary thorn in their sides, to make them respond to women's issues. But the form that it took in the end was that, in return for our government contract, they wanted control over the nature of our services. They wanted to see what we did in every public speaking engagement. They wanted to see the outline and be able to approve it. They wanted to be able to research sexual assault that happened to the women who had called us, and they wanted access, therefore, to our records, and they claimed it was for supervisory purposes, and to evaluate us. The usual bullshit. So they wanted every tenth file. We said no. That came to a major showdown.

Much of the battle occurred through the media, and she said, "It was big news for several months in our province."

> In those days you could still have a columnist or a reporter — and you still sometimes can — who can actually follow the story. So we kept the reporters informed, about what the struggle was, what our point of view was about it, what they needed to know about us, how to be in touch with us. Always answered their calls, always answered promptly.
>
> And we also tried to stay together as a coalition, not let them divide us. We continued to meet as a coalition, put joint positions together in relation to the government. And within that, we tried to take our responsibility as the centre that was in the urban area — we had more money, more power, more access to the media — and we tried to be protective of the smaller centres.
>
> In the end, of course, they were the big shots, and they cut us off.... All but two of us went down. Rape Relief survived, and the Nanaimo centre survived for a long time, but the others went down and were replaced by less progressive centres, over time.

Rape Relief activists predicted at the time that the attack on their work was a prelude to something bigger. Certainly the province's attack on the rape crisis centres helped to create division among feminists, as not all in the women's movement agreed with Rape Relief's refusal to see itself as a service and its choice to resist state interference absolutely and militantly. The next year, the predictions by Rape Relief activists proved true. It became clear, according to Lakeman, that "the SoCreds were getting ready to do the first wave of big cuts to government services and to social services and to NGOs. I really think we were their testing ground." The provincial government initiated a "restraint program," including significant budget cuts and many associated legislative changes. In response, labour and community groups mobilized under the banner of "Solidarity." The women's movement played an important role in the struggle, particularly through a large coalition called Women Against the Budget. Many feminists recognized these changes as not just about cutting expenditures. Women Against the Budget member Ruth Annis was quoted at the time as saying, "The attack on feminist services, like Transition House and the Women's Health Collective, is a political attack.... Feminist services are more than social services. They politicize women. This is what they want to stop" ("Women slam" 1983). The resistance reached sufficient size and intensity that many were calling for a general strike, including many feminists. However, organized labour, which was an important part of the mobilization, struck a deal on its own with the province and after that the resistance collapsed. It is not clear how the story might have been different had there been louder, stronger, more unified resistance to the attack on Rape Relief the previous year.

In the aftermath of the defunding of the B.C. Coalition of Rape Crisis Centres, the provincial government was still left with the problem of how to respond to violence against women. However opposed the government might have been to feminist politics, the victories won through organizing by women over the previous decade meant it could not just go back to ignoring the problem. Initially, Lakeman said, "they replaced us with what, in a labour struggle, you would call scab labour." Eventually, as many governments in North America have done, the province moved away as much as it could from an approach that talked about and responded to gendered relations of power.

> They created the "victim services" model rather than the women's services model, which has been repeated across the country. There's a couple of forms that that has come in. One is victims' services which are attached to police departments and answer to police departments, and there are victim services that are attached to crown counsel's office, and that answer to crown counsel. The ones that are attached to crown counsel are kind of useful. They tell women

how the court system works, and they tell women how to be good witnesses. Since they want to win the court cases, that's not a totally bad idea.[12] But victim services attached to police departments are a sneaky, dirty trick, because the whole point is that you need an independent advocate to put pressure on the police and the rest of the system. These are really women's auxiliaries working for the police, who carefully make sure you don't put any pressure on the police department. So they are anathema to us.

The B.C. government (and many others) also ended up creating services not attached to the criminal justice system.

The other thing that they did was to allow for the emergence of some "specialized victim assistance" which had a bit more autonomy, almost like a rape crisis centre, but you'll notice the degendered and depoliticizing name. That's still a problem in B.C. We still have specialized victim assistance, and they still don't like to pay for rape crisis centres and transition houses.

But the thing about feminism is, eventually we get your mother, we get your daughter, we get your sister, we get your friends, so some of those specialized victim centres have radicalized along the way, and are now more like independent rape crisis centres than they were ever meant to be. And independent rape crisis centres are re-emerging. And Vancouver Rape Relief continues to survive.

When the NDP was re-elected in 1991, Vancouver Rape Relief had to make the difficult choice of whether to reapply for state funding. It was "a very tough decision" but they ultimately decided it was a step they needed to take.

We decided to cooperate enough to try and get the salaries, partly because we were needing to accelerate integration in terms of class and race, again. We still had a high percentage of working-class women, but we very much needed to get more women of colour into the collective and onto positions of power within the collective. It was obvious that it was harder for women of colour to volunteer at the level that white, middle-class women, or even white, working-class women could volunteer. It became clear that we had to have some kind of an affirmative action strategy, and we thought probably salaries were an important part of that. So we went for the salaries, telling ourselves that a percentage of those salaries would always go to women of colour, and that we would accelerate the hiring of women of colour and Aboriginal women, to make ourselves obviously available.

Lakeman's Lessons

With all of the contradictions and all of the pressures of relating to the state, Vancouver Rape Relief still survives, still sees its mission in a highly politicized way, and still engages in the struggle for equality. And so does Lakeman. She draws a number of lessons from this persistence.

> You can't make the government's decisions for it. You've got to decide what you're trying to do, and hope like hell you succeed at it. If you start sucking up to The Man before you've even opened your doors, forget it, you're finished, it's over, you're not going anywhere. If you think that service to one woman is going to make her life better, you're mistaken. Nothing could be a greater disservice than to actually reduce her to a service recipient, when really she's trying to be part of an international uprising. It's just a terrible thing to do to somebody.
>
> It's probably misinformed, but I had an image from growing up of Mao[13] collecting up peasants, moving across China in a revolutionary army. I know lots of people will tell me what's wrong with Mao's revolutionary army, and I know plenty of what's wrong with it, but there was something right about it, too. It was an uprising of millions of people in a situation that required uprising. Part of what they did right, it seems to me, is refuse to disempower the broken. You had to be patching people up and feeding people and gathering people up and resisting, all at the same time. That's the model for me. Every woman who calls Rape Relief has something to offer the struggle. She has a story to tell, which I will use — with you, or with a conference, or with a classroom, or alone — trying to figure out what to do. Her story is valuable. She, physically, can and will do mutual aid with other women who call us.... We are a self-help, mutual aid group by just sitting down, discussing this topic. As women, we have no escape. These are the conditions of our lives for the rest of our lives, and you've only to admit it. I stand a chance of increasing my own survival by listening to her, and making common cause with her.
>
> A lot of people will tell you that it's unfair to ask the client, the woman, the caller, to do anything. In their minds, she is meant to be the recipient of a charity, and I think that's a terrible, terrible, terrible way to operate, and very counterproductive in terms of revolutionary practice. My own position is that when a woman calls us, she is asking us to join in her action. She doesn't call a feminist organization by accident. She calls knowing she's calling a feminist organization, and she is deciding — she may use the rhetoric of "get

help" but what she's really doing is calling for a truth-teller, calling for an ally, calling for public assistance on an action, calling for fellow travellers, calling for strategy discussion, calling to add numbers to hers. We are responding to that call. If you get your head around that, then you feel much better about saying to her, "You know, I have another woman who's asking for something you've got," and putting them in touch with each other so you're constantly growing a movement. And she understands herself as being aided by the movement, not by some great, genius councillor. Not by some Joan of Arc, but by an ordinary feminist whom she could be.

At the time that I started this work, I would have said I was completely naïve, I had led a particularly protected life, and I had no understanding of violence against women. Certainly my father didn't beat my mother, and I hadn't been hit by men. I still haven't been hit by a man.... Within a couple of weeks of being at Rape Relief, I found myself having nightmares, rape nightmares, which a lot of people do after they first start the work. Somehow, I think doing wife assault work [in Woodstock] wasn't as "in my face." I wasn't married, so I didn't think I was going to be beaten up by a husband. But all of a sudden, doing rape work, I realized this violence was meant for me, and then I had to contend with the consciousness raising that went with it. I was the kind of woman who liked going to bars. I was saucy and lippy and I was sexually charged, and I liked all that stuff. So I was at risk, and I knew I was at risk.

That was very good development for me. Now, I see the revolutionary potential. I see this as a struggle that can't be reduced to the economic answers of socialism. That it can't be separated from the history of anarchist struggle. That you can't achieve women's liberation without dealing with violence against women, and you can't deal with violence against women without dealing with women's liberation. You can't. It's not solvable. You can't deal with violence against women without transforming the state. You can't deal with violence against women without dealing with racism, and the class divisions between women. You can't. There's no short cut. We have to actually get on with the business of developing women's equality.

Notes

1. This is not at all meant to portray women who experience abuse as ignorant of their own circumstances or as passive victims waiting for privileged benefactors to enlighten and save them. Even in the most horrific circumstances, women experiencing abuse have no choice but to do intensive practical theorizing about their experiences and by doing so they develop many different strategies

to respond to them (e.g., Sev'er 2002). However, because abuse tends to thrive in and reinforce the isolation of women from each other, the very urgency of the circumstances that lead women to become experts in understanding and navigating gendered relations of power in their own lives may present tremendous barriers that keep such theorizing and action very isolated and local.

2. The violence that men experience is very serious and in many cases it is also deeply connected with men's experiences of oppression related to things like racialization, poverty, non-conforming gender expression, and queer sexualities. The experiences of people who identify as trans or genderqueer or who otherwise do gender in ways that are significantly different from dominant norms also experience gender oppression, including violence. This chapter, however, takes its cue from the politics of the interview participant herself and largely focuses on violence experienced by cisgender women, especially at the hands of men and through the workings of patriarchal institutions and social relations.

3. For a feminist analysis that in part discusses how attachment to intimate spaces is organized around and facilitated through a pervasive patriarchal way of doing (hetero)sexuality, written by an author held in high regard by the interview participant in this chapter, see Dworkin 2007.

4. For more on the social gospel in this era, see Chapter 1 of *Resisting the State: Canadian History Through the Stories of Activists*, Allen 1973, and Socknat 1987.

5. For more information on the Catholic Worker Movement, which still exists today, see www.catholicworker.org.

6. To hear some of Lakeman's memories of this conference, go to www.talkingradical.ca/audio/lakeman_conference.mp3.

7. For feminist analysis that is radically critical of the state response to violence against women and also critical of the dominant feminist orientation with respect to the criminal justice system and that comes to different conclusions than Lakeman's about action, see for example A. Smith 2005 and Incite! Women of Color Against Violence 2006.

8. To hear some of Lakeman's memories of Take Back The Night organizing, go to www.talkingradical.ca/audio/lakeman_take_back_the_night.mp3.

9. Dworkin was a prominent feminist in the United States whose work was focused on violence against women. See, for example, Dworkin 1997 and Dworkin 2007.

10. I have seen and heard other origin stories for Take Back The Night (e.g., Appignanesi 2007: 409) and have been unable to decisively determine the exact path by which this important form of action took such a hold of feminist imaginations in Canada and elsewhere. Undoubtedly, the work in Vancouver was early and important.

11. In more recent years, Vancouver Rape Relief has been at the centre of a controversy based on its refusal to allow a trans woman named Kimberley Nixon to become part of its collective. This dispute has been written about extensively in publications, on email lists, and on websites that ground themselves in feminist and/or queer politics; it will not be discussed here.

12. In the years after the interview, the right-wing B.C. provincial government of Gordon Campbell withdrew all funding from court-based victim services.

13. Mao Tse-tung led the Communist Party of China to victory in the Chinese Civil War in 1949 and led the People's Republic of China until his death in 1976.

Chapter 4

Women Against Violence (Part II)
Shree Mulay and Sadeqa Siddiqui on Feminist Anti-Violence Activism in Montreal

It might not have occurred to me to investigate an organization that identified itself as a "community centre" as a possible site for finding long-time activists, but an activist colleague of mine was emphatic that Montreal's South Asian Women's Community Centre, or SAWCC, was an important place to check out when I was in the city to do interviews. When I called them, they suggested I talk to Sadeqa Siddiqui. She, in turn, put me in touch with Shree Mulay.

The interview with Mulay happened first. It was in an aging but well-appointed row house owned by McGill University and converted to offices, including those of its Centre for Research and Teaching on Women. Old-fashioned patterned paper covered the walls at the second floor reception; after I stated my business I was sent up a further flight of stairs to Mulay's office. It was big and felt very academic — lots of papers on the desk and bookshelves packed just beyond capacity with books, many of them important feminist titles of the past few decades.

Mulay grew up in India and moved to Canada in 1964 to pursue a PhD in Biochemistry. It was the flurry of activity against U.S. military involvement in Vietnam that provided the first context for her to become politically active as a student. She eventually decided to remain in Canada and become a citizen. In the mid 1970s she was part of a group called the Indian People's Association in North America, which originally formed as a response to repressive activities by Indira Gandhi's government in India. In Montreal, members decided there was a need for a group specifically organized around the needs of immigrant women from South Asia, a group that later became SAWCC. Over the years Mulay has pursued a successful academic career and at the time of our interview was a professor in the Department of Medicine at McGill University and the director of the centre in which the interview was held. She has been active in the women's movement at the local and national levels, and over all of those years has sustained her involvement in SAWCC.

The interview with Siddiqui took place in the SAWCC offices at the end of my visit to Montreal. I was working in the agency sector myself at the time so SAWCC felt familiar, with its well-used but functional furnishings, its cubicles and almost bare meeting room. It was after hours so I only saw

Siddiqui herself, but I could imagine the mix of camaraderie, service-oriented bustle, paperwork, and occasional moments of frustration at the magnitude of the circumstances faced by many of the women that the organization supports. Siddiqui came to Canada from Pakistan with her husband and family in the late 1960s. Her political involvement began when she got a job with SAWCC in 1983, and she has been active ever since, as the organization has expanded its field of activities to include participation in the women's movements in Quebec and in Canada. At the time of the interview she was coordinator of SAWCC.

Seeing Difference

Both the last chapter and this one discuss struggles to end violence against women. In choosing to do this — to have two separate chapters organized around violence against women — I am not only signalling that I think it is an important issue; I am also effectively declaring that I see the existence of some difference or differences, some specificities, that have political meaning in the respective stories. Any time your words or actions group things together or separate them — treat them by the labels you give them or the ways you relate to them as if they were meaningfully alike or substantially different — you are saying something about what matters about those things and what the relationship between those things is or should be. This is a very political thing to do but it is also something that is unavoidable even in the most casual of conversations. The question, both in general and with respect to these chapters, then becomes "what" and "why."

To my mind, the simplest form of the answer is this: If a difference is somehow involved in shaping people's lives in important ways, then it should matter to me. If it is not involved in shaping people's lives in important ways, then I don't need to give it quite the same political attention.

For something to be "important" in how it organizes people's lives means it has to play a role in shaping our access to resources, opportunities, and control over our lives and bodies and communities. That is, it is a marker related to where and how we experience privilege and where and how we experience oppression, as in the various social relations of power named in the Introduction. Certainly gender and race are both produced by social relations as important markers with social meaning. Both are important in how our lives are organized.

Though there are many ways to arrive at these insights, for many of us they have emerged from the mix of movements that erupted in the late 1960s and 1970s. For many of these movements, in many different ways, appreciating the political importance of difference and acting on it in the service of liberation were crucial, and it is debate and even active conflict within and between these movements that have informed many analyses of difference that you can find today. An important way for me as an individual to begin appreciating the political significance of difference has been reading the words of women — both racialized and white women who identify as feminists and women of colour who prioritize women in their politics but organize and name their politics in other ways. The writings of radical women of colour have been particularly important in that ongoing journey for me.

One of the most crucial contributions of the women's movement in that era was the idea that the social world and our lives are organized according to gender: that there are important ways that institutions, other people, and language shape our lives depending upon our gender (and, indeed, are organized in ways that *produce* gender as a social relation); that, politically, gender matters; and, that women are oppressed and they must struggle to end that oppression. Feminism pointed out that existing political projects like liberalism and the various flavours of socialism of that era claimed a certain kind of universal relevance. The former is organized around the idea of "citizen" and the latter around "worker." Yet when examined closely, they were very clearly responding to the experiences of (particular groups of) men while erasing the experiences of (other men and) women. A key component of feminisms has been rejecting that erasure of women's experiences of oppression and an insistence on making that oppression visible and working to end it.

It was not long, however, before some women began to point out that as important as it was to recognize gender as a difference that is politically important, a political project with a too-simple idea of "woman" at its centre also has the potential to erase other kinds of difference and make certain specific experiences seem as if they were universal while marginalizing other people and other experiences. In practice, in the early stages of the so-called "second wave" of feminist movement in the early 1970s, many feminist spaces and much theorizing and action in Canada often centred on the specific experiences of middle-class, white, heterosexual, able-bodied, cisgender women, though individuals whose lives and politics challenged that norm were present from the very beginning. Especially from the 1970s, there were collective challenges within the women's movement from working-class women and lesbian women about the ways in which their experiences of oppression and choices about resistance were erased or at least marginalized in much of what was going on. Beginning in the 1980s, women with disabilities began to do the same sort of thing (Driedger 1993). Also in that decade, organized efforts by racialized women in Canada began to present crucial collective challenges to the women's movement in terms of racism.[1] More recently, trans[2] and genderqueer people and their allies have been challenging for expanded notions of gender and gender oppression.

At the most obvious level, all of this is to say that me recognizing that there are politically meaningful specificities to the ways in which racialized women experience violence and organize against it has very little to do with me. Rather, it is simply recognizing that there is an important history of struggle in which racialized women themselves have identified that specificity, so I had better listen.

Understanding Difference

This kind of listening is a beginning, though, rather than an end. Exactly *how* difference matters in any situation is a political question, and not necessarily a simple one to answer. Opening our eyes to the reality that difference can have political significance when it goes along with differences in power helps us escape one trap, but it opens up a whole range of new pitfalls.

One important example was already given above — how movement spaces and practices organized around simplistic understandings of "woman" can erase and marginalize women whose experiences of oppression are about more than gender alone. Analogous dynamics have historically operated in labour movements, queer movements, peace movements, anti-racist movements, disability rights movements, and pretty much any other you could name. All have exhibited internal differences in privilege and oppression and a need to struggle to make movements actually work for the more oppressed among those in whose names the movement claims to work.

Another manifestation of the same thing can be the ways in which those of us who are privileged in a certain way think about groups that are oppressed. For example, a common way in which racism shapes how white people think about racialized people is that we often understand the segments of humanity defined by racial categories in incredibly simplistic, homogenous ways. Brown skin comes to define the entirety of the people who bear it, and everything else about them fades into the background.

Take the categories of "South Asian" and "South Asian woman" that are important in this chapter. "South Asian" as it is usually used is a category that encompasses over a billion people, with a region of origin currently divided into several states and many regions of diaspora, with complex caste and class hierarchies, several major religions as well as longstanding traditions of secularism, dozens of languages, as broad a spectrum of political orientations as any other large chunk of humanity, diverse sexual and relationship practices, and so on. Even without further probing of the processes that lead us to understand "communities" as natural and inevitable (see below), it is because of the breadth of experiences encompassed by the term "South Asian" that it makes sense to recognize that in any Canadian city "there is not one South Asian community but many South Asian communities" (Agnew 1996: 209).

However, another political challenge that comes with the recognition that difference matters is the way in which recognizing difference in particular ways can be used as a tool for controlling people. Multiculturalism has been an important terrain for communities to struggle against some aspects of the oppressions they experience (e.g., Kobayashi 2008). However, Canadian feminists Himani Bannerji (2000) and Sunera Thobani (2007) among others have written about how the Canadian government's use of the state policy of multiculturalism is as a tool that recognizes difference but in a specific way that serves to preserve a broader status quo in Canadian society, with racial and other relations of oppression modified somewhat from previous forms but still very much intact.

Bannerji argues that this oppressive deployment of multiculturalism by the Canadian state depends on particular understandings of "tradition" and "culture" and "community." These ideas are actively encouraged by the state and are often embraced by elites, particularly elite men, within racialized communities. "Tradition" and "culture" are understood in ways that make them seem detached from history, from class, from struggle, and as essential to authentic membership in communities. From the complicated, contradictory, historically grounded ways of being and doing in the countries of origin of non-indigenous racialized people, certain features get extracted but not others — often features that emphasize patriarchy, control, and conservatism, and that help to erase and marginalize difference and mute class struggle within racialized communities.

Bannerji (1999: 268) writes,

> It is not that ideology invents particular socio-cultural features, found among many, but rather it centres some and erases others which might contradict the centrality of the selected ones.... It is the whole discursive organization that is distortive or untrue, not particular features as such, and it is in their establishment as "essential" that the harm is most palpable.

In the words of another Canadian feminist, Vijay Agnew (1996: 211), it is not unusual for community groups organized and funded through state practices of multiculturalism to "present gender roles prescribed by the culture as an unchanging reality rather than as something transformed by politics and economics." The pressure in this direction by the Canadian state, along with other features of official multiculturalism, construct discrete, "essentialized" communities organized around this specific ideological version of culture-based difference. The "community" as it has come to be understood under official multiculturalism is seen as absolute and essential, while in fact it is only one possible form of social organization in which racialized people could exist in Canada. As a result, Thobani (2007: 175) writes,

> Immigrants who might have self-identified along any number and

combination of possible identities, including those of class, gender, and age, instead find themselves to be overdetermined culturally, over and above all other aspects of their identities. State-sponsored multiculturalism compels them to negotiate and comprehend their identities on very narrow grounds, discouraging and possibly foreclosing the possibility of alliances that might allow a systemic challenge to white dominance, patriarchy, and global corporate capitalism.

All of which benefits white Canadian elites.

However, some argue that as important as embracing difference created by relations of oppression has been in many circumstances to organizing against that oppression — claiming "woman" as politically meaningful has been central for many in organizing against gender oppression, for example — in a way it just keeps people trapped. We cannot ignore how difference has shaped our lives, they argue, but our goal should be ending the power of such categories completely. Yet another Canadian feminist, Nandita Sharma (2006: 158), argues that uncritically embracing the differences into which we are organized, even when it is a basis for resisting oppression, "does not produce diverse and varied ways of living so much as it shapes our consciousness of the authenticity, and therefore the naturalness, of parochial forms of power." She calls for us to "rid our imaginations of the negative dualities of always-colonizing systems and the identities that they produce" and heed "the call to base our feelings of commonness on shared experience," not through some liberal denial of the existence of difference infused with power but through deliberate organizing to overthrow it (ibid.: 165).

It may not be entirely clear how to turn such a vision of transcending difference infused with power into reality. However, it is important to see in the history of organizing by anti-racist feminists in Canada a mandate

> beyond the politics of difference to show that it is not our identities or location that create change but our vision for the future. The question we must ask is do we have a vision for the future which can bring all women together in a common politics — the politics of inclusion — fighting for a common cause, for freedom for *all* women regardless of race, colour, class, or sexual orientation. (Carty 1993: 16, emphasis in original)

Not a politics of fragmentation on the basis of experience, nor one of false unity on the basis of erasure and oppression of some, but a complex unity reached through political struggle and through dealing openly and in liberatory ways with how relations of oppression organize the difference that divides us.

How It Matters

There are many areas where racialized women, including South Asian women, have identified specificities in their experiences around violence. I am sure I am missing some, and presenting others in an unnuanced fashion, but this list is at least a beginning of some of the areas to think about when considering this issue.

Feminists have clearly shown that the state does an abysmal job in general at responding to the violence men do to women (Lakeman 2005). Far beyond this, though, racialized women from many backgrounds face the histories and present day realities of the state actively *imposing* violence and other aspects of oppression on them and on racialized people of all genders. Chapter 1 mentioned some of the historical and contemporary realities of state violence against indigenous women and men. The Canadian state also has a long history of visiting violence upon racialized people in other parts of the world (Engler 2009; Gordon 2010). Indigenous people, people of African descent, and other racialized people in Canada continue to experience harassment and violence at the hands of police, courts, and other state officials (Agnew 1996: 202; Brown 2004; Smith 2004; Tator and Henry 2006). Regulation of migration to Canada by the settler state has always had aspects that are oppressive in terms of nation of origin, racial background, and gender (Agnew 1996; Sharma 2006; Walia 2006; Thobani 2007). Particularly since September 11, 2001, people identified as South Asian, North African, Arab, and/or Muslim have been subjected to increased harassment from state authorities, intelligence agencies, border agents, and others (Thobani 2007: 217–247; Razack 2008).

Given this role of the state as a source of violence in their lives and communities, some groups of racialized women — though definitely not all and not the group that is the focus of this chapter — largely reject making demands on the state as a basis for organizing against violence, and instead focus exclusively on finding approaches centred in radical, grassroots community mobilization (A. Smith 2005; Incite! Women of Color Against Violence 2006; Incite! Women of Color Against Violence 2007). Debate among racialized women and their allies about how to respond to state violence politically and strategically is ongoing, but racial oppression and violence in part produced by state relations shape the social landscape in which those processes of decision-making are grounded.

On the personal level, experiences of racism, legacies of violence produced by state relations, and histories of pervasive racism from police shape the ground upon which racialized women make decisions about how to respond to experiences of interpersonal violence, including if and how to relate to police, courts, and other elements of the state. If they do go to the police and if their case reaches the courts, their experiences of racialization impact how they are perceived and responded to by the agents of the court system around issues of believability, vulnerability, "rapability," consent, and so on (Razack 1998). The legal system also frequently manifests racism in how it deals with issues of culture, by taking them up in ways that reinforce racist stereotypes (Rudrappa 2007). One way that courts have sometimes done this is by excusing, in racist ways, patriarchal behaviours by racialized men as being "just part of their culture," thereby becoming less responsive to the experiences of racialized women. As well, in some cases when an immigrant woman decides to leave an abusive relationship, the legal systems in North America and in the woman's country of origin may both become involved, at times in conflicting ways, and there are few resources available to support women in navigating this (Dasgupta 2007: 216–217).

For racialized women who have migrated to Canada, the state also creates violence in their lives and their communities through the ways in which immigration is organized. A key instance of how the Canadian state has organized the lives of immigrant women into dependency and vulnerability to violence since the late 1960s is the "family class" sponsorship through which many enter the country. When a family is immigrating, generally one adult is designated as the primary immigrant and that person sponsors the rest of the family under immigration rules designed to allow family reunification. Even when both adults have applied as independents and when both are reasonably qualified to enter the country in that way, there are many instances of women having been unilaterally designated as "dependents" on their husbands by immigration officials. This is reinforced by the rules they must follow after they are in the country. Sponsored "dependents" are barred from using many social services and social programs for a period of ten years and must rely on the person sponsoring them to meet any and all needs, which enforces a very real, material dependency. This is true even after they have formal citizenship, and despite the fact that they must pay taxes to support those very services they are barred from using. Sunera Thobani (2007: 138) writes,

> Sponsorship regulations have played no small role in the popular construction of immigrant families as overly patriarchal and of immigrant women as family bound, dependent on their families and cultural communities ... [and] it also increased their dependence on their families as sites of refuge from racism within Canadian society. The state's organization of immigration thus reinforced this conflictual relationship: on the one hand, patriarchal structures were strengthened as a direct result of state policy; on the other hand, these families often became the only sites of support against the racism these women encountered.

As Thobani notes, the role of family and community can also be different for racialized women in Canada, in that those spaces, even if they are oppressive in other ways, can be crucial sites of protection from the racism of the broader society. This can make decisions about how to respond to abuse within the family even more difficult. As well, the need for solidarity against racist oppression can also lead to different kinds of pressures on racialized women to be silent about experiences of violence at the hands of similarly racialized men (West 2005).

The state is also relevant as a provider and funder of services. Women who have recently migrated to Canada tend to experience social isolation and often face barriers not just to accessing but even to knowing about the existence of resources to address various needs, and the act of migrating cuts off their access to resources they might have used in their countries of origin to address problems, such as their extended families (Agnew 1996: 199–200, 212–213). As long histories of struggles in urban centres across the country show, there is also a history of experiences of racism, language barriers, and other barriers excluding women of colour from white-dominated social services (ibid.: 197). There is evidence from the United States that South Asian women have faced additional racist barriers in accessing mainstream services since the 9/11 attacks (Sthanki 2007). It is likely that something similar has occurred in Canada.

Of course experiences of racism are not limited to spaces that are directly associated with the state. Everyday experiences of racism and exclusion enacted by white Canadians constantly recreate and reinforce a sense of belonging in many of those white Canadians and a related experience of not-belonging among those who are racialized (Thobani 2007: 77–80). This is an important part of creating the grounding in which racialized women experience violence and from which they are forced to make choices about struggling against it.

Working Against Violence

Racialized women in Canada have taken a number of different approaches to responding politically to the oppressions they experience. One has always been participation within the women's movement, particularly since collective challenges from women of colour became visible in the 1980s but also before. In the context of responding to violence, for some women this has involved participating in the mainstream feminist anti-violence movement through a rape crisis centre, a women's shelter, or some other sort of organization. Such organizations are perpetually underfunded and struggling to survive, and it has been noted that frontline work by feminist anti-violence activists takes a serious toll on all women who do it (Martin 2006). However, women of colour working in mainstream shelters have also consistently faced interpersonal and structural racism there, and have had to struggle against those experiences for themselves and for women of colour who use the shelter (Kohli 1993; Agnew 1996: 217–224). This experience was related quite powerfully, in my interview with her and in her own writings, by Rita Kohli (1993),[3] who identifies as an older South Asian lesbian woman with visible and invisible disabilities.

Another option that racialized women have always taken is to engage in struggle on their own or in the context of their communities, whether that is the centuries of resistance to colonization by indigenous women or the important work done by enslaved and free African-descended women for almost as long in supporting themselves, their families, and their communities (Bristow et al. 1994). In terms of formal organizations by and for immigrant women of colour, the first appears to have been the Caribbean Club, a group of single Caribbean women employed as domestic workers who came together in 1958 in Toronto (Das Gupta 1996: 17).

Such groups and programs began to appear more commonly in the 1970s, and especially in the 1980s. Each has its own history, of course, but a few features seem to have been fairly common (Das Gupta 1996; Agnew 1996). Most began with women of colour organizing themselves to address the needs they experienced and saw around them. Many chose to seek funding — which usually ended up being inadequate — from the state. While this provided access to much-needed resources to meet basic needs, such funding has never been without risks. One study of such organizations found that a "desire to keep their funding" often led to a "more pragmatic, uncritical approach adopted by community groups" (Agnew 1996: 171–172).

Though this was far from universal, in many instances in this type of organization, the women working in them were middle-class and the women using the services were working-class women of the same background (ibid.: 149). Many of the groups had a focus on language training and employment-related issues, and acted as a liaison to try and reduce some of the barriers faced by immigrant women and women of colour in accessing services from mainstream organizations, including mainstream feminist organizations. A more open focus on violence against women of colour began to be more common in the late 1980s or early 1990s. Many of the women involved in this work would not have identified as feminist, which may be as much a comment on feminism as about the politics of these organizers, but some would have. Regardless of the label, the focus was on empowering women (ibid.: 153).

Mulay

Shree Mulay was born and grew up in India. She was one of three children, all girls, as was her mother, so from the time her father died when she was twelve or thirteen, she lived in a very woman-centric environment. She moved to Montreal to study biochemistry in 1964. Soon after arriving she attended a demonstration in Washington, D.C., opposed to the Vietnam War and subsequently became involved in anti-war activities in Montreal. As did so many women involved in anti-war activism in that era, Mulay became aware that the group's activities were organized in sexist ways.

> You could see the differentiation made between men and women — what tasks were appropriate for women, who made the decisions, and what women would do in that context. I think it very much heightened my awareness of the disparity in decision-making and power-sharing between men and women.
>
> What I used to react to, as I remember, is when certain kinds of tasks would be allotted to women — such as stuffing the envelopes for meetings, going door-to-door collecting signatures — and the men in the group would be the ones to discuss the larger implications of the war and prepare the pamphlet that was to be written for distribution and so on. I resented that quite a bit.

At the time, Mulay's intent was to return to India when she completed her studies. This kept her focused on her academic work and made her feel a bit more distanced from the anti-war activities than many others swept up into social movement activity in that era. She completed her PhD in 1968 and a period of time followed in which she attempted unsuccessfully to obtain work in India, between short post-doctoral positions in Canada. She recalled, "That temporariness in my mind affected my participation in Canadian politics and Canadian social movements to a great extent." However, because of where she could find work, she eventually decided to remain in Canada, and in that era with her qualifications she had no difficulties in obtaining Canadian citizenship. "The moment I decided to apply for Canadian citizenship, my attitude changed."

During her earliest years as a citizen in Canada, Mulay was busy with paid work and she had two children. However, she also stayed in touch with others who had attended the Indian Institute of Technology, a group of elite educational institutions in India that specialized in technical fields. Many students from these institutions came to North America for further studies, and they and some other professionals from South Asia living on this continent formed an informal social network. Many also happened to have politics broadly in sympathy with the left, and in 1975 a number of these people formed an organization called the Indian People's Association in North America (IPANA).[4] The group's informal founding conference was held in Montreal. Mulay said,

> The group was formed directly in response to the National Emergency declared by the Indian Prime Minister, Mrs. Indira Gandhi, in 1975. The National Emergency basically abrogated all civilian rights. So this particular group began to do work on the question of civil liberties in India, and bringing the question of the poverty of Indian people to the fore, because Mrs. Gandhi's slogan was *Garibi Hatao*, which is "remove poverty." Her slogans were progressive but the actual implementation of what was actually done was *garib hatao*, which means "remove the poor."

Civil liberties in India remained the focus of the group until the National Emergency was lifted in 1977.

At that point, the participants in IPANA started to look around and figure out what they should do next. Immigration from South Asia to Canada had shifted from the earlier predominance (in most regions) of middle-class professionals to a much more working-class profile. As the members of IPANA asked "how do we become relevant here" and "not only for what's happening back there," those that lived in western Canada decided "to support the migrant farm workers in B.C." In Montreal, Mulay and some of the other members became particularly concerned about "immigrant women, women facing isolation" and they "decided as a group that there should be something which deals specifically with immigrant women and South Asian women." She said,

> We began to meet informally in 1980.[5] And it was really to say, "Oh, isn't it terrible. We have to do something about it." That was the general approach, because we had, ourselves, seen what was happening to many of the women who were coming. And these were people who were coming in under the family class, who would be virtual prisoners in their homes. It took a long time to reach an agreement as to what should be done. We decided that the only way to find out was to actually go and talk to people. So again we decided to go into those areas where there was a concentration of South Asians. We would go to shopping centres, just engage people in conversation to find out if there was a centre, what would you want in a centre like this. We also went door-to-door. There is one particular district in Montreal which basically consists of people who are mainly South Asian working class. They work in the factories — Montreal has had a huge garment industry in the past. It was partly talking to people, but also partly observing.

So it was that kind of discussion that led to a decision that we should have a centre where women can come and take language classes. You have to remember that no language classes were offered at that time [for women who entered as family class immigrants], either in French or in English.

They also wanted the centre to be "a place where women could gather, a place where there was some possibility of people calling in if they were in difficulty. From that evolved the charter or mission statement for the centre." So they had a mission and a strong core of volunteers, but not yet a solid plan for the work that they wanted to do. They managed to get funding from the Canadian and Quebec governments for five contract positions before they had any office space — the group was still meeting in people's homes. Luckily, at that point Mulay ran into an old friend who worked for one of the big social service agencies in Montreal. They had a few empty rooms in one of their buildings, and were willing to let the new centre use them. The formal opening of the centre was in 1981.

Siddiqui

Siddiqui's journey to SAWCC took a different path than Mulay's. She immigrated to Canada from Pakistan in the 1960s with her husband and family. In 1983, Siddiqui was not thinking about becoming an activist or about working to empower women; she was just looking for a job. Nonetheless, Siddiqui said,

> I had interest in the sense that from my childhood I saw my mother was very active in the community, so something was with me to help people and all that. But when I came to Canada, I thought that I left all of those things, those problems, behind.… When I started working in this organization, I realized that women are bringing the same sorts of problems here with them.
>
> My first job [with the centre] was only for five months to work on a project. After finishing that project I never left this organization, because this is the work that I wanted to do.

According to Siddiqui, the centre approached their work in a way distinct from many mainstream organizations. "They take one problem at a time." However, at the centre, "You don't just work on one aspect of women's problems." She used the example, "If the husband is beating her, then why is she in this situation?" Starting from that kind of question foregrounds all of the ways in which the causes of such an oppressive predicament weave together in how such situations are actually experienced. Early in Siddiqui's employment at the centre, the two biggest issues she saw were economic dependency and experiences of violence, and she saw them as part of the same problem: "[My] first thoughts were how to help them get out of that poverty and that dependence and get out of that violent situation." This kind of holistic understanding of the lives of racialized women can result in action of many different sorts, depending on the resources available, the inclinations of the women involved, and the barriers to particular approaches both within and outside of the groups that are taking action. The centre has had to navigate all of these issues, and their concrete actions in support of the everyday struggles of racialized immigrant women have varied depending on circumstances, opportunities, and barriers.

The angle that the centre tackled first was that of financial dependence. In part this was because it was a problem seen as integral to all of the other problems that women were facing and in part because there seemed to be an opportunity, back in 1983, to have this line of work supported by money from the state. They wanted

> to create opportunity for women to earn money by using the skills they have. We know that women have some kind of ability in them, skills in them. Almost all South Asian women can sew and cook at home; they make everything at home that they have no need to go out and buy, like clothing or handicrafts — anything. We thought that that would be the project, to take those skills and develop them into a business venture.

The initial vision was quite extensive: "Under one roof we wanted to have a seamstresses service; we wanted to have a small boutique with handicrafts; and a fast food take-out, a small café sort of thing." However, at this point the centre was still very new, and they were unable to obtain the resources to plunge immediately into realizing the full scale of this vision. So they started smaller.

> The first successful thing that we did was to have women coming to the centre and that created an interest to develop some kind of thing, to think about: "Yes, I can make things. I have the skills. I can make money with this." We had four or five women who were really good and interested in cooking, so we taught them to do catering, how you could develop it yourself, what is needed to provide food for parties and so on. So they learned that.... We did not have the kitchen facilities so we went from home to home, to each woman's home, once or twice a week, and we started preparing recipes and teaching all of these women how to use those recipes so that if one woman was not available then the others could use them. Learning each other's recipes, ways to make food in an efficient way and how to serve the food, was part of the training.

As time passed, they moved to preparing sit-down dinners for groups from the centre's membership, and then to advertising the service in the larger community and catering parties. The organization was quite informal: the centre fronted the money for the food, then when the women were paid they would pay the centre back and split the balance amongst themselves. It led, in turn, to other opportunities: women doing catering on their own, one teaching cooking classes, even a group of ten who were awarded a contract to run a cafeteria for a year.

> It worked the same way for sewing.... People donated two sewing machines to the centre and some women already had machines. So what we did was we took orders from universities and colleges for uniforms — karate uniforms, judo uniforms — and the women would make them.

Barriers and Divisions

Though this work could be framed as service-oriented rather than political, and thus be eligible for state funding, it had very political outcomes for the women whose lives it touched in that it provided them with opportunities to develop significantly greater power over their own lives. This line of activity was uncontroversial among those women whose work made the centre a reality and in the larger community. However, in order to honour the holistic vision motivating many women working at the centre, more than just this single dimension of women's experience had to be addressed. It was some of these other strands of activity that resulted at times in opposition both within the centre's own ranks and from the larger South Asian communities in Montreal.

Perhaps the most serious division within the centre around questions of how to orient their activities occurred in the mid 1980s. Mulay remembers that SAWCC "almost collapsed."

> It collapsed because there were these two aspects: women who were very committed to feminism and saw the need to bring up political issues [and others who felt differently]. One of them, for example, was dowry deaths.[6] In India, dowry deaths were rampant and they still continue to this day. We started a signature campaign which was addressed to Mrs. Gandhi, Prime Minister of India, and we collected lots and lots of signatures with the idea of delivering it to her, which was done.... But this was seen as a very political move. And within the group a schism developed. Those who felt that we should just focus on providing social services, and others who felt that politics was important, that political lobbying and all of that

needed to remain within the organization. These two have always been the tensions within the organization over the period of time. And within the organization they play out in different ways. So you may have the organization sometimes swinging more toward service delivery and other times more toward doing politics around social issues. In '85 one of the persons who had been with us right from the start decided that she did not agree with the others.

Then followed some of the nastier sort of infighting that can happen within an organization, including manipulation of by-laws, intense personal conflict, and the involvement of the courts. Though the woman championing the services-only orientation was at one point elected president of the centre, ultimately the court decided that the women who wished to keep a political orientation in the centre could not be arbitrarily excluded from it and could not be deprived of the centre's membership list. Mulay said that the situation

> was a tremendous setback because one of the consequences was that the free space that we had been given, they no longer wanted to have to deal with all of this fighting within the organization. So they basically gave notice that, "You have to find your own premises."

After the court ruling that did not favour her approach, what the centre's president at that time

> did, basically, was she found a place in a terrible location, in the middle of a shopping centre, and called the annual general meeting and resigned at that meeting. She submitted an annual report which was distributed very widely to the government, to our employers, accusing us of having a different political agenda, that we were radicals, that we were trying to front this organization to achieve extreme left wing politics. The organization could have collapsed because all of the funding disappeared at that time. Governments don't like to support organizations that are bickering within.

In response, "many of us took the decision that we won't let the organization collapse." Extensive private fundraising and volunteer labour kept the centre going. They paid their way out of their lease and found cheaper space, and "from then on the organization actually managed to make a gradual comeback financially."

Perhaps a more enduring challenge was not opposition to a holistic, political, and feminist orientation within the ranks of the centre, but opposition from certain segments of the broader South Asian communities in Montreal. In particular, Siddiqui identified that there was pressure within South Asian communities in Montreal and in North America as a whole to stay silent about violence against women. From the original British colonization of India to today's War on Terror, South Asian peoples have been attacked and their domination by white and Western people justified in the dominant imagination by racist claims about South Asian men supposedly being savage and inherently misogynist and about South Asian women supposedly needing to be protected by white/Western intervention (Razack 2008). Research in the U.S. context has shown that the need for racialized communities to survive and struggle against relations of racial oppression has historically resulted in what some have called a "political gag order" around violence against women, which can make it even more challenging for racialized women to speak up about violence they experience (West 2005). Siddiqui added, "This was always a family matter." Even she herself, before starting to work at the centre and seeing how much of a problem it was, "never thought that a woman would experience that kind of situation in Canada."

Initially the centre avoided addressing the issue directly, as a tactical approach to staying more connected to the community. For the first ten years of the organization's existence, the word "women" was actually not in the name — it was simply the South Asian Community Centre. This was consistent with the experiences of many other organizations of and for immigrant women through the 1980s, whose participants were certainly aware of the problems but who chose to navigate the obstacles in front of them by taking a less direct approach.

However, when faced with direct appeals for support, the women running the centre could not say no. It was an instance of support for a woman experiencing violence that resulted in a flare-up of community outrage in the early years of the centre. According to Mulay, "The way it got SAWCC into difficulty was that there was a woman who had been battered for a number of years and she came to the centre saying, 'Help me, I'm just desperate.' She had three children." Siddiqui remembered,

> The first time we received this call — actually, it was not a call, but one woman was brought to the centre by the shelter home. It was the only shelter in Montreal at that time. That woman was brought by the shelter worker and the police because she had difficulty with English and French. They wanted to know what exactly happened to her. She was all bruised and burned and had cut marks.… From that day on, I said, "Yes, that sort of situation we have to work with."

In the specific case at hand, the centre had to figure out on the fly how best to offer support. Mulay said,

> So SAWCC said, "It's very clear, you should leave your abusive

114 – Gender and Sexuality

> husband." She was ready to do that but she just did not have any resources. So that was the first time that SAWCC found out how to go about finding help for somebody to get them on social assistance, finding them a lawyer, etc. You have to do it once to know exactly what you can and cannot do.

It was this offer of direct support that resulted in backlash from some sectors of the community. According to Mulay,

> The husband filed a case against SAWCC for alienating his wife from him. He laid some heavy charges. SAWCC was named as one of the accused in this whole process. He had a case against his wife and also a case against SAWCC. But, of course, it was thrown out of court because it didn't make any sense at all. What it did was it gave SAWCC a reputation in the community of being an organization of radical feminists, bra burning feminists, man hating feminists who really wanted to break up every single marriage.

The centre persevered, however, and began strategizing about how best to offer support to women who needed it in this sort of environment. Siddiqui said,

> After this case we realized that there are women around here who were going through this situation. We wanted to start a small group talking about the situation. Because women would not have come out and talked about their situation unless they were sure people understood. We needed to open the discussion to make women aware of the situation. But how were we going to bring them out and talk about it? So in small gatherings and small groups we started talking about family situations, women's rights, what resources were available, what the shelters were. We just wanted women to know that in Canada there are many services available to women victims of family violence. When you learn the language, when you study and work, then you need to know what rights you have. We described what the shelter was for and all of that and slowly women started coming in to talk about their family situation.

The process of rebuilding the reputation of the organization in the South Asian communities at large was slow. According to Mulay,

> I think the women who had received services from the centre were our best advocates in being able to say that we were not at all insisting that they should all leave their husbands, that it was only one of the options that was offered to them in the delivery of our services.

Mulay also identified the importance of the particular approach to doing feminist politics embraced by SAWCC: though they are a feminist organization, they do not exclude men from their services. Only the actual board of the organization is women-only, but things like language classes and support for refugees are open to everyone.

In the late 1980s and early 1990s, organizations by and for racialized immigrant women across Canada began to speak about issues of violence more openly. SAWCC played an important role in this process by organizing a conference for South Asian women from across Canada and the United States in 1991. Siddiqui identified it as "the first conference in North America where South Asian women talked about violence against women." As well, she said, "many men who attended the conference understood the situation in the community." One of the initiatives to come out of this conference specifically in the Montreal context was an effort to bring leaders from the South Asian communities and their organizations into discussions about violence. At the time, many women experiencing violence sought help from religious or organizational leaders, and not all of these were dispensing advice that, in SAWCC's opinion, was in the best interest of the affected women. In the fashion of conservative elite men everywhere, Siddiqui said that some of these leaders needed to "understand that violence is not just happening because the woman is annoying her husband or not doing household chores, or not serving him." SAWCC was able to foster dialogue about how best to respond to women in South Asian communities who were experiencing violence, as well as to build credibility as an organization that could respond to the problem.

Making Change

Creating opportunities for women to end their financial dependence, directly supporting survivors of interpersonal violence, and facilitating discussions around issues of violence in Montreal's South Asian communities were all important. However, Mulay, Siddiqui, and the other women in SAWCC realized that this was still not enough.

One further response to these problems was exerting quiet pressure on the state behind the scenes to try and change some aspects of how racialized immigrant women's lives were organized into states of dependence in the first place. One site where this happened was around rules barring most immigrant women from eligibility for employment training programs, which reinforced their dependence on their husbands. Governments are most likely to pay for employment training for those people who are already receiving money from other programs paid for by that level of government, so federal programs are targeted to people on Unemployment (more recently, Employment) Insurance while provincial programs are most likely to be open to people on welfare. Once they become employed, that reduces that level of government's expenditure on support programs. Yet many racialized immigrant women who entered the country under the family class were, in Siddiqui's words, "sitting home." She clarified, "When I say 'women sitting home' I mean women who are economically depending on their husband and have never been in the job market or on welfare." They are not eligible for unemployment or welfare benefits because of the terms of their immigration sponsorship and they have a great deal of difficulty finding employment because they have no previous experience doing waged work in Canada. SAWCC began by exerting pressure in meetings with funders to accept one or two women who had been "sitting home" into a training program. Siddiqui said,

> After that, next year, we said, "Look, because of this program, those who were sitting home are now working, because these are the women who have the qualifications and now they are coming out." So, slowly, they accepted them. At one point I had twelve women, all of whom had been sitting at home. This way we showed the government the rate of success of getting into the job market. Some of them started working at the centre here, some of them started working in other places. That's all. There was no big campaign. It was a very slow process. This is how it happened.
>
> With that, many women have found jobs and become independent.

Behind-the-scenes lobbying only gets you so far, however. To get farther requires more openly political action, and that is most effective not as one small organization in one city but as part of a larger movement. On December 6, 1989, Mark Lépine went on a rampage at Montreal's École Polytechnique and killed fourteen women who were engineering students there, proclaiming both aloud and in a letter left behind his hatred of feminists.[7] The shock of this event led to organizing by women across Canada, particularly in Quebec, and it also encouraged women in South Asian communities in Quebec to begin to network more actively around issues of violence. The conference in 1991 came from this increased networking, and it was this conference, said Mulay, "that actually meant that we came on the radar screen of the Quebec [feminist] groups." Up to that time, the centre had been largely focused only on the South Asian communities while the broader women's movement had shown little interest in them.

Still, it was a long way from beginning to be aware of each other's existence and activities to actually working together.

Siddiqui said, "First of all, there's this organization called Fédération des femmes du Québec [FFQ]. Up until 1990 the Fédération des femmes du Québec was not open to women from cultural communities. It was controlled by white Francophone women. It was so hard to get into that one."[8] To do so, she continued, "We developed a group among ourselves with the leadership of Madeleine Parent[9] and Fatima Houda-Pepin," who later became a Liberal MNA in Quebec, to help bridge the divide.

Mulay remembered that Parent

> essentially introduced us to the FFQ, facilitated the discussions between the FFQ and SAWCC. The reason why it needed to be facilitated is that FFQ has had a very strong position about national independence of Quebec. As far as immigrant groups are concerned, their affiliation is with Canada.[10] So immediately it raises all kinds of divisions. An Anglophone women's organization that does not support the independence project of Quebec doesn't fit very well within the FFQ. So that discussion, and Madeleine facilitating that discussion, was very, very important because people in SAWCC trusted her. And the FFQ also trusted her judgement considerably. So in 1992 the FFQ held a conference called "Une société pluriel" or something like that, or "Un forum pluriel." And in that they wanted to bring more immigrant women but they had no connections with immigrant women.

Siddiqui remembered that the informal group facilitated by Parent and Houda-Pepin

> forced the Fédération des femmes du Québec at that time to let us be part of their annual general meeting and conference. We wanted to be part of their round table, and we wanted to give presentation[s] in their workshops on the issues concerning women of colour. We mentioned to them that our presentations would be in English and they should make arrangements for translation, and they did. That was our first introduction to meeting with FFQ. It went very well.
>
> After that, we became members of FFQ. It took a little bit longer, one or two years, to be recognized as full members.... Now they like us to be part of their organization. In a token way, still, but it is there. It is like they recognize the importance of bringing other women into their organization.

These initial discussions "evolved into the Bread and Roses March,[11] which took place in 1995," said Mulay. Under the leadership of well-known feminist Françoise David, the FFQ decided to push the Quebec government to take action on women's poverty. They planned a multi-day march in late May and early June from Montreal to Quebec City, ending in a large rally in front of the National Assembly. This happened to be the same year as the Parti Quebecois' sovereignty referendum, which was scheduled for the fall.

Many expected that the desire to cultivate women's movement support for the referendum campaign would make the government more open to listening to the demands of the march. It was in formulating those demands in the months leading up to the march that SAWCC women made their presence felt. Siddiqui remembered,

> The demands were on the table and everybody was discussing them but there was no consideration of the difficulties of immigrant women. We said, "Where are we? We have disappeared in there. Yes, we understand all of your demands which are ours too, but how about issues specific to immigrant women in Quebec?"
>
> They said, "Okay, you have your own meeting and bring your demands from there." Then we brought our women together and prepared our demands to include in with the others. It became part of the demands and it is still in the Quebec demands.

The process among immigrant women focused on four demands: the recognition of degrees and training received abroad; funding for women to take French-language classes, including an allowance equivalent to that provided for men taking such classes; a reduction in the sponsorship period from ten years to three years, to make it easier for women to leave abusive relationships; and operating funding for women's centres based in racialized and immigrant communities. Mulay particularly emphasized the significance of the third demand:

> Until 1995 you had to be sponsored for ten years, which meant if you came as a dependent, for ten years you were supported by your husband or spouse or whoever had sponsored you, and you could not apply for an independent position, which meant that social services, language training services were inaccessible to women who had been brought over as dependants.... And actually the Quebec government accepted that particular demand and reduced the sponsorship period to three years and women became eligible for the language courses right away. These were all very positive changes.

The success of this march lead Quebec feminists and feminists in the rest of Canada to organize a similar march with a pan-Canadian focus on women's poverty in June of 1996, in which SAWCC also took part. Over roughly the same period that SAWCC was challenging barriers to participation in the mainstream women's movement in Quebec, it was also part of a similar challenge at the National Action Committee on the Status of Women (NAC), the main coalition of feminist organizations at the federal level. Though it is beyond the scope of this chapter to talk in depth about this important and very difficult instance of anti-racist organizational change, what matters here is that SAWCC again played an important role in inserting the concerns of racialized women into this space, and again an important mediating role was played by Madeleine Parent, who at the time was the regional representative of NAC in Quebec. An important early lobbying effort that involved SAWCC occurred in 1992. According to Mulay,

> They had chosen fourteen cases of women — and the number was deliberate because, as you know, there were fourteen women who were killed at L'École Polytechnique — so they took fourteen cases of women who were denied immigration to Canada on humanitarian grounds. And this was specifically looking at the whole question of gender discrimination. There were women from the South Asian sub-continent who were part of that particular initiative, and SAWCC was very much involved with that particular case, putting forward, lobbying for them, going to the Justice Department, going to the Quebec immigration, becoming part of that national campaign.

Mulay went on to become a member of the executive of NAC for three years in the mid 1990s, and women from SAWCC became regular active participants in NAC activities.

In the late 1990s, Quebec feminists also became a driving force behind an even more ambitious project: the World March of Women. Siddiqui became a part of the committee coordinating the World March, and it again became an opportunity to push for greater responsiveness to the needs and demands of racialized women.

> When I became part of this World March coordination committee I realized that I was the only woman of colour there. We pushed the FFQ to bring more women from cultural communities. "You are not doing outreach to immigrant women, especially to Anglophone immigrant women and allophone immigrant women."
>
> They asked us to find someone from our community do this job for a few months and contact with cultural groups. Though I felt really bad that it became our job — "We have to do it, they can't do it," sort of thing — then we realized that something had to be done. "If they're asking us to do it, let's do it." This person contacted immigrant women from ethno-cultural communities and informed them about the World March and encouraged them to participate in it. And some of them became part of that march.

The hard work of countless women around the globe made the World March a success. It focused on issues of women's poverty and violence against women. It culminated in October 2000 with local actions around the world and a rally at the United Nations headquarters in New York City. In Canada, intense organizing of the almost one thousand groups that participated in the campaign in more than two hundred communities across the country — coordinated by the committee of which Siddiqui was a part — culminated in a demonstration of 35,000 people on Parliament Hill on October 15, 2000. Almost a quarter of a million Canadians signed cards supporting the campaign directed at the U.N. (Krapper 2000).

These efforts by the women of SAWCC not only contributed to change in the broader women's movement and to efforts by the women's movement to create change in the broader society, but they also were very significant to the development of SAWCC itself. Mulay said,

> When your vision changes from one of being a local organization to one connected to a large network, you begin to look at policies a little bit differently. Therefore, presenting briefs, participating in policy making, I think was an important next step for SAWCC. I'm not saying it was successful at all levels, but just making that shift, that transformation — that you are connected to a whole network of organizations, not only South Asians but other women's organizations, immigrant organizations, whether they're in Toronto or whether they're elsewhere — that was important.
>
> [As an executive member of NAC] I was able to bring what was being discussed nationally to the local level, and from the local level to the national level. And that's a very powerful two-way street to be involved in and to be part of.
>
> It began by the case of these refugee women, but it grew in other ways so that for the first time representatives from SAWCC — excluding me because I was on the executive, but many other women — started going to the national lobby. You begin to see how the government functions, what are the issues that can be brought, what is the forum at which it can be brought, what is a successful tactic, what is not a successful tactic. These are very, very important lessons. You cannot learn them by reading about them in textbooks. You have to do it in order learn it. You might make mistakes, but you learn from that particular process.
>
> My perception is that it is related to coming of age for the organization.

According to Siddiqui, SAWCC's political work is far from over. "Still we are fighting with the Quebec government to give women a chance to develop, to improve their skills, and recognize degrees that they have from their home country. Still we're fighting."

And in terms of the relationship to the broader women's movement in Quebec and Canada, she said, "No, it was not easy. And still it is not where we want it to be.... It's still an ongoing struggle." Still, she believes that what has been achieved is very significant. "Our women who were receiving our services became part of these marches. It's like we broke their isolation. We exposed them to the mainstream society, mainstream women.... It's like solidarity is built."

Meanwhile, conversations among racialized women and their allies about how best to respond to both gendered violence and the violence of the state are ongoing. Though there are important differences in the ways in which non-profit, community, and activist organizations have formed in the United States, Canada, and Quebec, increasing attention is being paid in grassroots spaces in Canada to discussions originating from communities in the United States around some of these questions and to novel experiments in how to navigate the contradiction between the need for resources and the strings to which state and non-profit resources are often tied (Ng 1990; A. Smith 2005; Incite! Women of Color Against Violence 2006; Incite! Women of Color Against Violence 2007). Older organizations like SAWCC continue their important work to meet needs and mobilize women while younger activists, including significant leadership from young women of colour, have been experimenting in Canadian contexts with ways of organizing among immigrants and refugees that explore new approaches to addressing basic needs, mobilizing people, and challenging the violence organized into immigrant and refugee lives by the Canadian state (Scott 2006).

Notes

1. Racialized women have also collectively challenged anti-racist movements in terms of sexism.
2. "Trans" is often used as an inclusive term to indicate people who are sex or gender non-conforming in one or more of a range of ways, including people who identify as transgender, transsexual, cross-dressers, intersex, or two-spirit.
3. In an article based on her own experiences and those of past and present immigrant, Jewish, and women of colour shelter workers in Toronto, Kohli (1993: 414–415, emphasis in original) concludes that, for those groups of women, jobs in shelters "have not been *empowering*. The silencing, invisibility, fear of reprisals, the greater demand for accountability, profound sense of betrayal, powerlessness, implicit coercion and punishment speak of grievous contradictions between the feminist mandate of shelters and the actual practice therein."
4. To hear some of Mulay's memories of IPANA, go to www.talkingradical.ca/audio/mulay_ipana.mp3.
5. To hear a more extended account of Mulay's memories of the founding of SAWCC, go to www.talkingradical.ca/audio/mulay_sawcc.mp3.
6. Leti Volpp (2005: 41) writes: "Dowry murders take place when a new wife is murdered, usually burned to death, in connection to escalating dowry demands."

The way that these murders often get talked about in the West, including by many mainstream feminists, ends up contributing to dominant racist imagery of non-white people as inherently "violent" and "savage." However, Volpp (ibid.) points out that dowry murder is roughly analogous to domestic violence in the North American context, and "death by domestic violence in the United States is numerically as significant a social problem as dowry murders in India."

7. For a brief feminist account of Lépine's actions and the text of the letter that the *Globe and Mail* described as a "suicide" letter but that feminists have argued is more accurately characterized as a "femicide" letter, see Pierson 1993: 115, 168–169.
8. To hear some of Siddiqui's memories of SAWCC's early relationship with the FFQ, go to www.talkingradical.ca/audio/siddiqui_ffq.mp3.
9. For an account of some of Madeleine Parent's earlier activities in Quebec, see Chapter 2.
10. No group is monolithic, of course. There were referendums on Quebec sovereignty in 1980 and in 1995. Mulay herself voted in favour of sovereignty in 1980 but against it in 1995. She said that in the earlier period, the Parti Quebecois "had a very broad social democratic vision" and so she supported their efforts at independence. "As the years evolved and as they stayed in power for a longer period of time, I could see how there was erosion of that particular ideal." She supported their efforts around protecting the French language but was deeply disturbed by a number of anti-union moves by the PQ government in the early 1980s. She was also concerned that "the Quebec government began to become increasingly xenophobic and racist." Public and governmental discourse became more and more hostile to immigrants. Protecting the French language was sometimes used as a justification, but it was clear to Mulay that "it didn't matter if the immigrant spoke French or not" and that the increasing hostility was directed at racialized people regardless of what language they spoke. "From a national social democratic vision it had shifted to one that was just purely nationalist. I've seen what terrible things it has done in India, and I did not want it repeated here."
11. To hear some of Siddiqui's memories related to the Bread and Roses March and the World March of Women, go to www.talkingradical.ca/audio/siddiqui_marches.mp3.

Chapter 5

Living Rooms, Bedrooms, and the Streets
Chris Vogel and Richard North
on Gay Liberation in Winnipeg

It's a story as old as time: Boy meets boy, they fall in love, and then set out to change the world.

I was set to hear one particular telling of that story from Chris Vogel and Richard North. I walked toward their home along tree-lined streets through an older residential neighbourhood in urban Winnipeg. As I made my way past parked cars, shovelled walks, and corner stores, I looked around me and reflected on the nature of urban space and on how it is shaped by social relations and in turn shapes our lives. The housing stock that is available plus many other details of how urban space is put together shape the choices we have for organizing our domestic living arrangements, how we get around, and how we get food in cities, among other things. And I didn't know it at the time, but there were features of urban design that were instituted in the early twentieth century in part to suppress opportunities for sex between men (Maynard 1994b). There are a great many neighbourhoods I would find more constricting and depressing than Vogel and North's — that is to say, suburbs — but there was still a sense of mandated conformity that building codes, the social relations embodied by the automobile, social expectations about "normal" living arrangements, the drive of capital to maximize profit, and a host of other factors have all imprinted on almost any fragment of North American cityscape.

Yet I also knew that their part of the city was not just streets and buildings, but that it had been home to many activists from many movements over the years and had long been an important part of the landscape in Winnipeg's rich, radical past. There was something reassuring in the knowledge that nothing can be imposed absolutely, that hidden within these similar houses on similar streets were people with an unknowable range of visions and desires — desires to arrange life differently in all sorts of ways, big and small, if only the will and the means could be found to do so. And I was lucky enough to know that I was about to be welcomed into one of those homes to hear about how desire contrary to dominant norms in at least one important respect had found expression in the lives of Vogel and North, in the face of intense obstacles.

Chris Vogel is a white man who grew up in a prairie family with a long history of support for the left-leaning CCF and later its successor, the NDP, and is a career civil servant with the Province of Manitoba. In the interview, he spoke smoothly and confidently, and often with a certain self-deprecating humour, whether the topic was his 1974 marriage to Richard North, the Manitoba NDP's long hostility to gay rights, or bickering among activists within the movement. North, a son of middle-class white Ontario, spoke a little less and a little more tentatively but with no less conviction as he talked about his time managing one of Winnipeg's few gay club rooms or about his fifty-nine day hunger strike. The two met in Winnipeg in the early 1970s and became both a couple and gay liberation activists soon after. For Vogel, it went something like this:

> Having met Rich and expecting to live with him provided one answer to the question I had been asking myself all through my teens after I realized I was gay.... So the domestic situation seemed to be taken care of, but now there was the whole rest of society to deal with.

Of course "the whole rest of society" was not exactly a welcoming place for men who desired other men, and it still isn't. The relentless, pounding message might be summarized as, "You should not exist. And if you do exist, you must be invisible. And if you are not invisible, you must be punished." But these two specific young men met in a specific time and place, one that gave them some options that were rather rare, historically speaking. Not only could they be together and try to change the world but they could try to change the world in ways that had everything to do with them being together.

Sexuality Matters

It would be easy to write this chapter, and to read it, much more narrowly than it deserves. "Boy meets boy, they fall in love, and then set out to change the world." Seems obvious, right? And on a certain level it is. But the issues at the centre of this chapter weave through the rest of social relations far more than many people suspect.

I grew up in a family that was relatively liberal in an apolitical and intellectual sort of way, but not one in which there was any openness or comfort about sexual issues on a personal level. When I first encountered issues of same-gender desire presented in blunt and politicized ways, along with people who themselves were unapologetically and openly queer,[1] it was not just that I suddenly had to deal with the impact of years of heterosexist and homophobic messaging from peers and the culture at large. I also had to deal with the anxiety and confusion that came from sexuality, *any* sexuality, being openly present, admitted, and discussed. Of course, sexuality is something we all experience, but it is deeply personal — however joyful or painful our own relationship to it, it is clear that our sexual histories, our desires, our aversions, and our experiences of sexual trauma weave deeply through who we are. It is capable of evoking immensely powerful reactions, both positive and negative. Because it is so personal, it is very easy (for some) to lose sight of the fact that sexuality is also relentlessly social and public.

As an example of the social power associated with sexuality, take my experience of making choices in writing this chapter. Despite an interest in making some use of both my own journey and anecdotes from the experiences of people in my life to try where possible to personalize ideas that have the potential to be abstract and alienating, there are whole vast swaths of that raw material that I am simply not going to consider using in this instance. That is because, even at its most vanilla, banal, and ordinary, sexuality and the strong stigmas that adhere to it can be used and abused in powerful ways. Some of this is as simple as me not wanting to risk provoking undesired conversation with older relatives after they read this; much is because people close to me have made certain choices about where and where not to share histories of sexual trauma or of joyfully embraced dissenting practices[2] related to sexuality and relationships (including, for some, same-gender desire), and it is not up to me to add even a scintilla of risk to their experience. This decision could be individualized, psychologized — it could be read as fear or cowardice or shame, on my part or on the part of others whose choices I am respecting. Certainly an ongoing struggle with shame is part of my journey and part of the journeys of many others.[3] To stop the analysis there, though, is to largely miss the point: Shame and fear do not arise from nothing. We have to be taught to feel ashamed; consequences must loom for us to become afraid.

Through laws, religious decrees, social relations that produce and enforce "normal" masculinity and femininity, the dominant media and popular culture, potential barriers to accessing the money all of us need to live, and the whispering of neighbours, sexuality is regulated and constrained, especially for women but also for men. Your ability to access welfare or pension benefits might depend on what relationships you have or used to have, and whether you have organized them according to what the government says is "right" and "normal." You might lose your job or custody of your children if institutions with power deem your sexual choices unsuitable. Your erotic practices and ways of structuring the relationships in your life might cause no harm and bring you happiness, but that will not necessarily stop a neighbour from refusing to talk to you, your community from shunning you, or your religious organization from expelling you. You might even be jailed by the state or beaten and killed by vigilantes taking the disdain and disapproval and loathing they see directed at you from all sides to what they consider to be the next logical step. And for women, your choice *not* to be sexually active in a given instance or in general, or to share your sexuality only with other women, is all too often met with sexualized violence from men. In all of these ways, people are pushed toward "straight" and "normal," and dissident ways of doing sexuality and relationships are either prevented or forced into secrecy.

Many different kinds of refusal to go along with dominant, oppressive, mandatory understandings of "normal" for sexual and relationship practices can result in such regulatory consequences, mild or severe. A traditional marriage with someone of the "wrong" racial background,[4] "kinky" sexual practices, premarital cohabitation, refusal by a woman to grant sexual access to a man who expects or demands it, open and honest arrangements that involve romantic/sexual partnerships with more than one person simultaneously,[5] expressions of assertive and adventurous sexuality by women, and even just having an intense but platonic friendship with someone not of your gender have at moments in the past and can still face consequences of one sort or another. So, of course, can having a sexual/romantic relationship with someone of the same gender. Since the 1970s, the organization of our lives in ways that assume and promote heterosexual relationships (of a certain sort) and erase and punish same-gender desire and same-gender relationships has been called "heterosexism" (Bunch 1987).[6]

Things that regulate, repress, and limit people's ability to express and enjoy sexuality often play a role in supporting other social relations of power. For example, the widespread reality of male sexual violence against women not only works at a social level to limit women's choices around and enjoyment of sexuality but also creates fear and a legacy of trauma that plays a much broader role in perpetuating the subordination of women (Brownmiller 1975). Other feminists have pointed out that social relations that make heterosexuality compulsory are not just oppressive to lesbians but are integral to the ways in which the oppressions of all women are organized (Rich 1994).

As well, the deep visceral reaction that sexuality and sexual topics evoke means that fears, phobias, and prejudices can be easily manipulated to push other agendas that do harm to oppressed groups. For example, the common contempt against women who act on a vigorous and diverse sexual appetite (but not men who do the same) is often mobilized by lawyers for the male accused in sexual assault cases in their introduction into the courtroom of the sexual histories of the women who have been assaulted, in order to make them seem to judge and jury to be less credible witnesses or less worthy victims. There also tends to be a sexual component to the racist images of people of colour that exist in the mainstream culture, part of the way people of colour are seen as "other" and "lesser" (DeGroot 1989; Ware 1992: 169–224; Valverde 1991; Lawson 2002). This includes specific issues where sexuality and racism intertwine, like the development of the dominant North American conception of "African AIDS"[7] and more general constructions of particular identities in the white imagination, like the "erotic and exotic" South Asian woman and the "sexually predatory" Black man. This last example, in turn, can be one strand of the racism that leads to few white people objecting to or even acknowledging the existence of racist policing that targets Black (and other racialized) communities and individuals. It is a common theme of the right-wing side of debates about welfare to try and inflame disapproval of and desire to regulate the sexuality of poor women, particularly poor women of colour, by demonizing single mothers (Duggan 2003).

When seen in this light, it becomes obvious that sexuality is very much public as well as private for all of us, and that the physical and emotional depth with which it is felt helps to give it a great deal of social power as it winds together with all of these other issues. For the most part, we in North America do not do well at genuinely discussing sex. The influence of heterosexism and homophobia mean that this is emphatically more true when it comes to genuine discussion of queer sexualities. Most of the time, sexuality is commodified and turned into a site of domination by the patriarchal and heterosexist practices that we are all exposed to from the time we are born, by the painful tentacles of shame, and sometimes by direct violence. Nonetheless, as hard as it can be to see it through all of that distortion, the regulation of the sexual and relationship lives of gay men is not just about gay men, and is deeply tied to issues that affect us all in one way or another.

Same-Gender Relationships in History

In every human society, there are those who engage in sexual and/or romantic activities with people of the same gender. In Chapter 1, I mentioned that ways of doing gender among indigenous nations were diverse and different from European practices, and that attacks on them and imposition of European and Christian practices were integral to colonization; the same was also true of indigenous ways of doing sexuality (Roscoe 1988; Stevenson 1999; Roscoe 2000; A. Smith 2005). There was widespread acceptance in many indigenous societies that women or men who dressed as and/or did the work of the other gender either belonged to that gender or to a distinct third or fourth gender. There was also acceptance of some kinds of samesex erotic practices, though all of this was organized quite differently from the modern North American understandings of hetero- and homosexuality.

In the European Christian tradition, official hostility toward same-gender erotic relations is longstanding (Richards 1991). Over time, same-gender sexuality has been vilified as a sin, then a crime, and more recently as a sickness, with the earlier labels never completely disappearing from the culture. Yet, all along, people have felt and found ways to act upon such desires. According to court documents, the first recorded instance of sex between men among the colonizers in what later came to be Canada was a man in

New France who was convicted for his activities in 1648 (Kinsman 1996: 98). From similar sources we can also learn about sporadic high profile instances such as the scandal that erupted in 1838 around George Markland, Inspector General of Upper Canada, because of his sexual liaisons with other men (Maynard 1994a: 122).

Despite this official hostility, there have been plenty of times and places in European and settler North American history where lots of people were quite tolerant of same-gender sexuality, even when no one openly contested the dominant messages that such things were "sinful" or "deviant." For example, law reforms instituted initially in France shortly after the French Revolution of 1789 and subsequently in other parts of Europe decriminalized same-gender sexual activity, though it had been recriminalized in most of the continent by the end of the nineteenth century. Some women and men in elite European literary circles in the early parts of the twentieth century were quite open about such things (Thurman 1999). Research has shown a "relative indifference" to same-gender erotic practices among large portions of the European working class in the same era (Tamagne 2000).

As people became more likely to live in cities and to support themselves by wage labour rather than family farming, desire for same-gender sexual intimacy began to result in networks of people brought together by that desire (D'Emilio 1992; Maynard 2004). In North American cities like New York and Toronto in the late nineteenth and early twentieth centuries, not only were there active networks of men who desired men and of urban spaces that these men created, appropriated, and put to delightfully subversive uses, but there were also plenty of places, particularly in working-class immigrant neighbourhoods, where men could, with imperfect but considerable safety and without segregating themselves from people read as "normal," live queer ways of doing gender and sexuality (Chauncey 1994; Maynard 1994b; Maynard 2004). These gradually forming networks and new ways of living led ultimately to the evolution of gay and lesbian identities as we know them today, though the process tended to be different and later for women because of their experiences of gender oppression and the existence of additional social barriers to women finding paid employment and to living independently of fathers and husbands. Queer networks became more extensive and visible in Canada in the years after the Second World War.

People who engage in sexual and romantic relationships with those of the same gender have always had to have ways of responding to their oppression. Often in the past and still too often in the present, secrecy and public denial of self and activities has been an essential tool for self-preservation. That has not been the only response, however. Spontaneous, collective resistance in the face of police repression has been recorded at least as far back as eighteenth-century England. Historian Alan Bray writes that when "a molly house[8] in Covent Garden was broken up in 1725, the crowded household, many of them in drag, met the raid with determined and violent resistance" (quoted in Kinsman 1996: 53). Germany was unique in the nineteenth century in having an organized homosexual rights movement. In the years after the Second World War an organized movement that described itself as "homophile" emerged in North America, particularly the United States. Its initial leadership briefly consisted largely of radicals who came out of the Communist Party and other places, but in the harsh environment of the Cold War they were quickly overthrown by more moderate voices (Hay and Roscoe 1996). This movement relied heavily on sympathetic experts who were or seemed to be from outside the gay community, such as psychiatrists and lawyers, to advocate for things like decriminalization of homosexual activity and a particular vision of equal rights, though by the late 1960s such organizations had become more vocal and more self-reliant. Law reform based on the liberal but still disapproving model most often put forward by such professionals made advances in North America and Europe in this period, and in 1969 the Liberal government of Pierre Trudeau passed a law reform bill which, among other things, decriminalized sex between two men under certain circumstances (Kinsman 1996: 262–278).

Vogel and North

It was in this time period that Vogel and North came out and got active. It is crucial to understand that this moment not only involved signs of liberalization around sexual issues in the mainstream (however modest those signs might have been) but also uprisings of many oppressed peoples and groups in North America and around the world. Therefore, though Vogel spoke of his family of origin as a politicizing influence (he felt affirmation growing up for "deliberate, controversial, unorthodox action to make things generally better" through his parents' support for the CCF government of Tommy Douglas in Saskatchewan and its struggles to introduce socialized hospital insurance and then medial insurance) he also placed great emphasis on being a student at this particular historical moment:

> We were both children of the sixties. To the extent that I was politicized by something, it was the experience of being at the University of Manitoba in the 1960s. I was caught up with the fervour of teach-ins and being against the Vietnam War, and considering the administration of the university to be stupid and incompetent and right-wing. Unlike the fifties, which were ultraconventional and authority was accepted without question, the sixties, the late sixties in particular, suggested the opposite — that newer ideas were better than old ones, that younger people were brighter and more ethical

> than older ones, that people could cause social change and that they should, that there was a moral imperative to fix up the mess. There was a mess and it should be fixed up and we were the ones to do it. It seemed to us that we knew everything at the time. *[laugh]*
>
> I was far from being the most left-wing person in my circle of friends. In fact, I was comparatively conservative. I had joined the NDP campus group (which was a good deal more progressive than the rest of the party, as it turned out) and participated in some demonstrations. I was more a follower than a leader. I don't know if I ever conceived of anything. *[laugh]*

The many examples that were in the air helped the desire for liberation to spread, and all it took was a spark to turn the struggles of lesbians and gay men in new and more militant directions. That spark occurred in North America on June 27 and 28, 1969. In New York City, a riot was ignited by a police raid on a gay bar called the Stonewall Inn (Carter 2004). Though such raids happened so frequently that they were routine, this time the clientele of the bar — which included "all segments of the gay and lesbian community, including a strong representation of the more marginal elements," particularly queer men who were poor, racialized, street-involved, and/or did gender in very feminine ways — fought back (ibid.: 77). It is this event that is commemorated across the continent in Pride celebrations every year. According to gay liberation activist and movement historian Tom Warner (2002: 61), after Stonewall, "gay and lesbian groups sprang up across Canada like flowers in spring."[9]

North said that, unlike Vogel, he had "never really done anything" political before, though he "admired these people who did progressive things and stood up for causes that they believed in." He was drawn into political action by the visible presence of this movement that spoke specifically to his realities, and the flourishing of other sorts of visibility that went with it. "Becoming involved in the gay movement," he said, "was my way of being a progressive." And certainly for both men, the emergence of this new movement was crucial in shaping the politics they have carried ever since.

Vogel came out as gay in late 1971 and North in early 1972, but it was only after a trip abroad together, in which they had a chance to see the flourishing of gay politics and culture in the broader world, that they became politically active in gay liberation. North remembered,

> We went to Europe together that winter and I think we probably were politicized by going to Europe, at least for me. I really hadn't travelled much at all. There was very little gay scene in Winnipeg at that time. We went to gay bars in the various cities that we went too. One thing that particularly sticks in my memory is that on the

plane back from London there was a woman who had a sweatshirt on that said "Gay is Good." This was early 1973, so that was pretty early on, and I really admired her courage in doing that. I suspect that for me that was a bit of a turning point, seeing somebody do that. When we came back the following spring we got involved in the campus gay group at the University of Manitoba.

That group, called the Campus Gay Club, had been founded in February 1972. In the early post-Stonewall years there were a number of kinds of groups focusing on gay issues that emerged in Canada — including some that were similar in organizational form and approach to the homophile groups that had existed in the United States in earlier years — and particularly in Vancouver and Toronto there were groups that embraced a kind of militant liberationist politics that was primarily committed to alliance with revolutionary formations among other oppressed groups. The Campus Gay Club, which changed its name to Gays For Equality the following year, was of the model that seemed to end up the most sustainable, with a primary focus that was specific to gay issues and a commitment both to social change activism and to providing services and social spaces for the emerging gay community. Though groups in most cities ended up gravitating toward this form over the years, there was still a significant range of politics within and between different groups across the country. A gay liberation activist in Toronto, Ken Popert, writing in 1975 about the founding of the National Gay Rights Coalition (called the Canadian Lesbian and Gay Rights Coalition after 1978) commented that the different political orientations within the new coalition could "be conveniently tagged as religious, service-oriented, rights-oriented, anarchist and leftist," and that the "civil rights grouping," which largely controlled the formal proceedings at the conference in question, included central participation from Winnipeg Gays For Equality (quoted in Warner 2002: 156).

Gays For Equality also seemed to be similar to most other gay liberation groups in that era in terms of who was and was not present and participating. The membership of the successor organization to Gays For Equality that exists in the early twenty-first century is at least half women, and according to Vogel its staff and directors are mostly women, but that has not always been true. He said that, though they did attend some of the demonstrations, back in the 1970s and 1980s "there weren't very many women involved with the group. There were at first, but they quickly became active in feminist or lesbian organizations separately.... The gay liberation organizations then were comprised almost entirely of men." He explained this by pointing out that many lesbians "had lots of experiences with men being very sexist and horrible, and some of those were gay men. They had, no doubt, some very unpleasant experiences." The more general experience that they shared with heterosexual women of oppression *as* women, including the highly gendered nature of experiences around sexuality and sexual violence, led many lesbians to a much different politics than most gay men in that era. As well, participation from queer people of colour and indigenous people was minimal. Canadian academic Kathleen Lahey (1999: 14), in writing about the history of lesbian and gay struggles with the legal system, has noted,

> Dramatic differences in the specificities of lesbian and gay experiences, together with the effects of gender hierarchies and attitudes toward race, class, and ability issues, meant that racially identified lesbians and gays often felt marginalized by activist groups and that lesbian and gay activists often found it difficult to work together.

A further obstacle to organizing in the early 1970s was the fact that secrecy and invisibility had been such crucial survival tools for most lesbians and gays, because much of what Gays For Equality actually did had to do with creating visibility for gay men (and to a lesser extent lesbians) and their issues. As Vogel recalled, "When we got going in the early years, gay liberation terrified most gays and lesbians. They would get screaming, spitting mad about it at times. They considered activists to be misfits, dangerous."

Given the intensity of the constraints that they faced, Vogel said, "In the early years, there were relatively few things we could do to draw attention to discrimination and the other problems imposed by prejudice on homosexuals."

One tactic to create visibility for issues is through demonstrations. However, the wariness of or even hostility to actively seeking visibility by many gays and lesbians contributed to the fact that, especially in smaller cities, demonstrations and other public events by gay activist groups in that era tended to be quite small. Vogel joked, "There were so few of us, we only looked good in close shots. The camera couldn't back up much before you realized how few of us there were." At least in Winnipeg, as North wryly noted, "Our first demonstrations, the majority of the people weren't gays and lesbians — they were Trotskyists." That term refers to one flavour of revolutionary Marxist organization that was enjoying a resurgence in the early 1970s, particularly among young people. Vogel felt that mainly they "were trying to convert us, of course, to at least buy their newspapers if not join their organizations." However, though it might not have been a big factor in Winnipeg, in places like Vancouver, Toronto, and a few other cities, queer members of Trotskyist groups actually played an important role in founding gay liberation organizations and advancing the early struggles (Kinsman and Gentile 2010: 243–301).

Another very early effort to raise visibility for queer people and struggles was to create a poster and plaster it all over downtown Winnipeg. North recalled, "We ran it off on a silkscreen. It was a phoenix rising from a fire. What did it say?"

"It was very wordy," Vogel replied. "There was a lot of text. I know because I cut it all out. *[laugh]* For hours and hours I cut out that thing!"

North said,

> It was, "Gays demand liberation from — " *[pause]* What was it that we were we being liberated from? "Stilting sex-role structures, blah, blah, blah." I can't remember what was on it, now. *[laugh]* But the idea was the phoenix rising, escaping from the sexual repression of the past and the sex-role structures that people certainly in the fifties felt very constrained by.

It was routine for posters that the group put up on campus to be torn down, presumably by other students or staff who were hostile toward lesbian and gay liberation, so this one they stuck all over construction hoardings in the downtown using wallpaper paste. This seemed to be quite successful, and they continued to use postering as a technique, including one with the word "Homosexual?" in very large print and the number of Gays For Equality's counselling and information line underneath. Postering was, as North said, "one of the things we could do" with minimal resources.

In those days, visibility through the mass media was not generally forthcoming. Vogel said,

> They wouldn't talk about homosexuality. Most people couldn't even say the word without choking. And it had been media policy, up until then, never to mention it. In order to accomplish anything there had to be media attention paid to the issue.

To get past this reluctance, along with the stand-by of holding a demonstration,

> We could maybe hold a panel discussion and hope somebody would come to that. We always did press releases. Maybe do some stuff at elections. We held demonstrations and, in 1974, hosted a National Gay Conference that included the first gay march in Winnipeg.

Other events in those years included Pride celebrations in 1974 and 1975, though they were then discontinued in Winnipeg until 1987. Vogel started a group called the Council on Homosexuality and Religion, which involved a number of sympathetic ministers and lay people, and for about ten years they put on regular church services, did educational events, and produced religious publications. Every year, speakers were brought to the local college and universities, and lesbian and gay writers were invited to do public readings, often sponsored by the Canada Council. This included a full festival of queer authors one year in the 1980s.

Vogel said,

> All of that media visibility, in turn, provided other opportunities. People would do more serious treatments academically or in the media. We would be invited to speak to students at schools, colleges, and universities. Once we got some media attention, other opportunities arose, and it was more or less in proportion. It became a topic, an issue. It was worth doing for its own sake, these public events and demonstrations and so on, but you got rewarded much more widely by other opportunities to initiate discussion.

However, as any activist has experienced, relying solely on the dominant media can be a deeply frustrating way of achieving visibility, particularly when you add in the mainstream distaste for subjects related to homosexuality. Vogel, North, and the groups they were a part of also did what they could to *become* the media.[10] They produced many pamphlets and brochures, though not always without difficulty. One produced by North in 1975 was called "Understanding Homosexuality." Vogel related,

> When we tried to get it printed, a printing firm in Steinbach refused to do it, and we picketed their office. I believe that this was the first gay demonstration in Manitoba. We found another printer and over the years we printed in total 15,000 copies that were distributed locally and to other groups in the country.

They also became involved in community-based broadcast media, initially in 1978 with a radio program called *Gay Christian Forum* and later *Gaysweek* on the local campus radio station. When the station closed down, they moved over to community access cable and produced more than 750 episodes of *Coming Out* between September 1980 and November 1994, when the cable company severely restricted the resources it devoted to public access programming.

Gay liberation activists also had some options for seeking visibility not open to activists in other movements. In 1970, a gay activist at the University of Minnesota named Jack Baker publically married his partner, and later was brought to Winnipeg to speak by the Campus Gay Club. This inspired Vogel and North to follow his example; their attempt to get legally married on February 11, 1974, was the first widely publicized same-sex marriage in Canada (Persky 1982).

Vogel said,

> We qualified, we considered, to get married, and we did it perfectly

legally in the hopes that we would be successful. Well, I guess I didn't suppose that we would be, but one never knew. There was nothing in the legislation that said that we couldn't be.

North added,

> We didn't really enter into it as a personal thing at all; it was very much a kind of activist thing to do to try and get some positive publicity.... But also on a personal level I'm very glad we did it, actually.

Vogel said that North

> produced a tremendous ceremony with all kinds of music and readings. We found out that when our families and friends came to it ... there was that part of it, too — the personal part, the celebration, the announcement, the general recognition that this was now the new status of your life. In addition to the educational benefits, the media benefits, the people who attended then became involved and engaged in the movement because they had a personal interest.

Marriage of people of the same gender has remained highly visible in Canada into the early twenty-first century, though as a result of a great deal of struggle it has transitioned from an isolated personal and political action by one couple into the formal decision to allow same-gender couples admission to the privileges connected to the state-regulated institution of marriage. In the more recent media portrayals of the issue, the visibility centres around controversy that is often posed as being between queer people and centrist, liberal, and left-leaning heterosexual allies on the one side, and hardcore social conservatives on the other. However, the issue has never been quite that simple. For one thing, beyond family, friends, and co-workers, when Vogel and North married in 1974 there was precious little support for same-sex marriage even among more progressive elements of the heterosexual mainstream.

As Vogel said,

> At an early stage, we discovered that marriage was clearly going to be the last battle even for heterosexuals. One of the candidates to whose town-hall meeting we had gone in 1973 came by our door after that, campaigning. He said that he supported amendment of the Human Rights Act to include homosexuality as a prohibited ground for discrimination. We said we supported him and he went on his way. Then the knock on the door came again — he was back having to tell us, spontaneously, that he didn't support same-sex

> marriage! *[laugh]* I think that is when I realized, "Oh shit. This is clearly stuck in some people's minds as the most heterosexual thing of all, the one thing to which they are going to cling after they have given us equality in every other way." It was going to be the last line they drew in the sand.

What might be less intuitively obvious to readers not familiar with queer politics is that whether access to marriage as it currently exists is a useful goal has been highly contested within queer communities. In 1974, according to North,

> there was at least as much criticism and lack of support amongst gay people in the movement. Probably the most support we got was from straight people. Certainly getting married in 1974 was considered a pretty conservative thing to do by most people who were involved in the movement. It was also quite difficult for people to be openly gay in those days, so it was only the more radical people who were involved in the movement — they were almost all leftists of one stripe or another, and marriage was not the thing to do.

Critics of heterosexual marriage as a social institution (though not necessarily as a personal choice made by people navigating the pressures of their own lives) have pointed to its role in how sexism, heterosexism, oppressive regulation of sexuality, and even capitalist social relations are maintained and reproduced. The queer community and the movements associated with it, along with the broader political culture, have shifted significantly since 1974, and now the majority of people who are out as lesbian and gay probably see equal marriage as an important political accomplishment, whether or not they are personally interested in taking advantage of it. However, though they would never support the exclusion of queer people from any benefits accruing to heterosexual people, a minority of voices in queer communities in Canada continue to question whether access to an otherwise unchanged state-regulated institution of marriage is really the most liberatory goal. In particular, there are concerns that prioritizing access to marriage as it currently exists might reinforce the marginalization of the rich diversity of ways that queer people have constructed their relationship lives, and that it provides a means by which sexuality will continue to be regulated and behaviours that give pleasure and cause no harm will continue to be sorted into "legitimate" and "illegitimate," those that are acceptable and those for which you will be shamed or otherwise punished. Various more creative political approaches to provide access to the benefits currently associated with marriage have been suggested (Warner 1999; davis 2005; Epstein 2005; Duggan and Hunter 2006: 221–238).

Vogel and North themselves are unconvinced by such criticisms, and in fact remained unconcerned that many other activists in lesbian and gay struggles in the early 1970s were critical of their use of marriage as a tactic. Vogel countered by saying, "Well, maybe, but everybody else thought it was pretty remarkable at the time. *[laugh]* Wasn't like it was being done every day!"

Beyond Visibility: Resisting Punishment

Combatting the historic invisibility of people who desire others of the same gender was in part meant as a challenge to the heterosexual mainstream, but Vogel emphasized that a big part of how it created change was indirect, via its impact on other gay and lesbian people.

> My conviction is that what really works in changing public attitudes is that people come out to their family and friends. The forum of success for gay liberation is the living room, not the courts or the streets or the legislatures. These other things that groups like ours did motivated and reassured people so that they would come out. We provided an inspiration, an indication that it was needed. Even when events like the onset of AIDS or things we did provoked negative reactions, that was a good thing because it forced people to feel that they had to do something.

However, as the above brief discussion of marriage illustrates, visibility on its own can only go so far. Change in the living room can be important for shifting the social mood, but institutions and relations that are organized in ways that marginalize, oppress, and punish queer people for refusing to be invisible must still be challenged and transformed.

Vogel and North acknowledged being lucky because, North said, "We haven't had in Winnipeg the kind of rabid opposition that they have had in lots of other places, at least not on a sustained, organized level." They also had relatively little to report in terms of vigilante violence by gay bashers. However, taking opposition to queer sexual and relationship practices — particularly those that refuse to be invisible — to the level of interpersonal violence has historically been integral to gay experience. For example, interview participant Richard Hudler, who was active with a group called Homophile Association of London Ontario (HALO) for many years, reported that violence and vandalism was a fact of life for the bar run by HALO. He recalled,

> We couldn't keep windows because vandals kept breaking them. I remember at one point we just covered them with plywood. We decided we had to do something so we could continue operating, so we just boarded the windows up. Then eventually when we did

renovations we got it so that they would open, but there was a grille so stones couldn't come through. And it was always a problem. Eventually we didn't like the look of just the grilles so we took them down and installed shatterproof glass, because we still got problems with stone-throwing and broken glass. Even when we got the shatterproof glass, they did; I don't know what they used, but they managed to break the windows. It cost three hundred dollars or something to replace every one. It was quite an expense. Then there's a picture somewhere of the back of the building where somebody had written "fag." It had to be painted over. There were often things like that happening. There was another time when they tore the porches off the building and we had to replace them.

Similarly, police repression has long been a fact of queer life in Canada. Police raids on gay bars had been happening from time to time for many years, and between the mid 1970s and the mid 1980s, many cities across the country saw an increase in police raids on gay community institutions such as bars, publications, and bathhouses[11] (Warner 2002: 99–118). Often, these actions were accompanied by homophobic behaviour from individual police officers and in some cases by media campaigns orchestrated by the police that attempted to link gay community spaces in the public mind to various kinds of criminal activity, for the most part with no evidence ever presented and no charges related to those activities ever laid. Again, Winnipeg's gay community was largely spared this sort of ordeal: Vogel observed that "bathhouses have never been raided here, and there have always been bathhouses." Resistance to the "biggest and most terrifying of the raids" against gay baths in that era, which occurred in Toronto in the early 1980s, was unexpectedly massive and militant and created sufficient pressure that eventually large-scale police raids of this sort ceased for the most part, though individual arrests for similar activities continue to be made occasionally (ibid.: 110). The changes in the law sought by activists to disarm the ways in which "the *Criminal Code* coordinated the enforcement of heterosexuality" remain to be won (G. Smith 2006: 66). Canada also has a long history of queer people being targeted in various ways by the apparatus of the national security state from the 1950s until at least the late 1990s (Kinsman and Gentile 2010). As well, some queer publications that could be produced and sold perfectly legally within Canada continue to be stopped arbitrarily by customs officers when attempts are made to import them.

Another source of punishment of deviations from the mandatory heterosexual "norm" involves the regulation of sexuality and relationships by institutional mechanisms less spectacular than massive police raids or angry crowds of bashers, but perhaps more pervasive — things like the refusal of the Province of Manitoba to recognize Vogel and North's 1974 marriage, even after they took the Province to court. At one time, immigration legislation prohibited gays from entering Canada, but lobbying by groups across the country, including Gays For Equality, resulted in the federal government removing that provision in 1975. Another example was refusal by the NDP provincial government of the application by Winnipeg's first gay club to incorporate, which it had to do to get a liquor licence. Vogel recalled that the attorney-general at the time was quoted in the newspaper as saying something to the effect that "while homosexuals should not be hounded and pilloried, they should not have the same legal rights as everybody else." During election campaigns over the following period, Vogel and North went to all-candidates meetings and asked questions. Vogel recalled,

> One of the questions we asked was about this refusal of the government to allow this group to incorporate and get a liquor licence. Some of the NDP candidates disagreed with the attorney-general which, for the first time, suggested progress was possible.

Though eventually incorporation and then a liquor licence were granted, this was the sort of incident that encouraged activists across the country to turn their attention to seeking formal mechanisms for responding to discrimination by institutions and governments. In Canada, one major legal tool for such things for many groups is the human rights codes of each province and the federal government. In the 1970s, it was not clear how lesbians and gay men could best use the human rights codes. However, there was broad agreement across both the moderate and radical wings of the lesbian and gay liberation movement that finding ways to do so, whether through inclusion under grounds already in the legislation or through the explicit addition of "sexual orientation" as a prohibited ground for discrimination, would be politically useful.

This was true in Manitoba as well, though the political environment faced by Gays For Equality was a little different than in most of the rest of the country. North said,

> We had an NDP government for many of those years.... The [Premier Ed] Schreyer government was terrible on this issue. Schreyer himself responded to a question on human rights protections for homosexuals at a town hall meeting on campus during the 1977 election by saying that anyone with this problem had no business speaking in a political forum. Of course everybody clapped and that was the end of that. In other parts of the country, like on the West Coast and in Toronto, the NDP was advocating on gay issues, but we had an NDP government that was hostile on the issue.

Vogel added,

> That has continued to be the case ever since. We first met with an attorney-general in 1974 (by this time it was Howard Pawley), but it wasn't until 1987 that they finally added "sexual orientation" to the Human Rights Code.

According to North, the struggle really heated up in the 1980s. By this point, NDP policy conventions in Manitoba had called for human rights protections for lesbians and gay men. NDP Attorney-General Roland Penner

> claimed in the early eighties that the existing legislation, the Human Rights Act, had general wording that already provided protection and he would not consider including sexual orientation explicitly in the legislation as a prohibited ground until it had been proven that the current legislation did not already provide protection.

So they proceeded to do exactly that. Vogel worked for the provincial government so in 1982 he filed a human rights complaint against the government on the grounds that denying spousal benefits to North was discrimination based on "sex." The idea was that if North had been a woman, he would have been eligible for benefits. The human rights tribunal and courts rejected that argument and decided, according to North, "that since sexual orientation was not explicitly mentioned, it was not covered." The refusal to consider discrimination on grounds already in a human rights code in this case and in a number of other cases across the country helped contribute to the movement's focus on getting "sexual orientation" explicitly included in human rights legislation in various jurisdictions.

North also pointed out that the lawyer representing the attorney-general had argued that sexual orientation was not covered by the Act.

> Despite this, Penner continued to deflect calls for amending the Act to explicitly prohibit sexual orientation discrimination by insisting that it was already covered somehow ... in spite of the fact that complaints under the Act were unsuccessful and that the government itself opposed an interpretation of the Act which provided protection.... It was a stalemate. It was very frustrating.
>
> My most radical act was in response to that. I went on a hunger strike in 1985. I ate nothing for fifty-nine days, consuming nothing but water, to protest the NDP government's refusal to amend the Human Rights Act. With the hunger strike, I was holding Penner's feet to the fire.... I was saying, "We are not playing games here. We are dealing with a fundamental issue of human rights. This has to be taken seriously. Your position had better be grounded in a truth that

you believe in, because this could be a life and death decision."

A hunger strike is the opposite of carnal indulgence. In those days, homosexuality was commonly associated with carnality and self-indulgence. A hunger strike is self-denial, a commitment to a cause, and also placed gay rights in the tradition of the struggles for equality by other disadvantaged groups. It was a statement that this was a minority group worth making a sacrifice for.

Vogel added,

> The hunger strike was accompanied by quite a strong media campaign. We made up a new document every day that had something to do with it, an open letter to the attorney-general, and distributed it to the media. The attachments were a variety of things: a list of all the churches that supported this, all of the organizations, all the businesses with non-discrimination policies.
>
> In one of the provincial elections we [had] distributed questionnaires to the candidates and Penner himself [had] said that he was in favour of amending the Act, so that was one of the documents that accompanied this open letter, and similar responses from other political leaders. I remember there were fifty-nine different documents that provided support. We organized panels — a religious panel, a labour panel, a legal panel. The comments of the panellists constituted the document for one of those days.

Vogel noted that, though "by itself it wasn't successful," other activists

> took the materials that we had been using, reformatted them more attractively, and used them right inside the party to agitate for a couple of years. It was becoming clear that the caucus had become a good deal more conservative than the membership, and that was causing a good deal of internal friction. And ultimately they so disrupted the internal workings of the NDP to the point where the cabinet and the caucus had no choice. I'm sure the only reason they acted in '87 was because they were concerned about re-election, because they depend so much on their members to get them re-elected.

After this change came into effect in Manitoba in 1988, Vogel and North launched a second human rights case. It wasn't enough: The human rights adjudicator and later a trial court ruled that denial of spousal benefits was not discriminatory based on "sexual orientation" because the word "spouse" was explicitly defined as being "opposite-sex,"[12] and they decided that it had not been the legislature's intent to equate same-sex relationships with spousal or opposite-sex common-law relationships. Only after the Supreme Court of Canada, based on the *Charter of Rights and Freedoms*, ruled in another case that "opposite-sex" definitions of "spouse" could, in fact, be considered discrimination based on sexual orientation were they at last able to win a court decision that denial of same-sex employment benefits violated the "sexual orientation" clause in human rights legislation. North was able to receive benefits, finally, in 1997.[13]

Existing Together

The search for visibility and struggles against punishment are vital, but they are, to a certain extent, about focusing energy externally. Though seemingly less glamorous and less exciting, a big part of the time that Vogel and North have invested in changing the world has not been focused outwards but rather has been devoted to the day-to-day work of creating community spaces and contexts for queer people to provide aid and support to one another. Gays For Equality morphed into the Winnipeg Gay Community Centre when, according to Vogel, it "had to move off campus because we were perfectly obviously not a student group and hadn't been for years," and it is now known as the Rainbow Resource Centre. Vogel stated proudly that through all of the years and all of the name changes, a basic thing like the information and support phone line has always been there and volunteers "have answered those phones every weekday evening from the fall of 1973." It also now offers an extensive library and archive, youth groups, anti-homophobia education for professionals and mainstream groups, services, and many other resources.

Other basic community needs included physical space and money with which to do things. When Gays For Equality moved off campus and became a community centre in 1982, it included a new club room called Giovanni's Room, which North founded and operated under the banner of the Oscar Wilde Memorial Society. Though in recent years, commercial bars have come to replace community-oriented club rooms in most cities, and Giovanni's is the only one that remained open in Winnipeg at the time of the interview, in its early years it was "very successful" and "the clubrooms and the income they earned allowed us to do lots of other things," according to North. He ran the club for six years, which he found both rewarding and "terribly exhausting, aggravating." By 1988, burned out, he left the running of the club to others, and though his participation in gay rights activism became less intensive and direct since, he has remained connected and involved.

Fundraising has always been central to Vogel's activities as well. These days, the Rainbow Resource Centre gets a modest amount of government funding on a project-by-project basis and is able occasionally to apply for grants from foundations, but an important kernel of the group's core operating money still comes from the community, just like it always did. They probably bring in more from direct mailing solicitations now, but they still get a chunk each year from the very first consistent method they had for raising funds back in the 1970s: holding community events. Vogel said,

> We started mostly by holding socials. It's like a dance: you rent a hall, get a temporary liquor permit, charge admission, sell drinks. We held gay socials from the very beginning. For years we weren't supposed to be raising funds, and the Liquor Commission did a variety of things to try and prevent you from doing that. We did it anyway. I must have sat on the door for over a hundred socials. Each time, I could hardly wait for the damn thing to be over. They used to go to one thirty a.m. Now they go to two thirty a.m. sometimes. Horrible. It just was the only way to get things done.

Both in fundraising and in social change work more generally, Vogel is an advocate of "dumb persistence."

> It doesn't matter what you did yesterday or last week or last month, it only matters what you are going to do next. And these things — whether it is a newsletter or a television program or holding meetings or educational events or getting a grant and creating a project – it is what you are going to do next that matters. Resting on your laurels never gets you anywhere. *[laugh]*

As for what comes next for Vogel, he said, "I don't really do anything else now except fundraising, because that is what we need the most." And in terms of where he might like to see the movement as a whole go, he wasn't sure. The most visible national struggle in recent years has been for marriage equality, and since this interview was conducted it seems to have been convincingly won. However, groups in different cities have been quietly working away at fighting homophobia and heterosexism in schools[14] and social services, trying to change laws related to sexuality, producing openly queer culture, fighting sexism and racism and ableism[15] within queer communities, extending resources to lesbians and gay men living in rural areas, and a few small groups in some cities continue to harken back to the original post-Stonewall visions of linking queer liberation to radical struggle for liberation from all oppressions.

Vogel seems quite willing to keep working away to support the struggle, wherever it goes. "I don't know what else there is, yet; maybe a higher degree of sexual liberation is yet to come." He continued,

> I think people should do what suits them individually and the government should butt out. I don't believe everybody should all do certain things; they should do what they want. If they want to have a very domestic, suburban, monogamous, middle-class, whatever-it-is

relationship, fine, that's what they should do. If they want to do some other things, well they should do that, too. The law is unnecessarily restrictive. The laws in the Criminal Code about sex and drugs and prostitution and just about everything are unreasonable and unnecessary, and people should be doing these things if they want. Some of us at least, and maybe most, were capable of covering the waterfront — we could push things like marriage and human rights that were seen as relatively conservative, middle-class things, while publicly expressing opinions that curled everybody's hair. *[laugh]*

Notes

1. "Queer" can be a controversial term and its meaning is often contested. I have chosen to use it deliberately for political reasons but readers unfamiliar with the politics need to be aware that it should be used with caution. Some people who identify as gay or lesbian, particularly from older generations and less urbanized areas, dislike it because their main experience of it has been as an attack from homophobes and bashers. Nonetheless, in the 1990s powerful efforts to reclaim the term came out of certain currents of activism grounded in communities as well as in academic discourse. The exact politics attached to the term vary and it has been criticized at times for reflecting the realities of relatively privileged gay men more than lesbian women, working-class and/or racialized queer people, or others who experience different nonconforming desires and/or gender expression. Nonetheless, it is seen by many activists as a site for forging politics that challenge moderate liberal "gay rights" approaches to social change, destabilize identity categories, and create space for possible unity among people who live a broad range of dissident sexual and relationship practices. See, for example, Duggan and Hunter 2006.
2. See Duggan and Hunter (2006: 182–183) for more on the utility of a framework of "dissenting practices" as a way to talk about non-normative ways of doing sexuality and relationships.
3. For a compelling elaboration of a politics of sexual shame, see Warner 1999. For some interesting analysis of shame in queer contexts that uses a cultural studies perspective, see Munt 2007.
4. For an extreme example from Ontario in 1930, as well as evidence of the widespread white opposition to white women being in relationships with racialized men at that time, see Backhouse 1999: 173–225. From the anecdotally related experiences of friends and acquaintances, interracial couples still at times experience hostility from white Canadian neighbours or passers-by on the street.
5. Arrangements that fit this general description have existed in many different ways, both liberatory and oppressive, across many different times and cultures. For information (from varying perspectives and of varying quality) on the current practice of "polyamory," a tradition organized around practicing non-monogamy in ethical and just ways, see, for example, Easton and Liszt 1997, Anapol 1997, Munson and Stelboum 1999, Ravenscroft 2004, and particularly Taormino 2008.

6. Interestingly, sexual regulation that divides people clearly into "heterosexual" and "homosexual," or variants thereof, is a relatively recent development in European and Euro-American societies. Before this particular binary division developed, distinctions between acceptable and unacceptable sexuality were more likely to label behaviours than people, and were more likely to revolve around whether the behaviour was procreative or not rather than the genders of the participants. A complete and detailed accounting of the historical evolution of sexual regulation is beyond the scope of this chapter, but a description of the historical emergence of heterosexuality as an identity and as a norm is available in Katz 1995. See Chauncy 1994 for a materialist account of shifts in the organization of sexuality in the New York context, which documents, among many other things, that the shift to the homo/hetero binary happened very unevenly and that there were working-class contexts where that paradigm did not dominate until the middle of the twentieth century.
7. For more on this, see Patton 1990.
8. Slang at the time for a pub frequented by men who had sex with men.
9. Also see Warner 2002 for a general overview history of queer movements in Canada. Much of the otherwise unreferenced material on Canadian queer movements in the rest of the chapter comes from that source. Though movement history is not their primary focus, material on Canadian queer movements can also be found in Kinsman 1996 and Kinsman and Gentile 2010.
10. To hear some of Vogel's and North's memories of producing media and publications, and about the ways the movement existed and that people within it related across the country, go to www.talkingradical.ca/audio/vogel_and_north_media.mp3.
11. Bathhouses are queer community spaces used by some men who desire other men to meet, socialize with, and sometimes have sex with other men. Sporadic bathhouse events organized by and for women have also occurred in some larger Canadian cities.
12. I generally try to avoid language that treats sex and gender as innate binary opposites, but for the sake of simplicity I am following the quoted sources and using the language of "opposite-sex" in this paragraph.
13. Information on struggles for legal rights and legal reforms by queer people in Canada can be found in the sources cited in note 9 and in Herman 1994 and Lahey 1999.
14. An important national survey of the experiences of queer youth found in 2009 that three-quarters of queer youth and 87 percent of trans youth felt unsafe in at least one place at school (EGALE Canada 2009). Verbal harassment due to sexual orientation was reported by 60 percent of queer students, and verbal harassment about gender expression was reported by 60 percent of queer students and 90 percent of trans students.
15. Ableism is the oppression and discrimination experienced by disabled people.

Chapter 6

Women's Liberation and the Lord
Shelley Finson on Feminism in Christian Churches

The damp chill in the air on that February morning probably had to do with being near the sea. I could not actually see the ocean from the front of the house occupied by Shelley Finson[1] and her partner, mind you, but then I could see no signs of the park, the major traffic artery, or the educational institution that I knew to be close by. All the mist left me was the short cul-de-sac and its houses, and an odd feeling of unusually intense residential isolation and quiet. The cab had dropped me off a few minutes early and I dithered in the slush, not sure whether it was better to risk interrupting Finson at breakfast or to remain conspicuously idle amidst the houses.

Finson answered my eventual knock and assured me I was right on time. Soon we were settled in a small downstairs room, talking about my project and the weather and the friend of hers who had put us in touch. Her voice was rich and still bore the marks of her English working-class childhood even though decades in the Americas had dragged her accent to the middle of the Atlantic. My first impression of her was of health and strength, but when I learned from her about the multiple bouts she had already fought with cancer, I realized I might be reading not so much physical well-being as a certain kind of poise and presence resulting from so many years of ministry, of teaching, and of bringing her activist, feminist, Christian faith into her everyday practices.

After leaving England, Finson lived for awhile with her remarried father in Jamaica, and eventually ended up in Canada in her twenties, in the late 1950s. She originally meant to stay only a couple of years. Circumstance and a search for meaning drew her into the United Church of Canada, first as a member and then as an employee. It was in the course of doing church-based, youth-focused community development work in Toronto in the late 1960s and early 1970s that she first encountered the women's movement. She remembered, "Gradually, I was consumed by this.... I needed to understand where my theology and this movement connected." She and an Anglican friend started a consciousness raising group for women church workers called Friends of Hagar, which became a space for mutual support and for taking action. In the late 1970s, Finson moved more and more into organizational change work, both through participation on task forces within the United Church and as coordinator of the interdenominational Movement for Christian Feminism (MCF). She was ordained in 1979 and began a long career as a theological educator in Toronto and later in Halifax. Though she did not take on the same kind of leading role in struggles by queer people within the United Church as she had for feminism, as a lesbian who was largely closeted in that context she was profoundly affected by the debates both before and after the decision in favour of ordaining "out" lesbians and gay men in 1988.

Paying Attention to Religion

Bodies shift our attention.[2] Even though so much about our social world is shaped by how the relations among people (and peoples) are organized, you can't touch or see or talk to a relation. You can only touch or see or talk to actual people. And, social creatures that we are, physical human presence cannot help but have an impact on us. At its most ordinary, this can mean something as simple as our feelings or talk shifting depending on which individuals are around us — Mom, our new boss, an ex-lover, a four-year-old we just met, and so on. What we say, what we leave unsaid, our vocabulary, our manner, our tone, the patterns of tension and ease in our bodies all change.

There are lots of ways this probably shouldn't happen. For example, despite years of working to be no less attentive to racism when in an all-white setting, I *know* something about the kind or quality of my attention to it still shifts when people of colour are also present. However, though there are ways we should vigilantly work to detach some of our ways of doing things from who is or is not around us in any given moment, there are other ways in which real, engaged, intersubjective relating demands that we be able to respond with great sensitivity to the people we interact with as whole people — that we learn to shift our attention to be respectfully, engagingly present with whomever we are interacting, and with whatever histories they carry with them.

I knew going into the interview that much of Finson's activism had been in the context of Christianity. So along with all the predictable ways that interacting with her shifted my attention, it also did so in a way that was unusual for me: it shifted the way I pay attention to religion.

To properly explain the "after," I need to digress a bit and talk about my "before." As with many people, my individual relationship to religion is complicated and contradictory. I grew up attending mainstream Protestant Christian churches in Canada — regularly, but far from every week. Religion was rarely a topic of discussion or a focus of attention beyond that. Despite this lack of overt attention to God in my family of origin, however, there are ways in which I have been profoundly shaped by the legacy of Scottish Presbyterianism on my mother's side, through all sorts of culturally informed everyday practices and ways of relating to aspects of life like work and pleasure.

As an adult, by and large religion is not something that I think much about and I feel no lack because of that. That is, of course, possible in part due to privilege. Many people in North America, especially Muslims and Jews and many non-Christian people of colour, experience oppression that at least partly focuses on their religion. In those circumstances, the pressure from the larger society to denounce or despise your faith is part of broader patterns of racism that target yourself and your loved ones, and religious community can be an important source of mutual aid and solidarity. I suspect that in those circumstances, indifference to the religion of your ancestors has a different feel and meaning to it than if it is the ancestral religion of the dominant group in society, as in my case. Also, in contrast with people who have been deeply wounded by, say, misogyny or colonization organized through a religion, I have not experienced religion in general or a specific faith as something that must be actively and persistently resisted for my own survival.

I experience other kinds of moments in my relationship to religion as well — interest, for instance, given how important it is to lots of people I know, to politics, and to social organization. As well, I have moments of negativity directed at religion, especially Christianity since it is where I come from and it is the dominant religion where I live. Some of that takes the form of unhappiness with the ways in which my Presbyterian heritage has shaped me. I am particularly likely to feel anger in a visceral way when Christianity (or, in some cases, another faith) is used to justify oppressive practices around gender, sexuality, and relationships. I also recognize that Christianity's very existence in the Americas is deeply colonial. Despite these moments of negativity and serious political misgivings, and despite the fact that I have great sympathy for the blanket personal and/or political hostility to Christianity by many who have been wounded by it in colonial, heterosexist, and sexist ways, the negativity I feel in my bones is more episodic and transient. I have collaborated politically with people who identify as Quaker, Mennonite, Muslim, traditional indigenous, Sikh, Catholic, Buddhist, other flavours of Christian, Jewish, Unitarian, and pagan, as well as lots of people who are not active practitioners of any faith.

All of which is to say that, by and large in my everyday life and in my political organizing, my experience of religion is one of personal indifference coupled with a genuine but somewhat distant interest and sympathy, and punctuated by moments of anger and political frustration.

Religion and Social Analysis

Over the years as I have learned about the world there has been a significant gap between religion and critical analysis, and between religion and social thinking. The faith contexts I existed in as a child contained little or nothing in terms of critical analysis of the world, and the spaces and texts through which I have learned to engage critically with the world have only sporadically and unevenly dealt with religion, faith, or spirituality. It has not been completely absent, so I already had some tools for understanding it when I met Finson; I just rarely used them. In the unthinking course of everyday life I was acting on an unarticulated understanding that treated religion quite simplistically. I mostly saw religion as a characteristic of an individual and assigned it a fairly peripheral place in understanding the social world.

In thinking back about how I've heard this topic talked about in casual conversation over the years, it almost always has to do with belief. The central question tends to be: "Do you believe that God exists?" Depending on who is in the conversation and how it is progressing, it can include things like "Do you believe that the Bible is the literal word of God?" or "Do you think human beings have a soul?" and even "Do you believe in the paranormal?" Of course there are highfalutin variations, like, "Do you think there is both a transcendent and immanent divinity?"

Such conversations are one window into the widespread tendency to construct religion as about how we as individuals orient ourselves toward various truth claims — that is, claims about what is true and what is false. Certainly many non-Christian faith traditions and pockets within Christianity do things quite differently, but the dominant ways of talking about religion in North America tend to treat this relationship to truth claims as fundamental.[3] This is true both of people who understand themselves to be secular as well as many Christians. It allows selves to be defined, others to be classified, borders to be patrolled: "Oh, he believes that? He's not a real Christian," or, "She really thinks that? Ugh, a fundamentalist in my workplace." It allows Christians to maintain the wall between true believers and the rest, and it allows at least a certain subset of people with secular worldviews to maintain a sense of smugness that they might not be able to sustain if they took a more critical and social approach.

One feature of such an approach is that it fosters a very individualistic understanding of religion. This is in the context of a broader dominant culture which, especially after the last three decades of attacks on social ways of seeing the world, bathes us in messages that push a very individualistic way of seeing ourselves and the world in every respect. Also, many Christian contexts, particularly the most politically vigorous strands of right-wing evangelical Protestantism, place a great deal of emphasis on a very personal, individual understanding of salvation. When, in such contexts, the question of Christianity and the larger society is raised, it still often takes a form that I would see as larger but just as privatized rather than truly social — that is, public figures and institutions and political tendencies are evaluated based on their orientation toward truth claims and compared to the orientation of the person or group making the comparison, but religion is rarely treated as a complex social phenomenon that must be investigated. And of course it should not be surprising when institutions of any sort, religious or secular, fail to encourage people to see their workings in a critical light.

In the Canadian context, there is an important exception to this individualistic take on religion. In conjunction with official multiculturalism, the mainstream understanding of white Canadians about racialized people who practice non-Christian religions is often so group-based as to be monolithic. This is really no closer to a nuanced and socially engaged understanding of religion, and it often becomes a primary element for constructing views of racialized people and communities that are simplistic, essentialist, and racist (Razack 2008: 145–172). (Related forms of social organization, enforced via ideas of "tradition" and "authenticity," have often been fostered in racialized communities by official multiculturalism, as briefly discussed in Chapter 4.) For some white Canadian Christians, it is the fact that these faiths are not Christian that marks the inferiority of those who hold them. Other white Canadians (both Christian and not) and the dominant national discourse exalt Canadians as uniquely liberal and tolerant, often understood in contrast with those racialized "others" and their supposedly illiberal religions, and so liberal tolerance itself becomes a marker by which white Canadians can maintain a sense of superiority that legitimizes the ongoing subjugation of racialized people (Thobani 2007; Razack 2008). This is particularly true of Islam since September 11, 2001, but is also applied to other non-Christian faiths held predominantly by racialized people.

The Substance of the Shift

With the material force of Finson's presence and the powerful illustration of her words, my attention shifted. It moved from the simplistic, individual, peripheral default position to one that was at least a bit more complex, social, and integrated with the rest of how I see the world — not something that was totally new to me, but not my normal at the time.

Appreciating the social character of religion requires little more than open listening to someone like Finson. Once she took up Christianity as a central part of her life, there was little about her that remained uninfluenced by the doctrines, practices, discourses, and institutional relations of Christianity; it was far from the only influence, but it was an important one. Because of the ways in which all of us have our behaviours regulated by the actions and reactions of people around us, being in Christian contexts played a very immediate role in shaping Finson's experience. Christian doctrine and discourses also served as sources of extra-local organization for her. As well, Christianity shaped how she understood herself; it was for her a source of membership in various collectives or identities — including "Christian," "minister," and "United Church member" — and an influence that shaped how she related to other aspects of her experience, including those associated with labels like "woman," "lesbian," "white," and "Canadian." And the interview demonstrates how Christianity was a major source of words, ideas, and imagery used by Finson in creating meaning about her life and the world.

The other key feature obvious from any religious life honestly told and respectfully heard is how complex it all is. People take it up in lots of different ways and it weaves in with other factors to organize our lives in lots of ways too. And as Finson's story illustrates, there's no guaranteed, single answer about whether (or in what context) it will be experienced as oppressive or liberatory. When she initially came to Christianity, Finson found meaning and empowerment and direction in important ways. However, she also came to appreciate that Christianity was one site and tool for her oppression as a woman and a lesbian and for the maintenance of unearned privilege related to being white and Canadian. Yet she also felt that Christianity had the potential to be a site and a tool for liberation in all of those areas.

You can see this contradictory role more generally in history as well. Christianity was all wrapped up in some of the worst things human beings have ever done to each other. This includes the mass burnings of women as witches in Europe; colonization and genocide in the Americas; the long and tragic history of anti-Semitism in Europe; the enslavement of Africans by Europeans; and more (e.g., Rumscheidt 1998: 62–88; Federici 2004; Thobani 2007: 43–47; Alfred 2005: 101–113). In each of those, whether as source of moral and political justification or through direct institutional collaboration, Christianity played a central role. Yet Christianity has also been part of survival and resistance by many enslaved Africans and their descendents in North America, as well as for shaping the actions of many early allies in anti-slavery work in England and North America. Lots of other important struggles for justice and liberation, especially in Central and South America, have happened under the banner of Roman Catholic liberation theology. Non-Christian faiths have also played an important part in organizing resistance to European colonial oppression around the world, though again never without contradictions. An important local example is the centrality of recovering traditional spiritual practices to the anti-colonial politics of many indigenous peoples in what is currently called "Canada" (Alfred 2005).

Finson spoke highly of a book by a former colleague in the area of theological education, Barbara Rumscheidt (1998), that examines the oppressive global social relations of neoliberal capitalism as they were experienced in the 1990s and the ways in which a kind of self-satisfied, uncritical sense of "good conscience" could be a central impediment to Christians in rich countries developing a critical understanding of the ways they are complicit in social relations that harm people around the world, including other Christians. Rumscheidt argues, however, that engaged Christian theological reflection of a particular sort and dialogue with those who are harmed by global social relations could also be central to Christians in Canada developing the kind of critical consciousness they would need to engage in active opposition to the ways that global social relations dehumanize, harm, and kill so many around the world.

The troubling, complicated roles that Christianity has historically played lead some to see the solution, both for guiding personal choices and as a standard for collective spaces, as secularism. However, it is not at all clear that secularism as it has evolved historically in the West and as it is understood in dominant discourse is much of an answer. For one thing, the dominant form of secularism in the West is clearly derived from Christian origins, yet that specificity gets hidden by claims that it is equal and universal. Secularism arguably disguises Christian hegemony rather than transforming it. Moreover, beyond very specific instances, whatever features in the dominant culture that allow social relations of power and oppression to continue to be seen as legitimate and normal do not seem to be fundamentally undermined by allegiance to either side of the Christian versus secular divide. Even worse, the rise of secularism was historically connected with the creation of oppressive circumstances too — the rise of the modern state form and of European colonialism, for example (Razack 2008: 145–172). In the twenty-first century, a simplistic glorification of secularism plays a role in justifying the so-called "War on Terror" and its associated war, empire, and domestic racism (ibid.). There is a need, I think, for those who accept the metaphysical truth claims of Christianity and those who do not (but whose realities have largely been shaped by the "Christian/secular" binary) to recognize our shared participation in a dominant and dominating culture that we must all work to transform.[4]

For the purposes of this chapter, based as it is in Shelley Finson's participation in social movement activity, the key example of the intersection of religion as a force of social organization with other kinds of relations is the different ways in which the organizing influence of Protestant Christianity in Canada has interacted with relations of gender oppression.

Christianity, Gender, and Sexuality

Christianity began slightly more than two thousand years ago at the eastern end of the Mediterranean Sea. The dominant ways of living in all of the societies in that part of the world in that era explicitly and emphatically empowered men over women. The early stages of what we now call "Christianity" began not as a radical break with the Jewish faith, as many Christian thinkers have opined over the years (in ways that often contributed directly or indirectly to theological anti-Semitism), but as a resistance movement within Judaism much like a number of others, which drew on Jewish prophetic traditions and other Jewish traditions of justice, compassion, and resistance to construct a radical practice against domination. As feminist theologian Rosemary Radford Reuther (1983: 26) has observed, in both its Old Testament and New Testament forms, "the God-language of the prophetic tradition is destabilizing toward the existing social order and its hierarchies of power — religious, social, and economic." In the era of Jesus Christ, widespread poverty and imperialist subjugation by the Roman Empire were the everyday realities of most of the Jewish people and this new religious movement was very much one of the oppressed resisting their oppression. The ways of being and doing embraced by what is often called in theological literature "the Jesus movement" and the earliest of Christian communities that followed involved significant, practical efforts among Christians to resist hierarchy and share important goods in common. There is considerable evidence that women played many important leadership roles in this movement, and the early Christian communities also included internal struggle around relations of gender oppression, which challenged (though did not overthrow) patriarchal relations within these communities in important ways.[5]

As time passed, this early practice changed dramatically. The details of the two thousand years between then and now would show many different ways of constructing ideas and ways of living by people who have identified as Christian, some radically egalitarian and others harshly hierarchical, but the dominant practices over much of that time have not been politically consistent with Christianity's beginnings. From its origins among Jews and Greeks drawing on Jewish tradition to resist oppression, in a scant few centuries Christian theological hostility to Jewish people was firmly established (Klein 1978). Despite anti-imperialist beginnings, by the later years of the Roman Empire, in the words of two Christian feminist theologians, there was a "Christian entanglement in imperial culture" and "Christianity became an imperial religion" (Rumscheidt 1998: 62; Reuther 1983: 28). Many Christians who oppose this development, including some in leadership roles within the United Church of Canada, identify its persistence into the present day (Empire Task Group 2007). And certainly in the realms of gender and sexuality, Christianity has been used in many times and places to justify oppressive sexual regulation and the subjugation of women.

In the present day, different people who give religion a central place in their lives and analysis, and who struggle for justice and liberation, have related to this legacy of Christianity in different ways. Some women who grew up within Christianity — for example, late feminist theologian Mary Daly — have decided that their religion is irredeemable and have, on feminist grounds, explicitly rejected Christianity and sought to elaborate a range of theologies and faith practices that they feel to be more radically reflective of their experiences as women. Some others who struggle for justice and liberation from a never-Christian perspective, and who struggle against oppressions that Christianity has played a major role in creating and enforcing, also see Christianity as irredeemable. For instance, Mohawk scholar Taiaiake Alfred (2005: 108–109), citing other indigenous thinkers, has said,

> Euroamerican arrogance comes from the monotheistic tradition of Judeo-Christian religions, which preach the "one right way."… Christianity became the state religion of the Roman Empire and thence the spiritual font and justification of imperial domination worldwide in the British and American empires. The monotheistic belief system and worldview is ideally suited to be justification for subjugation and genocide. It trumpets one right way; singularity; judgement and condemnation; the righteousness of believers, who are chosen people by birth or through conversion; the doctrine of suffering in the here and now for heavenly reward in the afterlife; and strictures against questioning authority.

Personally, I do not claim to know the extent to which Christianity can be a force for justice and liberation in the world, though I suspect any genuine attempt to make it more of one will have to listen long and hard to thinkers like Daly and Alfred. Rather, my job is to follow Finson's path through her engagement with the United Church of Canada.

Gender and the United Church of Canada

The United Church of Canada came into existence in 1925 when the Methodist Church of Canada, the Congregational Union of Canada, and much of the Presbyterian Church of Canada merged to form a single institution. The Church had roots firmly planted in the social gospel[6] tradition, a trend in Protestant Christian theology in the late nineteenth and early twentieth centuries that emphasized social reform in the interest of ordinary people from a range of perspectives, from relatively conservative to quite radical (Allen 1973; Horn 1980; Socknat 1987). The social gospel was a source of energy and inspiration for many people in social movements in that era and many strands of left politics in Canada, though some associated goals for reform were quite paternalistic and the majority of those who identified with the social gospel remained supporters of empire and never broke with colonial notions like the importance of "Christianizing" society and everyone in it. One feminist analyzing the history of the United Church has argued that the social gospel encouraged seeing society as the problem and the Church and its doctrines as only and always the solution, while allowing little space to critique the role of the Church itself as being part of various social problems (such as colonization, via its long complicity in residential schools, and gender oppression); an openness to this sort of internal critique began only in the 1960s and after (Trothen 2003).

Famous Canadian feminist Nellie McClung was a Methodist and, after Church Union, a member of the United Church, and she declared in 1915, "The church has been dominated by men and so religion has been given a masculine interpretation" (quoted in Squire 1979). Yet in some limited respects, the United Church was in the forefront of society around issues related to women's experiences. For example, it took positions that contraception and abortion were morally permissible decades in advance of their respective removals from the Criminal Code, and the first woman was ordained as a minister in the United Church (albeit after many years of struggle) in 1936 (Trothen 2003: 14–15, 23–28). However, all of this has occurred side-by-side with emphatic Church support for practices that feminists have identified as being central to the subordination of women. In numerous reports on gender and the family, the Church tempered its support for women's autonomy and well-being with positions reinforcing a particular, traditional gender role. More generally, it was a long and difficult process for the United Church to begin the shift away from seeing the form of particular relationships in the traditional patriarchal family as inherently good to paying more attention to the quality of those relationships.

In other words, though there were instances of what progressive Christians sometimes call "prophetic leadership" from the United Church of Canada, in some basic ways that institution was very much in synch with the broader society in terms of its participation in evolving relations of gender oppression and struggle against them. The only woman with a senior administrative position in the United Church at the time, Dr. Harriet Christie, said in 1970, "The church isn't any more closed to women than the rest of society, but it isn't giving any leadership.... We've worked like everything in other areas of discrimination, but we are ignoring this one" (quoted in Clarke 1970).

Finson's initial encounter with the United Church of Canada, however, occurred long before the resurgence of the women's movement in the late 1960s and early 1970s.

To Canada, Christianity, and Feminism

Finson's story begins not in Canada but on the other side of the Atlantic. She recalled, "My family of origin, my parents, I lived with until I was six. My father was a butcher. We lived in council housing in England. We were working-class British." Finson was three years old when the Second World War began, and she identified herself as "a child of the war." She was evacuated because of German bombing and her family was disrupted. Many of the children she lived with in those years were from communities even poorer than her own, until she ended up in her aunt and uncle's working-class household. She credited this childhood with giving her a sense of class consciousness and of "inequities." After her father remarried into a Jamaican family that was quite privileged in terms of class, she spent a few years living in a household where she "had servants and ways of being in the world that were quite different," which gave her an even broader picture of the ways in which class shapes people's lives.

In her mid teens, Finson returned to England from Jamaica. She spent time caring for an ill brother and working jobs that did not particularly captivate her. She said, "I didn't really have any direction." However, at some point she remembered that, "When I was a very young student in England we had a woman come from Canada to talk about Canada. She talked about geysers and Mounties and stuff." This intrigued her, so one day she "saw the Canadian embassy and went toddling in."

> I arrived in Toronto when I was twenty, going on twenty-one, and lived at the YWCA. I came for two years. The main thing I wanted to do was to sit in a coffee shop and order a coffee and doughnuts. I wanted to go shopping like June Allison and Doris Day, and have five boxes and go through the swing doors and drop the boxes and have Rock Hudson pick them up from the street. These are all impressions from movies. I had no real reason to come other than I didn't have anything else on my plate and I thought it would be fun to do, to come for two years.

Not long after she moved here, Finson's search for direction brought her in touch with the church that would shape so much of her life. In her youth, she said,

> I had been confirmed Anglican and I had to go to church when I was in Jamaica and I didn't particularly like it. I had occasionally gone to church when I was with my aunt but I was not particularly taken with any of it.

She began hanging out with a group of young people who attended

Queen Street United Church in Toronto. Through them, she became gradually more connected with the Church, initially because she felt she should rather than from any great passion. However, the Young People's Union in that particular church "was talking about ideas that were challenging; they challenged me intellectually. That is when I for the first time kind of became set on fire. I was beginning to smoulder away because I was excited about ideas."

Eventually, this smouldering and excitement led to Finson to complete a degree in theology. She went on to become a deaconess — a non-ordained ministry position in the United Church that at that time focused on pastoral care — and did a degree in religious education at Emmanuel College. Later she completed a Masters of Social Work, and much of her work was community development in poor communities in Toronto. It was in the context of her community work that Finson first encountered the women's liberation movement. As part of her Master's program,

> I had to choose a project, a piece of work, and I don't know why but I ended up in a project related to abortion. This project was an attempt to give women choice. I worked with this project because I was a community organizer, in the organizational development stream [of the social work program], and my task as a student was to help them develop a board and to develop the infrastructure so that this project could stay permanent and get funding and all of that sort of thing. Which I did as my project. I did my thesis in that area. My thesis work was the question, "Do the social agencies block women and do the free agencies, like Hassle Free Clinic and stuff, are they more permissive?" As it turned out, neither of those was true. Anyway, as I worked in this I visited with the various women's communities. I was really quite fearful. I remember going into the Velvet Fist[7] organization and feeling totally out of it and very unnerved, and not understanding very much. I heard about Laura Sabia,[8] but I was quite unnerved by it. But I felt it was important for me to be there, for some reason.
>
> I had a call from a woman friend who said, "Would you come and talk to my church about women in the church?"
>
> I thought, "Why would I want to talk about women in the church?"
>
> She was very embedded in the women's movement. I said I would do it since I was the only one she knew that was in the church. I scurried around and tried to find some resources.... I can't remember what I actually did. But I *do* remember listening to these women's stories. It was things like the women saying, "When my husband and

I go out, I get the babysitter. When I go out and my husband wants to go somewhere else by himself, I get the babysitter." It was that process of women sharing their lives that began to strike me. And, again, I started reading. I had not seen any of the feminist literature prior to this. The notion of justice for women or of inequities had not been introduced to me prior to this. I began to be interested in the women's movement and hung out there. I just went to whatever was going on. And with some friends; I found some other Christian women who were interested. Gradually I was consumed by this, in some ways. It was a passion for me. I needed to understand what it was. More importantly for me, I needed to understand where my theology and this movement connected.

Friends of Hagar

As was so often true in the women's liberation movement of that era, this shift in consciousness was not a journey Finson undertook alone. In late 1973, she visited with a fellow church worker, Edith Shore, who worked for the Anglican Church of Canada. "We were both sort of disgruntled with our work life in the church. We didn't have a lot of clarity but we just knew it wasn't quite as it needed to be."

An article published in that year offered numerous examples of the sorts of things faced by women working for the United Church (Clarke 1973). It told of the woman who was a national officer of the Church who, somehow, was always expected to serve the coffee at meetings. It mentioned the female Christian education director who was told at her first meeting after getting married to thank her husband for lending her to the committee. And then there was the national Church executive who, when she first approached the Church for employment, was sent to the office for clerical workers. And in terms of policies, examples included deaconesses who substituted at the pulpit for an absent minister getting paid half of what a man would get paid, and the male caretakers of big city churches automatically being put on the Church pension plan while it was not even offered to the women who worked as congregational secretaries. Or, as a colleague of Finson's summarized it a year later, "Women do most of the work of the Church and men make most of the decisions" (Morrison 1974).

Finson and Shore came up with the idea of gathering together other women who worked for churches to talk about their experiences.

> We formed a group called the Friends of Hagar.[9] There were about twenty or twenty-five of us and we would meet every three or four weeks. We would have Swiss Chalet chicken and tell each other our stories. Essentially, it was a consciousness raising group. That

> is all we did. We would go around and we would hear each other talk about how our life was in the Church. We politicized each other about structural dimensions of our lives, and began to see the similarities.
>
> We talked about things like being in a meeting and feeling invisible. You'd say something and nobody would say anything to it and then somebody, particularly a male, would say the same darn thing and it would be picked up.
>
> [Or, for instance,] I was working then in the Conference[10] office and a colleague would come in and say, "Good morning, girlie."
>
> I would say to him, "I don't want to be called girlie."
>
> "Oh, I'm just teasing you. I'm just being friendly. What's wrong with you?"
>
> It was very hard to respond to that without seeming picky.
>
> We groaned and moaned, really, about stuff that was painful, stuff that was annoying. Those groups were not "poor me, poor me," they were really essentially a politicizing process.... Most of us didn't have the structural analysis and certainly didn't have the support on the ground to do anything about it. We would chat and sometimes tell each other how to deal with things.

Along with a core group of women who participated, Finson estimates that as many as 100 or 150 women came in and out of the group. After the initial period it included not just church employees but also lay women. Finson was particularly appreciative of the one Jewish woman who regularly participated. Much initial Christian feminism made exaggerated claims about Jesus Christ being a feminist, and explicitly or implicitly framed that as a radical break from a supposedly irredeemable Jewish patriarchy.[11] The Jewish woman who participated helped them realize that "a lot of the early Christian feminism stuff was anti-Semitic" because of this sort of approach. In time, Finson said, they came to understand that while Jesus exhibited some anti-sexist qualities and practices, "he certainly wasn't himself a feminist." Moreover, "Was he the only one in the world at the time that saw those things? I don't think so. He got those [anti-sexist] ideas from somewhere," most likely other Jewish women and men in his cultural environment. Finson said, "The Jewish woman would help us sort that out."

As was often the case with consciousness raising groups, there came a point when politicizing talk grew into politicized action.

> We simply began doing workshops. We actually didn't have a name but one time we were doing a workshop and we were forced to come up with a name. Then we gave the name meaning because [in the Bible] Hagar was in the desert and was abandoned by the structure

> or the institution of marriage — all of the dimensions of her life we were able to make some identification with.
>
> We went to the Toronto Conference [of the United Church] and did a workshop, the Anglicans went off and did stuff with the Anglican Church, and so on.
>
> We did things like go and picket for the ordination of Anglican woman. We had a newsletter. That ran for about five years, I think. It went across the country and had quite a readership. Women sent articles. We began to identify the specific issues that were affecting our lives. The language issue became clear to us, in the sense that "God the father" was problematic, and being called "brothers of Christ" and stuff. We began to open up some of these doors.

By the mid 1970s, women were exerting pressure for the United Church and other Canadian churches to engage in systematic institutional change. This found expression in at least two different paths of action: an interdenominational project called the Movement for Christian Feminism (MCF) and a series of task forces within the United Church. Finson was involved in both.

The Movement for Christian Feminism

The MCF[12] formally began in 1975. According to Finson, it was funded with money from the United Church, the Anglican Church, and the Women's Inter-church Council. Later, it also received money from the federal government's Status of Women office. It had a board of about a dozen women who identified as Lutheran, Anglican, Presbyterian, United, and Catholic. Finson was hired as the MCF's coordinator.

One core activity of the group was community development — reaching out to women with shared concerns, letting them know they weren't alone, and bringing them together. Finson would go to different cities. She would, for instance,

> go to Owen Sound or to London. I would arrive and I would find a woman there who would bring me in. I would do a few radio programs and I would talk about the Movement for Christian Feminism. People would ask me questions about, "How can you be a feminist and a Christian?" And I would say, "Oh, well, it is not easy." It was a way of trying to touch the lives of woman who themselves, like me, were trying to make sense of their religious, spiritual, theological lives, and of this movement called the women's movement.

The MCF was also very active in participating in and sometimes organizing conferences on women and the church. Finson also found it important to connect with the secular women's movement, which at that time she often found to be a more receptive environment for Christian feminism than traditional church women's organizations. The MCF also served as a platform for prodding individual denominations to make some changes. Finson remembers, for example, that at one point they put some effort into analyzing sexism in the *Observer*, a monthly magazine of the United Church, and using those findings to pressure for changed editorial practices. The MCF also did considerable work with educators and students in Canadian theological schools. But "the major portion would be the work with the national offices" of the churches to get sexism on their agendas and to start them looking at institutional reform.

In Canada, Finson said,

> the churches came into the realm of concern for women backwards. They came in backwards; you had to drag them in. In the States I don't think that was necessarily true. I think there was a lot more leadership at the national level. But here initially they had to be dragged in, shamed in.
>
> I can remember, in the early days of the MCF, going to interview a very senior male bureaucrat. I had met an organization that was working with women bureaucrats and doing workshops with them to help them do structural analysis. This was fairly early, and I wanted them to do something, and they were willing to do something (for free, I think) with United Church or other bureaucrats. I went to see this senior man, to see if he would help support this. I had a document. I documented the organization, the purpose; I was well prepared. I can remember him listening to me go through what this would be. I gave him the document, he turned the document over, and he looked at me and he said, "Shelley, my son went to university with six other young men and out of those six young men, four of them are already divorced because their wives have left them." I was sitting there thinking, "Okay, what has this got to do with me?" But it had a lot to do with it, because it touched something in him. So I was then sitting there trying to say, "Do I care about your son's friends? It's not my problem here. *This* is my problem." But I was trying to listen. I dealt with that in whatever way I did and I tried to get him back onto this, and in the end he was fairly supportive. That's by way of example of them coming in very slowly.

Once pressure had resulted in a certain level of official buy-in from the institutional Church, initiative was largely removed from the MCF, at least in terms of Finson's church. She said,

> I think the MCF had organized and identified a lot of issues prior

to that, but it was the task force, particularly in the United Church, that did the structural work in terms of salaries and employment practices within the organization of the United Church.

The Task Forces

The first task force to examine issues related to feminist concerns within the United Church actually started slightly before the MCF got off the ground, but for years the task force process seemed to lack adequate resources and institutional commitment.

Finson said of the 1974 task force, chaired by Dr. Harriet Christie,

> I was on that and it was a painful, painful experience because they put every possible position on that question, on that committee. You had the bigot at one end and the radical at the other end. It was very, very painful.
>
> It was painful because you felt like you could never get anywhere because you had persons who held such strong different views that there was no place for compromise and you had to accommodate everybody. They must have felt the same about us at the other end of the spectrum.

The task force's mandate initially emphasized issues of organizational reform within the United Church without asking fundamental questions about the Church with respect to sexism — things like employment equity, representation of women on decision-making bodies, equal pay, and so on. They investigated things like why, thirty-eight years after the United Church first ordained a woman, there were only ninety women ordained and on the rolls of the Conferences of the Church, compared to three thousand men. And why there were only five women among the thirty-six officers of the General Council, the United Church's highest decision-making body, and only two Conferences had women as presidents and none had women as executive secretaries (Duncan 1975). They also worked with the *Observer* around sexist language and did some limited networking with women's movement organizations like NAC.

The group's work was interrupted by Dr. Christie's death in 1975. In response, Finson said, "that committee went quiet for awhile. Then it was resurrected." Finson chaired it for a period of time. The task force sought an expanded and extended mandate to pursue its work but was refused by the Church. Instead, the Church constituted a new group, which Finson also chaired. It did some important work in trying to change attitudes, explore the roots of sexism, and reflect on the theological basis for struggling for gender equity. Again, the group was disbanded after a relatively short period of work, responsibility was shifted to a different location within the national office, and a new (again fairly ad hoc) committee with a new name and a new mandate was formed and briefly functioned in 1978 (Trothen 2003: 89–93). Members of the subsequent incarnation of the task force "claimed that this constant name-changing and membership upheaval served to undermine and sabotage their efforts" (ibid.: 97).

But, Finson said,

> There must have been organizing brought to bear — probably the MCF and other organizations — that this subject would be a General Council initiative. The concerns would be institutionalized rather than as a peripheral kind of task force. It went into the system. There was a lot of organizing across the country through the Conferences, and the women particularly, to get this issue into the system with a portfolio.... It would have a staff. Earlier, it was just part of Harriet's portfolio, but this got a full-time person on board.

This decision was made in 1980. There was great surprise when the membership of the new Interdivisional Task Force on the Changing Role of Women and Men in Church and Society was announced by the Executive of the General Council because of the omission of two of the women with the strongest record of pushing for feminist change within the United Church, including Finson. She said,

> Daphne Anderson had been very instrumental in doing educational stuff in Vancouver and it seemed natural that she and I would have gone in on it since we had the history. But there was a feeling that I was probably — I don't know what they said, really. What does "too radical" mean? What does "too biased" mean? What does it mean?

One of the first acts of the new task force was to demand that Anderson and Finson be added as members, and to seek answers as to why they had been left off to begin with. The task force wrote (in two different contexts, both quoted in ibid.: 95, emphasis in original):

> What is the justice issue here? Can the church tolerate strong women? ... How, when did Shelley's name get dropped? Do we need to ask why people are so cautious of us?
>
> A *noticeable* pattern throughout history is that people who begin this process of asking fundamental questions, become ostracized at the point when their concerns are being acknowledged by the community. The effect is that the cutting edge of the movement is

dulled and irreversible divisions occur. Those who are asked by the community to "raise our awareness" often flounder because they are cut off from those who have prepared the way. We are asking that Shelly be appointed as an integral part of the task force, so that this will not happen to us.

As Finson recalled, "People across the county reacted strongly that I wasn't on it. It went back to the executive and was debated. It was quite heady stuff. We both joined it eventually."

The mandate of the task force included raising awareness and effecting changes in theology, language, attitudes, and practices in response to the changing roles and consciousness of women and with a mandate to recognize the "equal worth of women and men" (Trothen 2003: 93). Fairly quickly, the group recognized that their vision for their work went beyond shifts in gender roles and that regardless of what the Church wanted to officially name them, they would consider themselves to be "a task force on sexism" (ibid.: 95). Not surprisingly, their understanding of sexism was not just about individual behaviour but about teachings, attitudes, structure, and basic aspects of social organization. The task force completed a crucial transition from the emphasis of the first such group in the mid 1970s solely on matters of women's representation in an unchanged Church structure to a more radical critique of sexism in the institutional Church and in much Christian theology. As an integral part of their work they developed new feminist theological methods that emphasized a starting point in women's experiences, the political and theological importance of storytelling, and the development of new theological imagery such as the circle and the dance (ibid.: 98–100).

Institutional reform of the Church remained a high priority. A key area, according to Finson, was "the whole question of employment practices: All the departments were mandated to examine their employment practices as it related to women. It went right through the system." The task force collected copious data demonstrating the Church to be an unjust employer. Women, they found, were more likely to be paid less, to be confined to low-status job categories, and to be underrepresented in positions of power both as senior staff and as members of decision-making bodies at all levels. Barriers were identified and departments pushed to make changes (ibid.: 100–102).

Another key point of reform was that "stuff went into the system related to inclusive language, and Conferences and so on began to take votes on such things.... I think Conferences were expected to have an inclusive language task force." Sexist language was identified in Church documents and publications, in hymns, and frequently from pulpits across the country. Reforms included changing the sorts of ubiquitous phrases mentioned by

Finson above, like "brothers in Christ," to alternatives that did not erase half of humanity. They also extended to debates about the even more volatile idea of ending the use of conceptions and language for God that attributed masculinity. Judging by the letters and articles in the *Observer* through those years, this was perhaps the sexism-related issue that sparked the most intense controversy. The staff person for the task force, Mary Connor, was quoted as saying, "To say you don't necessarily want to hold on to the image of God as male is like putting a stick of dynamite in the middle of the church" (Clarke 1981: 29). However, the pages of the *Observer* frequently included letters oozing hostility to all aspects of women's liberation (as well as some in staunch support), and even the much less visible attempts to shift things like employment practices frequently ran up against resistance.

The work of the task force touched on other aspects of sexism as well. They produced educational material on pornography and on sexism in the mass media. They investigated questions of violence against women and sexual harassment, including discovering that at least one-third of all women in ministry in the United Church had been subjected to sexual harassment as theological students or as Church employees (Trothen 2003: 101). They cultivated an informal network of grassroots women in the Church. And they attempted during their mandate to present a visible presence for feminist theology at sessions of General Council. They succeeded in getting the General Council of 1984 to pass a strongly worded confession of the United Church's complicity in sexism but were disappointed in the lack of debate and concrete action resulting from this resolution. Still, as the mandate of the task force expired in late 1984, its members must have experienced at least some satisfaction in knowing the significant impact they had made on the life of the Church, even as much work was left to be done. One of their victories was convincing General Council to respond to the end of the task force's lifespan by creating a new Standing Committee on Sexism to pursue the reforms that the task force had begun (ibid.: 103–109).

Racism and Heterosexism

This task force not only deepened its analysis of sexism over the course of its mandate but also shifted its politics in other important ways. Finson said,

> We began to recognize the connections between race and sexism. That was a very important shift in perspective for us. Because, again, most of us understood issues in a very separate way and that whole recognition of the kind of structural connection of race, class exploitation, ageism, heterosexism — to be able to see those connections was very important.

Even by 1982, there was an increasing emphasis in the task force on the struggles of indigenous women. Some members of the task force began to see the importance of having working-class women and racialized women represented as members, though the group never reached a consensus on it. The task force also took strong positions in support of the struggles of lesbians and gay men (Trothen 2003: 96–97).

Finson's personal journey around issues of racism neither began nor ended with her participation on the task force. An important early shift in her attention to racism began a few years before the task force, while she was at a six-week feminist theological educational event involving a multi-racial group of women at a seminary in the United States. Finson remembered,

> I come from Jamaica and my stepmother is a woman of colour ... and I was raised with playing with Black children, my sisters and brothers. So I am trodding around thinking I am pretty okay, I am not racist in any way.
>
> We had some white women come in from the community to this event and they asked these Black women some incredibly inappropriate questions. Things like, "What is your life like as a Black person?" Terrible, insensitive questions.
>
> The Black women afterwards said to us, "Why didn't you challenge your white sisters?"
>
> And I thought, "What is wrong with the question?"
>
> We had this discussion. They kept saying to us, "Those things you are saying are racist." And, "Where is the racial dimension of your analysis?"
>
> I was having trouble. There was a Black woman there who I became quite friends with. She wrestled me to the ground on this. I was *insistent* that I was not racist. And not only this, but this woman went to Harvard, and she had more money than I did. Her family had lots more money than my family *ever* had. And what the hell was she talking about, me being racist? I had a great wrestle with her. Anyway, she and I went for a walk. It was a very hot day.... The corn was higher than me; it was amazing. We went through the corn and we came to a river. We sat by this river and we decided to take our shirts off, and we were sitting there. We heard gunshots. I looked at her and I knew at that moment that she was different than me. If those were hunters, they would see her as a Black person. Her experience of that gunshot was very different from mine. It was at that moment that I realized that I was racist.

Finson's navigation of her experiences as a lesbian followed its own trajectory as well.[13]

I suppose in the whole circle of stuff for me, the ideologies and the politicization, that my own being lesbian was essentially the last piece of that for me. It has been the most difficult. Not difficult for me as a lesbian — I have been lesbian forever so I am not uncomfortable with that — but it has been the most difficult for me to find my place in the larger society. I have been quite slow in that to be an active leader. The Movement for Christian Feminism was exciting and significant in my life but it was a very painful time. In many ways I was a lightening rod for a lot of anger. And a lot of women's pain. I think I just decided I wasn't going to pick up this other cause, I wasn't going to do that.

She said, "I lived as a lesbian but closeted for many years." For a long time, she had little access to lesbian or more broadly queer spaces and groups: "I had a partner and we lived happily and did our stuff, but we lived mostly inside heterosexual society." As the years passed, she was gradually able to build more community with other lesbians, including others who were Christian, through the women's movement and other spaces. She said, "Of course, gradually, heterosexism and its ideology became clearer for me. I and others, particularly Christians, began to raise awareness of ourselves inside the institution."

The push for change around queer sexualities began to be felt a little later than the feminist push, and the atmosphere was very hostile. In 1971, under the headline "Accept homosexuals; but don't approve of homosexual acts," the *Observer* could editorialize that homosexuals shouldn't complain too much because, in the opinion of the editors, "Acceptance as persons they already have" ("Accept homosexuals" 1971: 11). The editors went on to demonstrate their understanding of "acceptance" by saying, "We should recognize that the increase of homosexual activity is threatening. We believe to be homosexual is tragic." They concluded with a bizarre defence of the Church's long legacy of heterosexism and homophobia that claimed that it resulted in more great art and literature for humanity:

> It should be known that some of the world's most creative people were homosexuals. The sublimation of homosexuality has helped many persons to live rich productive lives. The Christian faith and community have contributed immeasurably to such sublimation. (ibid.)

Over the years the pages of the magazine became more open to articles and letters reporting on queer-friendly activities within the Church and pro-queer positions, and it clearly came to be seen as a justice issue deserving attention for certain people within the Church. Even so, when explaining a

1976 brief from a United Church department in favour of inclusion of homosexuality within human rights protections in Ontario, the brief's presenter felt it necessary to add the qualification, "We're not saying that we approve of homosexuality." And in 1979, an editorial in the *Observer* advocating respectful and open debate on the subject felt the need to caution, "We are not opening this discussion because we endorse homosexuality" (Clarke 1979: 8). A 1980 report by a United Church task force focused on issues of sexuality and relationships contained some moderately positive recommendations on gays and lesbians; these recommendations were among the most heatedly attacked both from within and outside the Church (Trothen 2003).[14] A toned down report issued in 1984 by a separate task force looking at sexuality was also attacked for similar reasons.

One of the central questions involved in how the Church should deal with issues of sexual orientation was around whether gay men and lesbians who were open about who they were should be permitted to become ordained ministers. Finson was not out at all in the context of the Church, yet heterosexism and homophobia were definitely at play during her attempts to gain ordination.

> I was ordained in '79 and I'd become a deaconess when I first graduated, which would have been in about '64 or '65. So I'd been a deaconess for a number of years. When I went for ordination, I had these years of ministry. I was written up here and there as the youth worker. I had lots of kudos.... But when I came up for ordination there was a bit of a question. In fact, I was turned down.... I was astounded. I remember going to them and thinking they'd like me and they knew me; these people all knew me. They turned me down on the basis of who they thought they knew and they thought they knew I was lesbian, I'm assuming.
>
> I was outraged. I was outraged! Because of my ministry. They said to me, "We don't hear your call." I said, "What the hell is a call? I have been working and responding to a call, and now you're telling me you don't hear a call? What call are you listening for?"... They wanted a different call, they wanted a more golden call or a silver call, a beautiful call. So I was outraged. Outraged! It took me a long time to process it.
>
> I had an interesting experience when somebody took me for lunch and said, "Are you ... ummm ... are you, you know ... are you lesbian? Because, you know, if you're lesbian, you know, I could sort of help to interpret this to the committee."
>
> I looked at her and I said, "You know, I only discuss my sexuality with people who want to sleep with me because otherwise it's

of no importance. Are you interested?" *[laugh]* When I picked her up off the floor — but anyway, I said, "It's not an issue here, unless everybody wants to talk about it, if that's why they want to know about who I want to sleep with."

I let it be known I was going to take in a tape recorder to the next interview and I was going to get a lawyer and sue them. Of course I didn't have a tape recorder and I probably wouldn't have, but I might have. They never raised this. I heard they were going to raise it, but they never raised it. But they did say, "We wonder about your call." I broke in a rage and I said, "How dare you. How dare you raise that for me!" I still have feelings. I think they were stunned by my anger. And I got through.

As the issue gained prominence in the 1980s, Finson was working as a theological educator, initially at the Centre for Christian Studies, an openly justice-focused institution then based in Toronto. By the time the issue reached a climax in 1988, she was at a more traditional institution, the Atlantic School of Theology in Halifax.

When I was in Toronto there were enough Christian feminists who were lesbian that there was a critical mass and so I had lots of support. I could raise issues of heterosexism/sexism in committees because I knew I had lots of support. When I came here, I didn't. There weren't lots of lesbian Christians. There were few, very few. I came here in '85. If you remember, in '88 the Church was dealing with the issue of the ordination and commissioning of gays and lesbians. And it wasn't friendly. It was not a friendly place. I can recount going to a presbytery and hearing some terrible, terrible stuff said about gays and lesbians, and not feeling able to speak. I was not accustomed to that. But I couldn't speak, I didn't have the courage. It was painful because they would sing, "Come in, come in, come in and sit down. We're all part of the family," when they'd just said they didn't want us.

Loraine MacKenzie Shepherd, another United Church minister who was closeted at that time, has written of the years surrounding the 1988 decision. She has criticized the Church's attempts at open and inclusive debate for lacking any awareness of how such a process opened people experiencing oppression up to verbal attacks on their personhood and even physical violence: "Everyone was welcomed into the discussion, but a simple inclusion of all voices did not provide lesbian and gay people, or people of colour, the safety necessary to risk speaking" (Shepherd 2002: 5).

Shepherd recalls her own experience as a minister to three smaller congregations in Ontario in those years:

> Anger erupted across the country and in virtually every United Church congregation. I found myself living daily contradictions as I ministered to people livid about the United Church's decision.... One congregation I served passed a motion forbidding homosexuals from ministering in their church. Because I was committed to empowering the voices of marginalized rural congregations, I helped them write a letter to the national Church expressing their dismay over the national Church's decision, while I preached about God's inclusive love and grace for all people. In contrast, the other two congregations of the multi-point pastoral charge I served refused to endorse the motion of the first congregation, because they were committed to an open, inclusive church. And in the meantime my partner and I made emergency get-away plans should we come home to a manse sprayed with homophobic graffiti. In its attempt to become inclusive, the church had become a dangerous place for me. (ibid.: 4)

Finson's ministry never involved being a pastor for a congregation, but the controversy in 1988 still touched her in intense ways at the Atlantic School of Theology. She said,

> The school had a terrible time debating this subject of the ordination. It showed everybody where they stood, and some of them were not nice, were cruel, ill-informed, bigoted. We did educational programs. I brought in a lesbian colleague of mine to do a workshop on working with gay/lesbian youth. We had various talks. But by and large the school was not well prepared. I don't think we prepared our students.

The tension of being closeted in such an atmosphere also shaped Finson's presence in the classroom.

> I would be afraid of bringing myself out in the class. I'm a fairly passionate teacher when I get inside the material, so my mouth runs away with me. So I'm saying, "There's Blacks and there's people of colour and there's Latinos and there's le- le- le-." I terrified myself. Sort of my own homophobia. I don't remember how long ago it was that I decided to give it up and get on with it.

She was inspired by a sabbatical spent at the Episcopal Divinity School in Boston.

They have an incredible number of gay and lesbian students, they have gay and lesbian faculty. Everybody is celebrated: All the Blacks celebrate themselves, all the Latinos, all the Asians, everybody. It's a great pot of diversity and nothing is that important, everything is brought into perspective. When I came back I came out to my faculty group. That was painful. They didn't know what to say, many. But, anyway, we get on.

Relentless Persistence

Through that frustration, through the Church's indifference to the needs of women, through the polarized anger in response to so much feminist challenge, through the misogyny from some pulpits, through the gross homophobia from colleagues and fellow Church members, through the refusal to hear calls for justice, Finson persisted.

What keeps me going is that, my faith. It's a faith stance. Jesus has challenged me. It's still there. "Bring in the new world, the new day." I'm drawn by other people's witness…. If I flag, I have to go and get on the street. I just have to go down to a picket, somebody picketing, and that will turn me on, get my head back on track again.

I've had cancer three times, three encounters with cancer. I can tell you that brings one up short in terms of life. I understand life differently a bit now. It's a substance, it's something that's absolutely real. It's not something I'm casual about or, "Life slipped by, isn't that interesting, it's now Thursday." I live life much more. I get up and I say, "Good morning day. I'm going to try to use this day. I'm going to live it. I'm not going to waste it."

A story: I listened once to a video about people in a revolutionary Latin American country. It was called *Revolution or Death*. It was the story of the people of that country who sent their children to the revolution, and had to because they were so oppressed by the regime, and they were killed. These children's bodies came home on the back of a truck and we saw it, and we all wept. It was a terrible, terrible movie. It was painful, all weeping away. The woman who was leading it said, "The mothers of those children do not have the time or the luxury to weep that you have." I think that's true. I mean, we don't have the time to beat our chests about, "Oh I'm so depressed. I'm so hopeless." That is a luxury. And I get there, but I have to get out of it. It's self indulgence. Of course I have my own personal needs, so go take care of them. Go to a counsellor, get yourself sorted out, but don't sit there and beat your chest about how bad it is and stuff when these people over there don't have the luxury to do that. Do it!

I always say it's better to do it and fail than not to do it. I did lots of things wrong, for God's sake. Many times I approached people inappropriately and hurt them or said the wrong thing and I felt bad and thought, "Oh, I wish I hadn't done that." But get on. At least I tried, I put [in] the effort. So I get quite angry with people who use, "My mother didn't love me, and so I just don't feel good about myself." For God's sake, take care of yourself. Go and find someone who will help you with that, but don't use that as a reason for not getting on and putting your shoulder to the wheel. I have not much patience for that.

That's what I would say: pick your spot, do your thing, learn about it, find colleagues, don't do it alone, and you will be blessed because you will know that you've touched people's lives. One person, you've touched them. And what's more important than that? What's more important than bringing life where there is no life, or bringing hope when there is no hope? What's more important? I don't think there's anything more important than that.

Notes

1. Finson passed away on February 3, 2008 (Journey 2008).
2. The following discussion has some political limitations. Some of my statements make claims about "religion" in general while others make claims about "Christianity" more specifically (while recognizing that both are incredibly internally diverse). I have done my best to identify the specificities of my (privileged) experience of religion while also trying to present some more general ideas, but there may be areas where I have generalized my own history, experience, and knowledge in inappropriate ways. As well, the discussion would be made much richer by a much more thorough integration of other religious traditions and ways of doing spirituality. I have done so in a sporadic way, but in some ways the shape of the discussion is limited by my overall choice to organize the analysis to flow largely from a combination of my own experience, the experience of the interview participants, and the dominant social relations in Canada. In this case, those might be characterized as secular (in some senses "post-Christian" might apply) left, Christian left, and mainstream Christianity, respectively.
3. The strand of my thinking in this passage owes quite a bit to my own appropriation of ideas from Jantzen 1999.
4. Again I would refer the reader to Jantzen 1999. I have a more complicated reaction to her ideas than just blanket endorsement, but I am convinced that Christianity and the secularism that has derived from it have important shared elements of discourse that celebrate death, and we need to collaborate in putting together an "imaginary" that celebrates life and emphasizes flourishing as a paradigm for understanding and acting in the world. Also, I want to be clear that I don't see efforts to change culture and imagination as somehow separate

5. from efforts to transform social relations in material ways — the two can only happen together.
5. For a much more elaborated feminist look at early Christianity, see Fiorenza 1979, Reuther 1983, Reuther 1985, and Schottroff 1995. See also many of the other items from the vast output of Fiorenza and Reuther over the years. For a more recent critical feminist analysis of Fiorenza (and three other feminist theologians) see Shepherd 2002.
6. For more on the social gospel in the early twentieth century, see Chapter 1 of *Resisting the State: Canadian History Through the Stories of Activists*.
7. This was a feminist publication based in Toronto.
8. Sabia was the president of the Canadian Federation of University Women and chair of the Committee for the Equality of Women in Canada, a national coalition of women's groups. She played a prominent role in lobbying for what became the Royal Commission on the Status of Women in 1967 (Griffin Cohen 1993: 6–8).
9. To hear some of Finson's memories of the Friends of Hagar, go to www.talkingradical.ca/audio/finson_friends_of_hagar.mp3.
10. A Conference is an administrative unit of the United Church of Canada, comprised of multiple presbyteries, which are in turn comprised of multiple pastoral charges, which may consist of one or a small number of congregations (United Church of Canada 2010). As of 2010, the Church had 2,250 pastoral charges grouped into ninety-one presbyteries, which in turn were organized into thirteen Conferences.
11. Finson specifically pointed to a 1971 article called "Jesus was a Feminist" by Leonard Swidler, a liberal Catholic theologian from the United States. In 2007, Swidler published a book of the same name, which in important ways has failed to address the criticisms of the original article. For a feminist look at early Christianity that explicitly works against this sort of reading, see Schottroff 1995.
12. To hear some of Finson's memories of the MCF, go to www.talkingradical.ca/audio/finson_mcf.mp3.
13. To hear Finson relate an incident of blatant homophobia in employment in the church — a different one from the one included below — as well as some of her memories of the ordination debate, go to www.talkingradical.ca/finson_church_homophobia.mp3.
14. The task force of which Finson was a part at that time also criticized this report but on the basis of its inadequate treatment of sexism.

Conclusion

Over the course of six chapters we have heard stories from nine different long-time participants in social movements in northern Turtle Island.[1] They have spoken of strikes and schools, confrontations and conferences, pleasure and anger. Starting from their words, I hope you have encountered history-from-below and ideas that are new to you, particularly with respect to gender and sexuality struggles that have shaped Canada. To draw this diverse material together, I want to step back a little and reflect on how the preceding pages might contribute to an enhanced understanding of the world and on what exactly we can take away from them.

Any long-term project of learning about the world such as writing a book is both a pressure and an opportunity to learn about learning about the world — to think through how we do it, to identify and work through inconsistencies as best we can, and to come up with an explicit foundation for building knowledge that we can feel confident in presenting to others.

In reality it was messier than this, but here's a sketch of the start of that journey for me: Time spent thinking about my own experiences. Time spent hearing and reading the experiences of others, some very, very different from my own. Then lots of effort put into figuring out how all of those different experiences could co-exist, and how I should re-evaluate my own experience based on what I learned from others. It involved figuring out first that these disparate experiences were connected, and then figuring out how.

Like I said, it was messier than this, and much longer — its beginning predates the book project and it continues still. But this kind of initial muddling toward an explicit analysis of learning about the world, of knowledge production, led to a few core realizations that are very relevant to the book you are holding.

The first is that producing knowledge is a result of an embodied person engaging in material practices in the world at specific times and specific places. I don't just suddenly know something — I have to hear it, feel it, see it, read it. It is physical. It is active. And it isn't some kind of magical, agentless happening, but rather it is a material act done by *me*. I read a book, I listen to my friend's story of workplace sexual harassment, I practice shooting a basketball.

Moreover, it is a kind of material doing that has, for all of its incredible variety, a general form: It begins when I encounter an input. This might be experience I have myself. It might be someone else's account of their experiences, via an interpersonal interaction or a text of some kind. Or it might be analysis, somebody explaining how *they* understand the social world and how *they* make meaning from the experiences that they have and hear about.

And when I encounter such an input, it doesn't just pour into my brain like water into a glass, but rather I have to take it up. There is an active process whereby this input is turned into meaning for me. In so doing, I put the input (including its source and context) into relation with the sum of the knowledge I have, to that moment, already produced from all of the earlier iterations of the cycle I'm describing here. This step might happen in a split second, as a smoothly integrated and unconscious moment in the regular flow of experiencing and acting in the world, or it might be something more deliberate and explicit than that.

Once I have put the input into relation with my existing knowledge, I may add it to what I already know in a straightforward way. Or I may discard this new input as uninteresting, unreliable, incomprehensible, indigestible, or wrong. Or it may cause me to modify my existing knowledge, to reconsider past understandings and synthesize new ones. I may reframe this input or fit it into new contexts. I may make connections that the source of the input couldn't anticipate or intend. The new knowledge may take the form of "facts" that can be clearly communicated, skills that can only be developed by doing, or some sort of more amorphous common sense or feeling about "how things work." Someone else when faced with the same input might take it up (or not) in very, very different ways.

Any and all knowledge we have is built that way, from toddlers learning not to touch hot things to high school students doing chemistry experiments to older adults evaluating current events in light of a lifetime of political involvement.

Implications

The description above illustrates how experience is our source of input for producing knowledge about the world, whether that is our own immediate experiences or our experience of hearing/reading the experiences and analyses of other people. The meaning made from past experiences also provides the basis for evaluating the meaning of new experiences. Consistent trajectories of experience translate into sustained patterns and directions for our individual journeys of knowledge production. And throughout the book I've shown that all of us have such sustained trajectories of experience — that is, that our experiences are socially organized in ways that are all about privilege and oppression. Therefore, our place in social relations, our history of experience of what I described in the Introduction as socially organized power-over, play a role in shaping how we can know the world.

A key early site for me to begin figuring this out was the issue of racism. I entered adulthood unaware that I knew very, very little about it. After all, even growing up in a mostly-white area of rural southern Ontario, I knew it existed and I thought I knew what it was. Except I didn't really. In hindsight,

I can see that formal schooling, the mass media, and informal pedagogy in the rest of life — all shaped as they are in the context of social relations that privilege white people and oppress racialized people and normalize that arrangement — produced and reinforced this ignorance in me. It is, I now know, a dimension of white privilege that my everyday life contained no pressures to develop accurate knowledge about racism and plenty of incentives not to do so, in stark contrast with people who are the targets of racial oppression, for whom developing practical knowledge about it is essential for surviving and thriving.

Eventually, though, inputs accumulated such that something sank in. I could tell from social dynamics at an interpersonal level, from the different ways that various people around me reacted to various things, from a few painful instances of making gaffes myself, that I was not getting something. I've never liked feeling ignorant and I especially don't like stumbling into saying things that hurt people, so this prompted me to start doing some deliberate learning, including both seeking out particular texts and paying attention to the people around me in new ways. This stage is imperfect, incomplete, and ongoing, but it did eventually lead to a modest reduction in cluelessness and some understanding of how racism is socially organized and socially produced. This, in turn, has led to me re-evaluating my own experiences and recognizing that they aren't some politically neutral default but are just as much produced by the social relations that oppress people of colour and indigenous people as that oppression itself.

It also led me to a better understanding of knowledge production when it comes to racism. That is, I came to appreciate that both my original ignorance and the path of my learning have been shaped by my place in social relations of racial oppression and white privilege. This requires that I recognize the limits that such situatedness places upon me. Reading books and listening hard are all well and good, but the journey of learning and the knowledge I can produce are still different — and, in important ways, more limited — than for someone whose knowledge production is informed by everyday experiences of racism. Yet because the social relations that produce racism also produce me, learning about racism isn't some noble gesture toward others (or "Others") made from a place of innocence, but very much about me and about a state of affairs of which I am an integral part; it is, among other things, about learning about myself, about my place in the world, and about how I can and must act in it. Again, this is all imperfect and in progress, and my capacity to just not get it remains intact, but that, at least, is the path.

This lesson is applicable much more generally: Knowledge production is shaped by all of our socially organized experiences — our experiences of all of social relations — in all of their complexity. This is really just a more grounded way of approaching the idea of standpoint that was raised back in the Introduction.

The learning process described above has some other implications as well. For instance, it is clear that building knowledge about the world that captures anything beyond our own very local environment can only happen in some sort of dialogue with other people, directly or via texts. Our lives are organized in ways beyond any one person's local, immediate experience, and to figure out how any of that works we need to talk and listen to other people. This allows us to build knowledge about the world far beyond what a narrow and constricting understanding of standpoint might allow for, and points toward ways to do that.

Another implication is that this understanding of learning also forces us to confront the limits of our own ability to know the world. Understanding knowledge production as a journey by an embodied person through a very complicated world makes it clear that we can never be sure we know it all. There is always some new voice, some new experience, some new analysis, waiting around the next corner to shake up our current understanding. It's not that this boxes us into a situation where nothing is true or where we can't really know anything, as some critics might wrongly accuse. We can know things and we do know things, and our very ability to use that knowledge to navigate the world is evidence of the realness and relevance of our knowledge. But it is neither as clear cut nor as absolute as we are generally taught.

Another core learning from listening to many different experiences and looking to many different analyses to try and understand them and how they relate to me is that, in fact, they *are* all related. This has not always been true. A thousand years ago, a sheep herder in the Scottish Highlands had his experience organized in ways that had no connection whatsoever to the ways that the experiences of a Mohawk clan mother were organized in northeastern Turtle Island or those of a small farmer in South Asia. That has long since ceased to be true. Different people have described it in different ways, but many thinkers agree that in the contemporary world all of our lives are connected to and organized through an overarching, complicated nexus of relations. These are relations that are not mystical or metaphysical, but rather they can be studied, learned about, described, and changed. Mind you, identifying the existence of those material connections is not to make any rash claims about their character. Unlike theorists who claim that it all boils down to one root cause, to a single central kind of relation — to capital, to patriarchy, to white supremacy, to the state, to some other single thing — I don't claim to be able to name this totality, to know in a definitive way how it works and what matters about it and what we should do about it.[2] This is something that is subject to ongoing learning, experimentation, challenge, and reassessment. Diverse traditions that pay attention to any and all of those aspects of social relations, and particularly to how they are interconnected, are important resources in this never-ending cycle of learning.

And finally, given the socially organized character of its experiential basis and the centrality of dialogue with other people, it's clear that knowledge production is emphatically social, for all of us, almost all of the time. It makes sense, therefore, that when people come together to work deliberately and collectively to intervene in the social world, such activity plays out in important ways in the field of knowledge production. Or put another way, people create knowledge through collective struggle.[3]

As we act collectively to change the world, our experiences shift, which shifts our ground for knowledge production. As well, movements and communities in struggle tend to be sites of intense dialogue and of deliberate, collaborative efforts to make meaning of the world — sometimes formal, sometimes not. All of these shifts in our experiences and these opportunities for dialogue are not random or neutral. They are, in many ways, specifically about challenging that which oppresses us. In the course of such challenge, whether successful or not, we produce knowledge about how oppressive institutions and more diffuse oppressive relations that we oppose are socially organized. We also build new knowledge among the "we" who are in motion about ourselves, including a greater sense of collective possibility and power. We build knowledge about the world that is and about the future worlds toward which our struggles are oriented. Moreover, it is through collective struggle that the knowledge that we already hold and the knowledge that we build as we struggle are given social enactment — we give social force to our knowledge, for instance, that we are human, we deserve dignity, and all of humanity deserves dignity too. Therefore if you seek knowledge about the world that has the potential to be transformative — that is about change and that can usefully inform efforts to create change — then the knowledge produced in and by movements is a crucial place to start. And what better way to engage with such knowledge than to talk to people who participated in the collective process of knowledge production.

Canadian History Through the Stories of Activists

These ideas about how we know the world have informed (and, indeed, developed in conjunction with) the research and writing of *Gender and Sexuality* and its companion, *Resisting the State*, both with the subtitle, *Canadian History Through the Stories of Activists*.

I began from the experiences of people long immersed in movements — the in-depth interviews with fifty long-time activists. Yet it soon became clear to me that the most useful way to honour these activists and their commitment to change was not just deep listening to their stories, but striving to understand how those stories fit into the social world — how the participants' experiences were socially produced and how their actions fed into collective movements that created change. Therefore I related to each story as a window, an entry point, a vantage to see the larger stories in which they were embedded. Or, I took each story as a node bound into larger networks, with thin tendrils extending outwards, wrapping and tangling around the tendrils from other nodes, becoming thicker, connecting in great densely intertwined webs. Whatever metaphor you prefer, the point is not just individual lives and memories, but the ways in which the participants' lives, like all of ours, tie into bigger networks of relations and flows of doing across a range of scales, and in which individual memories exist in interactive relation with shared histories.

In presenting the material this way, I had to make some choices. All of our lives are shaped by history and shape history in turn along so many axes that it would be very difficult to talk about them all at once; all the strands wrap around each other, interpenetrate, tangle, stick. To aid clarity and readability, in each chapter I've chosen only a few of the many possible strands to talk about. It is important to emphasize that which connections and how to draw them were *my* decisions. Taking responsibility for that (and for the many other ways an author exerts power over a text) is an important reason why I have made myself and my journey of knowledge production visible — not exhaustively so, admittedly, but in significant ways. However, in making my decisions about how to talk about larger flows of doing over time and about analytical tools for understanding the social world, I tried to be guided by the standpoints of the participants. That doesn't make the power to choose any less mine, but it gave me a framework that allowed me to be responsible to the people who shared their stories. I do not pretend to be other than I am; rather, I have proceeded on the basis that the embodied and dialogical character of knowledge production means I can enter into such processes guided by their accounts of their experiences.[4]

There are a few other general characteristics to the book that flow from the approach to knowledge production that informs it. It is, for instance, rather less linear than we are often taught to expect of histories. Rather than beginning at point A and narrating events of importance up to point B, it weaves back and forth through time according to the requirements of presenting the experiences of the participants and drawing the relevant connections to larger flows and ideas. It also makes it not only acceptable but expected that some important areas will be touched on more than once but from different angles and with different lenses. If you look across both this book and its companion, you will encounter more than once things like the origins of capitalism and the New Left upsurge in movements in the 1960s and 1970s, for instance.

This approach to knowledge production also implicitly contains the idea that broader listening to experiences and to analyses will result in knowledge that is more robust and useful. Certainly there are many more voices that would enrich it, but this book tries to follow that advice. And in terms of the ideas that I took up and tried to apply in relevant ways, I did not stay bound to any single tradition but attempted to be searching and acquisitive and synthetic, with an emphasis on seeking out connections. And, finally, this book does history in ways that are quite up front about being incomplete, as any telling of history must inevitably be. It is incomplete in that not only are there more voices that would enrich this book, but there are *always* more voices to hear from in understanding the trajectory of the social relations that produce us all. It is incomplete in the sense that there are *always* more stories of oppression and resistance. It is incomplete in the sense that tomorrow's history is *always* being produced as we move through the world today. However, most conventional history and even many kinds of critical history — much conventionally Marxist history, for instance — tend to advance a closed framework and a claim to greater finality than is ever actually warranted.

Nodes and Strands

Doreen Spence and Donna MacPhee's stories centred around their experiences as indigenous women confronting the ways in which the settler state's schooling, and dominant forms of knowledge production more generally, are oppressive toward indigenous peoples. An obvious choice for a larger historical flow that has shaped their lives and against which they have struggled is the settler colonization of Turtle Island. As with everyone else who lives on this continent, their lives would be unimaginably different in the absence of this long and complicated historical trajectory; as with other indigenous people in particular, they have had little choice but to navigate the oppressive character of this reality on an everyday level, which led them to more organized and collective forms of challenging colonization and racism. Within that historical flow, there are lots of potential connections to make to Spence and MacPhee's stories and acts of resistance. I chose three major ones: I drew attention to the tight relationship between colonization and the introduction of gender oppression to Turtle Island, and the ways in which struggle against gender oppression began not among settlers but against settlement; I talked about knowledge as a site and tool for oppression and resistance — mostly about the specific example of colonial oppression and anti-colonial struggle, but with relevance to many other struggles as well; and I sketched out some of the history of settler institutions in what is now "Canada" attempting to use schooling to exert power over indigenous peoples and indigenous people resisting.

Though Madeleine Parent's involvement extended over decades, from her start in the student movement to her long-term commitments to the labour and women's movements, she was most interested in talking to me about the Dominion Textile strike of 1946. It is important to note that her story, too, could not have happened without histories of colonization on Turtle Island. However, in the chapter I drew this connection only in passing. This particular struggle also happened in the context of waged work (mainly by women and children) that was organized in capitalist ways. For that reason, I connected the hardships they were struggling against to the tendency of this form of making and doing to push us to see and prioritize things over people and our doings. I touched briefly on the long and complicated history of making and doing on this planet coming to be organized in capitalist ways, and in particular its central historical dependence on racial oppression and on transformed and increased gender oppression. I tied the Dominion Textile struggle to a little of the history of politics at the level of the Quebec state, to the trajectory of workers' organizations in Canada and Quebec, and to the troubled relationship of many of those organizations to the efforts by women workers to stand up for themselves.

Lee Lakeman talked about collective efforts to resist the violence done to women by men in a small Ontario city and in Vancouver, British Columbia. I drew the connection between her struggles and the phenomenon of violence against women, particularly the ways in which it tends to be denied, ignored, and erased even in supposedly progressive or movement or pro-feminist spaces, though the movement of which Lakeman has been a part has made important steps to challenge that. Following the lead of her stories, I connected the struggle against male violence with struggles related to the state, and to the flow of struggle and historical context of the so-called "second wave" of the women's movement.

Shree Mulay and Sadeqa Siddiqui talked about their involvement in struggles against gendered violence among South Asian women in Montreal. I used this second chapter focused on violence against women to connect Mulay and Siddiqui's struggles to reflections on the political significance of difference, particularly but not exclusively with respect to race and gender. I drew this connection in general, in relation to struggles against gender oppression in Canada, and in relation specifically to struggles against gendered violence. This included connecting to ways in which racialization produces specific experiences of gendered violence; in particular, for many though not all racialized women, this means violence that is not just not remedied by state practices but is actively produced by them. I tied their struggles to broader histories of collective organizing by immigrant women of colour in Canada and the connection of that work (or not) to the mainstream women's movement.

The stories of Chris Vogel and Richard North covered decades of struggle by gay men and other queer people in Winnipeg. To effectively connect their struggles to the larger clusters of relations and historical flows they are produced by and co-create, I first had to talk about the ways in which sexuality is not just individual and private but is a relentlessly social phenomenon that ties into many social relations that we might be inclined to see as totally apart from it. Keeping their struggles at the centre, however, I explored the connection to histories of shifting organization of sexuality, histories of same-gender desire, and histories of resistance by queer people in Canada.

Shelley Finson's struggles were in a collective way focused on women in Christian religious institutions in Canada, particularly mainstream Protestant churches, and in a more individual way related to queer struggles in the same context. Again this involved sketching out the social character of something we usually treat individualistically: religion. I drew the connection between her efforts to create change and general histories of Christianity and its relationship to gender, and more specifically to the journey of the United Church of Canada around gender and sexuality in the twentieth century.

These, then, were the nodes from which I began and the strands of connection I followed to larger flows of doing and to tools for thinking about the world. From the stories of these activists, contextualized in these ways, we learn not only about their lives but also something about the oppressive character of the social relations in which we are all embedded. This tracing toward larger scales is not comprehensive, but it presents some useful information and ideas to understanding the past and the present of life in the territories currently identified as "Canada." It does not attempt to map the dense tangle of relations in detail, but it shows some things about how power has worked and changed when it comes to gender, racialization, colonization, state relations, capital, sexuality, and more. The book also lays out some important ways that people have challenged those experiences of oppression. In doing all of this, the book not only refuses the deceptively rosy picture of Canada we see in most classrooms and media but it also points toward hope, toward strength, toward paths of struggle through which we can create a better world. From these stories of struggle, we can understand how we got to where we are, and we can take up ideas and inspiration that we can all apply in moving toward a better tomorrow.

That is, again, not to claim that this is anything close to a complete account of the past or a comprehensive array of ideas and tools we might need for the future — not at all. I've already alluded to some of the many other voices whose experiences of oppression and of struggle would add to our understandings of social relations in Canada and of our choices in resisting.[5] Of particular relevance to a book looking at sexuality and gender struggles is the absence of any trans voices, along with voices of many other experiences and struggles grounded in racialization, sexuality, ability, class, and gender that are simply not present in these pages. I hope, however, that the stories, the histories, the voices, the ideas presented in this book are taken as an invitation for you, the reader, on your ongoing journey of knowledge production to seek out more voices to learn from, in your everyday life and through movies and books and radio and the Internet.

In particular, I invite you to read *Resisting the State: Canadian History Through the Stories of Activists*. After all, many of the stories in this book are about struggles that not only focus on gender and/or sexuality but that oppose the state in significant ways. What organized the colonial and educational oppression that Spence and MacPhee fought against; what has been a key source of support for tyrannical employers; what has responded as minimally as possible to the valiant activism opposing violence against women and indeed organizes the lives of many women (particularly racialized women) into violence; what has been a principal bulwark of heterosexist social relations, if not that cluster of relations and practices that we so often treat as a thing called "the state"? And in that other book you will encounter struggles that not only oppose the state (and many other oppressive aspects of social relations) but that are also gender struggles. You will find stories like that of Kathy Mallett, an indigenous woman who was an important leader in struggles by mostly other indigenous women in Winnipeg against the ways in which child welfare authorities attacked their communities and families. That is most definitely a gender struggle, as I have understood that term in this book. Lynn Jones's struggles as a working-class African-Nova Scotian woman in the community, in the workplace, and in the labour movement cannot be divorced from her experiences of gender. And Josephine Grey's work for the human rights of poor people, much of which has been with other women of colour living in poverty, is clearly a gender struggle too.

Ordinary

Yet I worry a little bit about whether I have struck the right balance in one particular respect. As I said, one of the things I want to accomplish in these books is to honour the people that I talked to — the great things that they have done and also the gift of their stories. Their experiences have included many different kinds of moments of resisting oppression and exploitation, from the very small-scale, individual, everyday moments that we all have whether we name them as such or not, to the much more public and collective expressions of resistance. Doing right by their stories means respecting the presence and importance of these many different moments. So it is just as politically crucial to recognize the significance of an individual resisting an instance of everyday racism on a bus, say, as it is to see the politics of organizing a massive demonstration.

However, from the start the goal of the project that resulted in these books has been to explore histories of collective and public resistance and knowledge production in the midst of it. One outcome of this focus — and one outcome of the tendency most of us have when reminiscing about our lives, to pay attention to the remarkable and extraordinary — is that I heard more about the big, memorable things than about the everyday things. This isn't necessarily bad, as the big stuff *is* important. Yet because being at the centre of big actions, big victories, or big defeats is not the norm for most of us, it risks obscuring the fact that such extraordinary things only happen because of ordinary people doing ordinary things.

I think most of my interview participants would agree that they themselves are very ordinary people who have mostly done quite ordinary things, even if the circumstances in which they have done them have on occasion been a little unusual. Even the most collective and public moments of resistance to oppression and exploitation are made possible because they are built upon countless small ones. They are built from many small meetings that are sometimes fun and sometimes boring and sometimes frustrating. They are made up of conversations, of taking your lunch hour to hand out leaflets on a downtown street corner, of lots and lots of e-mails and phone calls. They are made up of the little acts of support and affection and solidarity that a group of people who share experiences of racism or heterosexism do to keep each other strong in the face of the constant assault of everyday oppression. They are hours spent figuring out what government documents really say or painting signs or arranging rides for everyone. They are bake sales and yard sales and socials and letter writing. They are speaking up and they are listening. They are asking for donations and making donations. They are putting together child-care arrangements and ensuring the hall is physically accessible and figuring out how to get the DVD player hooked up correctly. They are making puppets and painting murals and writing media releases. They are difficult discussions about sexism. They are deciding whether you can afford to give up three hours of sleep to join an early morning picket line in someone else's strike. They are some really great parties. They are long bus rides and long speeches, and cool music and new friends.

Yes, the extraordinary moments do happen, but they happen because of lots of people doing lots of things that are completely ordinary. Things you could be doing. In fact, things you already do. If this book supports even a handful of people in thinking a bit more deliberately about how they can join the moments of refusal and resistance they already experience, the everyday activities (exertions of what I talked about in the Introduction as power to-do) they already engage in, with those of other people in order to create collective efforts for social change, it will have been well worth writing. As the Zapatistas, a group of indigenous peasants in southern Mexico who are engaged in ongoing struggle against neoliberalism, have observed,

"We are perfectly ordinary people, therefore rebels" (quoted in Holloway and Sitrin 2007: 58).

Notes

1. Much of this Conclusion is the same as in the companion book, *Resisting the State: Canadian History Through the Stories of Activists*, but some material toward the end is specific to this book.
2. Often in the book I've talked about "social relations" in general, with the idea that we have to figure out how they are organized in specific cases. I also like feminist sociologist Dorothy Smith's (1999; 2005) terms "ruling relations" and "ruling regimes" for use in this situation. I am uncertain of its origins, but I have seen some feminist sources use the term "kyriarchy" to capture this idea. African-American feminist bell hooks often uses some variation on the phrase "white supremacist capitalist patriarchy." Personally, I'm a fan of keeping our naming practices in this area unstable and open; I find it a useful reminder of the fact that challenging domination is a constant process of learning and experimenting.
3. A great deal of the published research and theory related to social movements is knowledge that claims to be *about* them but that is, in my opinion, of relatively little use to movements themselves. There is little that talks about knowledge production *by* them, *in* them, and from their standpoints. For some important work that takes the latter approach and that has informed my own thinking, see Frampton et al. 2006; Coté, Day, and de Peuter 2007; and Choudry and Kapoor 2010.
4. As per Note 12 in the Introduction, this means understanding standpoint not purely as in Harding 1988 but as in D. Smith 2005: 7–26 and Frampton et al. 2006: 7, 38.
5. See Note 18 in the Introduction.

References

Abella, Irving. 1974. "Oshawa 1937." In Irving Abella (ed.), *On Strike: Six Key Labour Struggles in Canada 1919–1949*. Toronto: James Lewis & Samuel, Publishers, pp. 93–128.

____. 1973. *Nationalism, Communism, and Canadian Labour*. Toronto: University of Toronto Press.

"Accept homosexuals; but don't approve homosexual acts." 1971. *The United Church Observer* 34, 6 (December), p. 11.

Acklesberg, Martha. 2004. *Free Women of Spain: Anarchism and the Struggle for the Emancipation of Women*. San Francisco: AK Press.

Adamson, Nancy, Linda Briskin, and Margaret McPhail. 1988. *Feminist Organizing for Change: The Contemporary Women's Movement in Canada*. Toronto: Oxford University Press.

Agnew, Vijay. 1996. *Resisting Discrimination: Women From Asia, Africa, and the Caribbean and the Women's Movement in Canada*. Toronto: University of Toronto Press.

Alfred, Taiaiake. 2005. *Wasáse: Indigenous Pathways of Action and Freedom*. Peterborough ON: Broadview Press.

____. 1999. *Peace, Power, Righteousness: An Indigenous Manifesto*. Don Mills ON: Oxford University Press.

Allen, Richard. 1973. *The Social Passion: Religion and Social Reform in Canada 1914–28*. Toronto: University of Toronto Press.

Amnesty International (Canada). 2004. *Stolen Sisters: A Human Rights Response to Discrimination and Violence Against Aboriginal Women in Canada*. Ottawa: Amnesty International (Canada).

Anapol, Deborah M. 1997. *Polyamory, The New Love Without Limits: Secrets of Sustainable Intimate Relationships*. San Rafael CA: IntiNet Resource Center.

Antrop-González, René. 2008. "Claiming our Humanity through Alternative Education in the Belly of the Beast." In Matt Hern (ed.), *Everywhere All the Time: A New Deschooling Reader*. Oakland CA: AK Press, pp. 149–158.

Appignanesi, Lisa. 2007. *Sad, Mad, and Bad: Women and the Mind-Doctors from 1800*. Toronto: McArthur & Company.

Armstrong, Pat, et al. (eds.). 2004. *Canadian Woman Studies/les cahiers de la femme: Benefiting Women? Women's Labour Rights* 23, 3/4 (Spring/Summer).

Backhouse, Constance A. 1999. *Colour-Coded: A Legal History of Racism in Canada, 1900–1950*. Toronto: The Osgoode Society for Legal History and University of Toronto Press.

Baillargeon, Denyse. 2005. "Textile Strikes in Quebec: 1946, 1947, 1952." In Andrée Lévesque (ed.), *Madeleine Parent: Activist*. Toronto: Sumach Press, pp. 59–70.

Bannerji, Himani. 2000. *The Dark Side of the Nation*. Toronto: Canadian Scholars' Press.

____. 1999. "A Question of Silence: Reflections on Violence Against Women in Communities of Colour." In Enakshi Dua and Angela Robertson (eds.), *Scratching the Surface: Canadian Anti-racist Feminist Thought*. Toronto: Women's Press, pp. 261–277.

Berton, Pierre. 2001. *The Great Depression*. Toronto: Anchor Canada.

Bishop, Anne. 2002. *Becoming an Ally: Breaking the Cycle of Oppression in People*, 2nd ed.

Halifax: Fernwood Publishing.
Brant Castellano, Marlene, Lynne Davis, and Louise Lahache (eds.). 2000. *Aboriginal Education: Fulfilling the Promise*. Vancouver: UBC Press.
Bristow, Peggy, et al. 1994. *We're Rooted Here and They Can't Pull Us Up: Essays in African Canadian Women's History*. Toronto: University of Toronto Press.
Brown, Maureen J. 2004. *In Their Own Voices: African Canadians in the Greater Toronto Area Share Experiences of Police Profiling*. Toronto: African Canadian Community Coalition on Racial Profiling.
Brownmiller, Susan. 1975. *Against Our Will: Men, Women, and Rape*. New York: Simon and Schuster.
Bunch, Charlotte. 1987. *Passionate Politics: Feminist Theory in Action*. New York: St. Martin's Press.
Butler. Judith. 1990. *Gender Trouble*. New York: Routledge.
Camfield, David. 2000. "Assessing Resistance in Harris's Ontario, 1995–1999." In Mike Burke, Colin Mooers, and John Shields (eds.). *Restructuring and Resistance: Canadian Public Policy in an Age of Global Capitalism*. Halifax: Fernwood Publishing, pp. 307–317.
Carter, David. 2004. *Stonewall: The Riots That Sparked the Gay Revolution*. New York: St. Martin's Griffin.
Carty, Linda (ed.). 1993. *And Still We Rise: Feminist Political Mobilizing in Contemporary Canada*. Toronto: Women's Press.
Chauncey, George. 1994. *Gay New York: Gender, Urban Culture, and the Making of the Gay Male World 1890–1940*. New York: Basic Books.
Choudry, Aziz, and Dip Kapoor (eds.). 2010. *Learning From the Ground Up: Global Perspectives on Social Movements and Knowledge Production*. New York: Palgrave Macmillan.
Citizenship and Immigration Canada. 2002. *A Look at Canada: 2002 Edition*. Ottawa: Ministry of Public Works and Government Services.
Clarke, Patricia. 1981. "Christian Feminism." *The United Church Observer* 44, 9 (March), pp. 29–31.
___. 1979. "Church and homosexuality: the issue won't go away." *The United Church Observer* 42, 10 (April), p. 8.
___. 1973. "Women's Lib hit the church, in a ladylike way." *The United Church Observer* 36, 10 (April), pp. 6–7.
___. 1970. "Harriet Christie: Woman in a Man's World." *The United Church Observer* 33, 4 (October), p. 12.
Clarke, Tony, and Maude Barlow. 1997. *MAI: The Multilateral Agreement on Investment and the Threat to Canadian Sovereignty*. Toronto: Stoddart.
Codjoe, Henry M. 2005. "Africa(ns) in the Canadian Educational System: An Analysis of Positionality & Knowledge Construction." In Wisdom J. Tettey and Korbla P. Puplampu (eds.), *The African Diaspora in Canada: Negotiating Identity and Belonging*. Calgary: University of Calgary Press, pp. 63–92.
Connell, R.W. 2005. *Masculinities*, 2nd ed. Berkeley: University of California Press.
Coté, Mark, Richard J.F. Day, and Greig de Peuter (eds.). 2007. *Utopian Pedagogy: Radical Experiments against Neoliberal Globalization*. Toronto: University of Toronto Press.
Dasgupta, Shamita Das. 2007. "Battered South Asian Women in U.S. Courts." In

Shamita Das Dasgupta (ed.), *Body Evidence: Intimate Violence Against South Asian Women in America*. New Brunswick NJ: Rutgers University Press.
Das Gupta, Tania. 1996. *Racism and Paid Work*. Toronto: Garamond Press.
davis, heather. 2005. "The difference of queer." *Canadian Women Studies/les cahiers de la femme: Lesbian, Bisexual, Queer, Transsexual/Transgender Sexualities* 24, 2/3 (Winter/Spring), pp. 23–26.
DeGroot, Joanna. 1989. "'Sex' and 'Race': The Construction of Language and Image in the Nineteenth Century." In Mendus, Susan, and Jane Rendall (eds.), *Sexuality and Subordination: Interdisciplinary Studies of Gender in the Nineteenth Century*. New York: Routledge, pp. 89–128.
DeKeseredy, Walter S., and Linda MacLeod. 1997. *Woman Abuse: A Sociological Story*. Toronto: Harcourt Brace & Company.
D'Emilio, John. 1992. *Making Trouble: Essays on Gay History, Politics, and the University*. New York: Routledge.
Driedger, Diane. 1993. "Discovering Disabled Women's History." In Linda Carty (ed.), *And Still We Rise: Feminist Political Mobilizing in Contemporary Canada*. Toronto: Women's Press.
Dubinsky, Karen, et al. (eds.). 2009. *New World Coming: The Sixties and the Shaping of Global Consciousness*. Toronto: Between the Lines.
Duggan, Lisa. 2003. *The Twilight of Equality? Neoliberalism, Cultural Politics, and the Attack on Democracy*. Boston: Beacon Press.
Duggan, Lisa, and Nan D. Hunter. 2006. *Sex Wars: Sexual Dissent and Political Culture, 10th Anniversary Edition*. New York: Routledge.
Duncan, Muriel. 1975. "You haven't made it ... until we've all made it." *The United Church Observer* 38, 9 (March), pp. 12–15.
Dworkin, Andrea. 2007. *Intercourse, The Twentieth Anniversary Edition*. New York: Basic Books.
___. 1997. *Life and Death: Unapologetic Writings on the Continuing War Against Women*. New York: The Free Press.
Easton, Dossie, and Catherine A. Liszt. 1997. *The Ethical Slut: A Guide to Infinite Sexual Possibilities*. San Francisco: Greenery Press.
EGALE Canada. 2009. "Youth Speak Up About Homophobia and Transphobia: The First National Climate Survey on Homophobia in Canadian Schools." At <egale.ca/index.asp?lang=E&menu=4&item=1401>.
Empire Task Group. 2007. *Living Faithfully in the Midst of Empire: Report to the 39th General Council 2006*. Toronto: The United Church of Canada.
Engler, Yves. 2009. *The Black Book of Canadian Foreign Policy*. Halifax: Fernwood Publishing.
Epstein, Rachel. 2005. "Queer parenting in the new millennium: Resisting normal." *Canadian Women Studies/les cahier de la femme: Lesbian, Bisexual, Queer, Transsexual/Transgender Sexualities* 24, 2/3 (Winter/Spring), pp. 7–14.
Federal-Provincial-Territorial Ministers Responsible for the Status of Women. 2002. *Assessing Violence Against Women: A Statistical Profile*. Ottawa.
Federici, Silvia. 2004. *Caliban and the Witch: Women, the Body and Primitive Accumulation*. New York: Autonomedia.
Fiorenza, Elisabeth. 1979. "Women in the Early Christian Movement." In Carol P. Christ and Judith Plaskow (eds.), *Womanspirit Rising: A Feminist Reader in Religion*.

New York: Harper & Row, Publishers, pp. 84–92.
Fitzgerald, Robin. 1999. *Family Violence in Canada: A Statistical Profile*. Ottawa: Statistics Canada.
Fleras, Augie, and Jean Leonard Elliot. 1999. *Unequal Relations: An Introduction to Race, Ethnic, and Aboriginal Dynamics in Canada*, 3rd ed. Scarborough ON: Prentice Hall Allyn and Bacon Canada.
Foster, Cecil. 1996. *A Place Called Heaven: The Meaning of Being Black in Canada*. Toronto: HarperCollins Publishers, Ltd.
Fournier, Suzanne, and Ernie Crey. 1998. *Stolen From Our Embrace: The Abduction of First Nations Children and the Restoration of Aboriginal Communities*. Vancouver/Toronto: Douglas & McIntyre.
Frampton, Caelie, et al. 2006. *Sociology for Changing the World: Social Movements/Social Research*. Halifax: Fernwood Publishing.
Francis, Daniel. 2010. *Seeing Reds: The Red Scare of 1918–1919, Canada's First War on Terror*. Vancouver: Arsenal Pulp Press.
Furniss, Elizabeth. 1999. *The Burden of History: Colonialism and the Frontier Myth in a Rural Canadian Community*. Vancouver: UBC Press.
Galabuzi, Grace-Edward. 2006. *Canada's Economic Apartheid: The Social Exclusion of Racialized Groups in the New Century*. Toronto: Canadian Scholars' Press.
Goldberg, David Theo. 2009. *The Threat of Race: Reflections on Racial Neoliberalism*. Marden MA: Blackwell Publishing.
Gordon, Todd. 2010. *Imperialist Canada*. Winnipeg: Arbeiter Ring Publishing.
Griffin Cohen, Marjorie. 1993. "The Canadian Women's Movement." In Pierson, Ruth Roach et al. (eds.), *Canadian Women's Issues Volume I: Strong Voices: Twenty-five Years of Women's Activism in English Canada*. Toronto: James Lorimer & Company, pp. 1–31.
Gullickson, Gay. 1996. *Unruly Women of Paris: Images of the Commune*. Ithaca NY: Cornell University Press.
Harding, Sandra. 1988. *The Science Question in Feminism*. Ithaca NY: Cornell University Press.
Hay, Harry (auth.) and Will Roscoe (ed.) 1996. *Radically Gay: Gay Liberation in the Words of Its Founder*. Boston: Beacon Press.
Henry, Frances, et al. 2000. *The Colour of Democracy: Racism in Canadian Society*, 2nd ed. Toronto: Harcourt Canada.
Herman, Didi. 1994. *Rights of Passage: Struggles for Lesbian and Gay Legal Rights*. Toronto: University of Toronto Press.
High, Steven, and David Lewis. 2007. *Corporate Wasteland: The Landscape and Memory of Deindustrialization*. Ithaca NY: Cornell University Press.
Hodgkin, Katherine, and Susannah Radstone. 2003. *Contested Pasts: The Politics of Memory*. New York: Routledge.
Hogue, Jacqueline. 1986. "Madeleine Parent: *une militante chevronnée*." *Canadian Woman Studies/les cahiers de la femme: Canadian Women's History/L'Histoire Des Femmes Canadiennes* 7, 3 (Fall), pp. 103–4.
Holloway, John. 2005. *Change the World Without Taking Power: The Meaning of Revolution Today*, rev. ed. London: Pluto Press.
Holloway, John, and Marina Sitrin. 2007. "Against and Beyond the State: An Interview with John Holloway." *Upping the Anti: A Journal of Theory and Action* 4,

pp. 51–59.
Holmes, Janelle, and Eliane Leslau Silverman. 1992. *We're Here, Listen To Us! A Survey of Young Women in Canada*. Ottawa: Canadian Advisory Council on the Status of Women.
Horn, Michiel. 1980. *The League for Social Reconstruction: Intellectual Origins of the Democratic Left in Canada, 1930–1942*. Toronto: University of Toronto Press.
Hull, Gloria T., Patricia Bell Scott, and Barbara Smith. 1982. *All the Women Are White, All the Blacks Are Men, But Some of Us Are Brave*. New York: The Feminist Press.
Incite! Women of Color Against Violence (eds.). 2007. *The Revolution Will Not Be Funded: Beyond the Non-profit Industrial Complex*. Cambridge MA: South End Press.
___. 2006. *Color of Violence: The INCITE! Anthology*. Cambridge MA: South End Press.
Isbester, Fraser. 1974. "Asbestos 1949." In Abella, Irving (ed.), *On Strike: Six Key Labour Struggles in Canada 1919–1949*. Toronto: James Lewis & Samuel, Publishers, pp. 163–190.
Jantzen, Grace M. 1999. *Becoming Divine: Towards a Feminist Philosophy of Religion*. Bloomington IN: Indiana University Press.
Jensen, Robert. 2005. *The Heart of Whiteness: Confronting Race, Racism, and White Privilege*. San Francisco: City Lights.
Jiwani, Yasmin. 2000. "The 1999 General Social Survey on Spousal Violence: An Analysis." At <harbour.sfu.ca/freda/reports/gss01.htm>.
Johnson, Holly. 1996. *Dangerous Domains: Violence Against Women in Canada*. Scarborough ON: Nelson Canada.
Josephson, Jyl. 2005. "The Intersectionality of Domestic Violence and Welfare in the Lives of Poor Women." In Natalie J. Sokoloff with Christina Pratt (eds.), *Domestic Violence at the Margins: Readings on Race, Class, Gender, and Culture*. New Brunswick NJ: Rutgers University Press, pp. 83–101.
Journey. 2008. "Shelley's Obituary." At <journey-shelley.blogspot.com/2008/02/shelleys-obituary.html> February 4.
Katz, Jonathan Ned. 1995. *The Invention of Heterosexuality*. New York: Penguin Books Ltd.
Kealey, Linda. 1998. *Enlisting Women for the Cause: Women, Labour, and the Left in Canada, 1890–1920*. Toronto: University of Toronto Press.
Kinsman, Gary. 1996. *The Regulation of Desire: Homo and Hetero Sexualities*, 2nd. ed., rev. Montreal: Black Rose Books.
Kinsman, Gary, and Patrizia Gentile. 2010. *The Canadian War on Queers: National Security as Sexual Regulation*. Vancouver: UBC Press.
Kivel, Paul. 2002. *Uprooting Racism: How White People Can Work for Racial Justice*, rev. ed. Vancouver: New Society Publishers.
___. 1999. *Boys Will Be Men: Raising Our Sons for Courage, Caring, and Community*. Vancouver: New Society Publishers.
Klein, Charlotte. 1978. *Anti-Judaism in Christian Theology*. Philadelphia: Fortress Press.
Kobayashi, Audrey. 2008. "Ethnocultural Political Mobilization, Multiculturalism, and Human Rights in Canada." In Miriam Smith (ed.), *Group Politics and Social Movements in Canada*. Peterborough ON: Broadview Press, pp. 131–158.
Kohli, Rita. 1993. "Power or Empowerment: Questions of Agency in the Shelter

Movement." In Linda Carty (ed.), *And Still We Rise: Feminist Political Mobilizing in Contemporary Canada*. Toronto: Women's Press, pp. 387–425.
Kong, Rebecca. 1996. "Criminal Harassment." *Juristat* 16, 6, p. 12.
Kostash, Myrna. 1980. *Long Way From Home: The Story of the Sixties Generation in Canada*. Toronto: James Lorimer & Company.
Krapper, Pamela. 2000. "On the road to women's equality: the World March of Women in 2000." *Briarpatch* 29, 10 (Dec–Jan), pp. 4–6.
Kulchyski, Peter. 2007. *The Red Indians: An Episodic, Informal Collection of Tales form the History of Aboriginal People's Struggles in Canada*. Winnipeg: Arbeiter Ring Publishing.
Lahey, Kathleen. 1999. *Are We "Persons" Yet?: Law and Sexuality in Canada*. Toronto: University of Toronto Press.
Lakeman, Lee. 2005. *Obsession, With Intent: Violence Against Women*. Montreal: Black Rose Books.
Lambertson, Ross. 2005. *Repression and Resistance: Canadian Human Rights Activists, 1930–1960*. Toronto: University of Toronto Press.
Lawson, Erica. 2002. "Images in Black: Black Women, Media and the Mythology of an Orderly Society." In Njoki Nathani Wane, Katerina Deliovsky, and Erica Lawson (eds.), *Back to the Drawing Board: African-Canadian Feminisms*. Toronto: Sumach Press, pp. 199–223.
Lévesque, Andrée (ed.). 2005. *Madeleine Parent: Activist*. Toronto: Sumach Press.
Little, Margaret Jane Hillyard. 1998. *"No Car, No Radio, No Liquor Permit": The Moral Regulation of Single Mothers in Ontario, 1920–1997*. Toronto: Oxford University Press.
Locke, Daisy. 2000. "Family Homicide." *Family Violence in Canada: A Statistical Profile, 2000*. Ottawa: Statistics Canada, pp. 39–44.
Lynd, Staughton. 1997. *Living Inside Our Hope: A Steadfast Radical's Thoughts on Rebuilding the Movement*. Ithaca NY: ILR Press.
Martin, Stephanie L. 2006. "Bearing Witness: Experiences of Frontline Anti-Violence Responders." *Canadian Woman Studies/les cahiers de la femme: Ending Woman Abuse* 25, 1/2 (Winter/Spring), pp. 11–15.
Maynard, Steven. 2004. "Capitalism, urban culture, and gay history." *Journal of Urban History* 30, 3 (March), pp. 378–398.
___. 1994a. "In search of 'Sodom North': The writing of lesbian and gay history in English Canada, 1970–1990." *Canadian Review of Comparative Literature/Revue Canadienne de Litterature Comparée* 21 (Spring), pp. 117–132.
___. 1994b. "Through a hole in the lavatory wall: Homosexual subcultures, police surveillance, and the Dialectics of Discovery, Toronto, 1890–1930." *Journal of the History of Sexuality* 5, 2 (October), pp. 207–242.
McCaskell, Tim. 2005. *Race to Equity: Disrupting Educational Inequality*. Toronto: Between the Lines.
McFarlane, Peter. 1993. *Brotherhood to Nationhood: George Manuel and the Making of the Modern Indian Movement*. Toronto: Between the Lines.
McKay, Ian. 2008. *Reasoning Otherwise: Leftists and the People's Enlightenment in Canada, 1890–1920*. Toronto: Between the Lines.
McNally, David. 2006. *Another World is Possible: Globalization and Anti-Capitalism*, rev. ed. Winnipeg: Arbeiter Ring Publishing.

Mies, Maria. 1998. *Patriarchy and Accumulation on a World Scale: Women in the International Division of Labour,* rev. ed. New York: Zed Books.

Miller, J.R. 1996. *Shingwauk's Vision: A History of Native Residential Schools.* Toronto: University of Toronto Press.

Monture-Angus, Patricia. 1995. *Thunder in my Soul: A Mohawk Woman Speaks.* Halifax: Fernwood Publishing.

Morrison, Cathleen. 1974. "Women Work — Men Make Decisions." *The United Church Observer/Toronto Region Insight,* September, p. IV.

Mulay, Shree. 2005. "The Importance of Being Madeleine: How an Activist Won the Hearts of Quebec's Immigrant and Minority Women." In Lévesque, Andrée (ed.), *Madeleine Parent: Activist.* Toronto: Sumach Press.

Munson, Marcia, and Judith P. Stelboum (eds.). 1999. *The Lesbian Polyamory Reader: Open Relationships, Non-Monogamy, and Casual Sex.* New York: Harrington Park Press.

Munt, Sally R. 2007. *Queer Attachments: The Cultural Politics of Shame.* Burlington VT: Ashgate Publishing Company.

Muscio, Inga. 2005. *Autobiography of a Blue-eyed Devil: My Life and Times in a Racist, Imperialist Society.* Emeryville CA: Seal Press.

Ng, Roxana. 1990. "State Funding to a Community Employment Center: Implications for Working with Immigrant Women." In Roxana Ng, Gillian Walker, and Jacob Muller (eds.), *Community Organizing and the Canadian State.* Toronto: Garamond Press, pp. 165–183.

Obomsawin, Alanis, dir. 1993. *Kanehsatake: 270 Years of Resistance.* National Film Board of Canada.

Olsen Harper, Anita. 2006. "Is Canada Peaceful and Safe for Aboriginal Women?" *Canadian Woman Studies/les cahier de la femme: Ending Woman Abuse* 25, 1/2 (Winter/Spring), pp. 33, 38.

Palmer, Bryan. 2009. *Canada's 1960s: The Ironies of Identity in a Rebellious Era.* Toronto: University of Toronto Press, 2009.

___. 1992. *Working Class Experience: Rethinking the History of Canadian Labour, 1800–1991.* Toronto: McClelland and Stewart.

Parent, Madeleine. 2000. "Remembering Federal Police Surveillance in Quebec, 1940s–70s." In Gary Kinsman, Dieter K. Buse, and Mercedes Steedman (eds.), *Whose National Security? Canadian State Surveillance and the Creation of Enemies.* Toronto: Between the Lines, pp. 235–245.

Patton, Cindy. 1990. *Inventing AIDS.* New York: Routledge.

Persky, Stan (ed.). 1982. *Flaunting It: A Decade of Gay Journalism from the Body Politic.* Vancouver: New Star Books.

Pierson, Ruth Roach. 1993. "The Politics of the Body." In Ruth Roach Pierson et al. (eds.), *Canadian Women's Issues Volume I, Strong Voices: Twenty-five Years of Women's Activism in English Canada.* Toronto: James Lorimer & Company, pp. 186–263.

Pratt, Sheila. 1979. "Native high school proving 'a real break' for Indians." *Calgary Herald,* September 10, p. B1.

Quinn, Herbert F. 1979. *The Union nationale: Quebec Nationalism from Duplessis to Lévesque.* Toronto: University of Toronto Press.

Ravenscroft, Anthony. 2004. *Polyamory: Roadmaps for the Clueless & Hopeful.* Santa Fe NM: Fenrid Brothers.

Razack, Sherene. 2008. *Casting Out: The Eviction of Muslims from Western Law & Politics.*

Toronto: University of Toronto Press.

___. 2002. "Gendered Racial Violence and Spatialized Justice: The Murder of Pamela George." In Sherene Razack (ed.), *Race, Space, and the Law: Unmapping a White Settler Society*. Toronto: Between the Lines, pp. 121–156.

___. 1998. *Looking White People in the Eye*. Toronto: University of Toronto Press.

Rebick, Judy. 2005. *Ten Thousand Roses: The Making of a Feminist Revolution*. Toronto: Penguin Canada.

Reuther, Rosemary Radford. 1985. *Womanguides: Readings Toward a Feminist Theology*. Boston: Beacon Press.

___. 1983. *Sexism and God-Talk: Toward a Feminist Theology*. Boston: Beacon Press.

Rich, Adrienne. 1994. "Compulsory Heterosexuality and Lesbian Existence." *Blood, Bread, and Poetry*. New York: Norton Paperback.

Richards, Jeffrey. 1991. *Sex, Dissidence and Damnation: Minority Groups in the Middle Ages*. London: Routledge.

Roediger, David R. 1991. *The Wages of Whiteness: Race and the Making of the American Working Class*. New York: Verso.

Roscoe, Will. 2000. *Changing Ones: Third and Fourth Genders in Native North America*. New York: Griffin.

Roscoe, Will (ed.). 1988. *Gay American Indians. Living The Spirit: A Gay American Indian Anthology*. New York: St. Martin's Press.

Rudrappa, Sharmila. 2007. "Law's Culture and Cultural Difference." In Shamita Das Dasgupta (ed.), *Body Evidence: Intimate Violence Against South Asian Women in America*. New Brunswick NJ: Rutgers University Press, pp. 181–194.

Rumscheidt, Barbara. 1998. *No Room for Grace: Pastoral Theology and Dehumanization in the Global Economy*. Grand Rapids MI: Wm. B. Eerdmans Publishing Company.

Sakai, J. 1989. *Settlers: The Mythology of the White Proletariat*, 3rd ed. Chicago: Morningstar Press.

Salutin, Rick. 1980. *Kent Rowley, the Organizer: A Canadian Union Life*. Toronto: James Lorimer & Company.

Sawyer, Alison. 1981. "Women's bodies, men's decisions." *Phoenix Rising* 1, 4 (Winter), p. 8.

Scher, Len. 1992. *The Un-Canadians: True Stories of the Blacklist Era*. Toronto: Lester Publishing Limited, 1992.

Schottroff, Luise. 1995. *Lydia's Impatient Sisters: A Feminist Social History of Early Christianity*. Louisville KY: Westminster John Knox Press.

Schreader, Alison. 1990. "The State-Funded Women's Movement: A Case of Two Political Agendas." In Roxana Ng, Gillian Walker, and Jacob Muiller (eds.), *Community Organizing and the Canadian State*. Toronto: Garamond Press, pp. 184–199.

Scott, Macdonald. 2006. "Fighting Borders: A Roundtable on Non-Status (Im)migrant Justice in Canada." *Upping the Anti: A Journal of Theory and Action* 2, pp. 151–159.

Sev'er, Aysan. 2002. *Fleeing the House of Horrors: Women who have Left Abusive Partners*. Toronto: University of Toronto Press.

Sharma, Nandita. 2006. *Home Economics: Nationalism and the Making of "Migrant Workers" in Canada*. Toronto: University of Toronto Press.

Shepherd, Loraine MacKenzie. 2002. *Feminist Theologies for a Postmodern Church: Diversity,*

Community, and Scripture. New York: Peter Lang Publishing Inc.
Simpson, Leanne, and Kiera Ladner (eds.). 2010. *This is an Honour Song: Twenty Years Since the Blockades*. Winnipeg: Arbeiter Ring Publishing.
Smith, Andrea. 2005. *Conquest: Sexual Violence and American Indian Genocide*. Boston: South End Press.
___. 2006. "Indigenous feminism without apology." *New Socialist* 58 (September-October), pp. 16–17.
Smith, Charles C. 2004. *Crisis, Conflict and Accountability: The Impact and Implications of Police Racial Profiling*. Toronto: The African Canadian Community Coalition on Racial Profiling.
Smith, Dorothy. 2005. *Institutional Ethnography: A Sociology for People*. Lanham MD: AltaMira Press.
___. 1999. *Writing the Social: Critique, Theory, and Investigation*. Toronto: University of Toronto Press.
Smith, George. 2006. "Political activist as ethnographer." In Caelie Frampton et al. (eds.), *Sociology For Changing The World: Social Movements/Social Research*. Halifax: Fernwood Publishing, pp. 44–70.
Smith, Linda Tuhiwai. 1999. *Decolonizing Methodologies: Research and Indigenous Peoples*. New York: Zed Books Ltd.
Socknatt, Thomas. 1987. *Witness Against War: Pacifism in Canada 1900–1945*. Toronto: University of Toronto Press.
Sokoloff, Natalie J., with Christina Pratt (eds.). 2005. *Domestic Violence at the Margins: Readings on Race, Class, Gender, and Culture*. New Brunswick NJ: Rutgers University Press.
Squire, Anne M. 1979. "In 50 years, how much progress for women as 'persons.'" *The United Church Observer* 43, 4 (October), p. 11.
Stacey, Judith. 1988. "Can there be a feminist ethnography?" *Women's Studies International Forum* 11, 1, pp. 21–27.
Stevenson, Winona. 1999. "Colonialism and First Nations Women in Canada." In Enakshi Dua and Angela Robertson (eds.), *Scratching the Surface: Canadian Antiracist Feminist Thought*. Toronto: Women's Press, pp. 49–80.
Sthanki, Maunica. 2007. "The Aftermath of September 11: An Anti-Domestic Violence Perspective." In Shamita Das Dasgupta (ed.), *Body Evidence: Intimate Violence Against South Asian Women in America*. New Brunswick NJ: Rutgers University Press, pp. 68–78.
Stimpson, Liz, and Margaret Best. 1991. *Courage Above All: Sexual Assault Against Women with Disabilities*. Toronto: Disabled Women's Network.
Swidler, Leonard. 2007. *Jesus Was a Feminist: What the Gospels Reveal about His Revolutionary Perspective*. Lanham MD: Sheed & Ward.
Tamagne, Florence. 2000. *L'Histoire de l'homosexualité en Europe: Berlin, Londres, Paris, 1919–1939*. Paris: Sueil. Quoted in David Berry. 2004. "'Workers of the World, Embrace!' Daniel Guerin, the Labour Movement and Homosexuality." *Left History* 9, 2, pp. 11–43.
Taormino, Tristan. 2008. *Opening Up: A Guide to Creating and Sustaining Open Relationships*. San Francisco CA: Cleis Press.
Tator, Carol, and Frances Henry. 2006. *Racial Profiling in Canada: Challenging the Myth of "A Few Bad Apples."* Toronto: University of Toronto Press.

Thobani, Sunera. 2007. *Exalted Subjects: Studies in the Making of Race and Nation in Canada*. Toronto: University of Toronto Press.
Thompson, E.P. 1966. *The Making of the English Working Class*. New York: Vintage Books.
Thurman, Judith. 1999. *Secrets of the Flesh: A Life of Colette*. New York: Ballantine Books.
Tombs, Robert. 2008. *The War Against Paris, 1871*. Cambridge: Cambridge University Press.
Tremblay, Sylvain. 1998. "Crime Statistics in Canada, 1998." *Juristat* 19, 9. Ottawa: Statistics Canada.
Trothen, Tracey J. 2003. *Linking Sexuality & Gender: Naming Violence against Women in The United Church of Canada*. Waterloo ON: Wilfrid Laurier University Press.
United Church of Canada. 2010. "Governance: Congregations and Courts of The United Church of Canada." At <united-church.ca/organization/governance/structure>.
Ursel, Jane. 1992. *Private Lives, Public Policy: 100 Years of State Intervention in the Family*. Toronto: Women's Press.
Valverde, Mariana. 1991. *The Age of Light, Soap, and Water*. Toronto: McClelland and Stewart.
Volpp, Leti. 2005. "Feminism versus Multiculturalism." In Natalie J. Sokoloff with Christina Pratt (eds.), *Domestic Violence at the Margins: Readings on Race, Class, Gender, and Culture*. New Brunswick NJ: Rutgers University Press, pp. 39–49.
Walia, Harsha. 2006. "Colonialism, Capitalism and the Making of the Apartheid System of Migration in Canada." Z-Net. At <zcommunications.org/colonialism-capitalism-and-the-making-of-the-apartheid-system-of-migration-in-canada-by-harsha-walia> March 4.
Ware, Vron. 1992. *Beyond the Pale*. London: Verso.
Warner, Michael. 1999. *The Trouble With Normal: Sex, Politics, and the Ethics of Queer Life*. Cambridge MA: Harvard University Press.
Warner, Tom. 2002. *Never Going Back: A History of Queer Activism in Canada*. Toronto: University of Toronto Press.
West, Carolyn M. 2005. "Domestic Violence in Ethnically and Racially Diverse Families: The 'Political Gag Order' Has Been Lifted." In Natalie J. Sokoloff and Christina Pratt (eds.), *Domestic Violence at the Margins: Readings on Race, Class, Gender, and Culture*. New Brunswick NJ: Rutgers University Press, pp. 157–173.
Winks, Robin. 1997. *The Blacks in Canada: A History*, 2nd ed. Montreal and Kingston: McGill–Queen's University Press.
Wise, Tim. 2005. *White Like Me*. New York: Soft Skull Press.
"Women slam BC budget." 1983. *Calgary Herald*, September 9, p. C8.

Index

Aboriginal peoples, (see indigenous peoples)
abortion, 83, 155, 157
Acquired Immune Deficiency Symdrome (AIDS), 126, 137
agency, 9-10, 17
Alfred, Taiaiake, 154
ally work, anti-oppression, 3, 10, 24, 83, 89-90, 117, 119, 166
American Federation of Labor (AFL), 52, 56-8
Amnesty International, 30, 72
anarchism, 6, 78, 95, 131
Anderson, Daphne, 163
Anderson, Doris, 77
Anglican Church, 146, 156, 158, 160
Annis, Ruth, 92
anti-poverty movements, 2, 18, 24
anti-psychiatry movement, 2
anti-racist struggles, 18, 24, 37-8, 44n6, 99, 102, 106, 108, 115-121, 143, 165-6, 180-1, 183-4
    other oppressions in, 100
    sexism in, 78, 121n1
anti-Semitism, 151, 153, 159
anti-war movements, (see peace movements)
Asbestos, Quebec, strike of 1949, 66, 68n18
Assembly of First Nations, (see also National Indian Brotherhood) 32
Atlantic School of Theology, 169

Baker, Jack, 134
Bannerji, Himani, 101
bathhouses, 138, 145n11
    police raids on, 138
Bishop, Anne, 10
Blackfoot Confederacy, 37
Blue Quills, Alberta, 37
Bread and Roses March, 117-8, 122n11
Breehan Bible College, 33
British Columbia Coalition of Rape Crisis Centres, 86, 90-2
British Privy Council, 76
Bryant, Anita, 86
Buddhism, 11, 148

burn-out,
    activist, 2, 142
business unionism, 57

Calgary, 18, 23-4, 33-4, 37-8, 41-2
Calgary Committee Against Racism, 38
Campbell, Gordon, 96n12
Campus Gay Club, (see also Gays For Equality; Rainbow Resource Centre) 131, 134
Canada Council, 134
Canadian Association of Sexual Assault Centres, 69
Canadian Federation of University Women, 76, 173n8
Canadian Lesbian and Gay Rights Coalition, 131
Canadian settler state, 18, 138, 182
    colonial character, 3, 4, 8, 13-14, 24-25, 30-2, 35, 38, 40-1, 49, 103, 151, 180, 183
    funding as response to struggle, 42, 78, 80, 82-3, 103, 105-6, 109-12, 142-3
    liberal mythologies of, 3, 7-8, 13, 182
    multiculturalism in, 101-2
    participation in empire, 103
    regulation of migration, 7-8, 13, 52, 103-5, 118, 118-9, 121, 139
    regulation of workplaces, 53-4, 183
    restricting access to social programs, 104, 115-6, 118
    role in sexual regulation, 18, 127-8, 134-42, 144, 145n13, 182-3
    role in violence against queer people, 138
    role in violence against racialized people, 12, 103-4, 121
    role in violence against women, 30, 35, 72, 75, 82-6, 103-4, 181, 183
    role in violence against workers, 54
Canadian Student Assembly, 54-6
capitalism, 1, 18, 20n7, 66, 102, 123, 136, 177, 182
    and Christianity, 151-2
    and colonization, 49-50, 52
    and land, 25, 49
    origins of, 49-51, 67n7, 179

and patriarchy, 17, 50-1, 67n8, 102, 181, 185n2
social organization of, 17, 46-52, 67n6, 181
struggles against, 2, 17-18, 48-9, 102
and white supremacy, 50, 67n8, 102, 181, 185n2
capitalists, (see owners of capital)
Caribbean Club, 106
Casgrain, Thérèse, 55
categories and oppression, 16-18, 68n10, 100, 102, 144n1, 149
Catholic Church, 35-6, 54, 59, 66, 78, 148, 160, 173n11
liberation theology, 151
and unions in Quebec, 56, 62-4
Catholic Worker Movement, 78, 96n5
Centre for Christian Studies, 169
Charter of Rights and Freedoms, 142
Children's Aid Society (CAS), 18, 30, 44n3, 82, 85, 125, 183
Christianity, (see also names of specific denominations; social gospel) 91, 146-8, 171, 172n2
and capitalism, 151-2
and colonization, 28-9, 31, 34-5, 50, 127, 148, 151, 154-5
and empire, 152-4
and feminism, 2, 146-7, 157-65, 173n5, 173n11, 182
hegemony, 11, 22n18, 148, 150, 152, 172n2
history, 153-4
and Judaism, 153, 159
and liberation, 151-2, 154, 171-2
and patriarchy/sexism, 29, 148, 151, 153-5, 157-65, 167, 173n11, 182
and queer sexualities, 125, 127, 133-4, 141, 148, 151, 154, 167-71, 182
and racism, 150-2, 166
and secularism, 152, 172n4
understood individualistically, 149-50
understood socially, 150-2
Christie, Dr. Harriet, 155, 162-3
citizenship, (see also immigration policy; immigrants) 104, 107
as core of liberal theory, 99
obtaining, 7, 13, 97, 107
civil liberties, 54-6, 108

Cold War, 66, 129
colonization, 3-4, 12, 22n18, 23, 31, 43n1, 50, 102, 113, 180, 182
and assimilation, 28-9, 30-1
and capitalism, 49-50, 52, 181
and Christianity, 28-9, 31, 34-5, 50, 148, 151, 152-5
and education, 23, 30-35, 37, 40-2, 44n7, 75, 180, 183
and gender, 17, 29-30, 43-4n2, 72, 75, 180-1
global resistance to, 77
indigenous women's resistance to, 17-8, 29-30, 75, 106, 180
and knowledge, 24-32, 37, 44n7, 180
resistance in education, 37-43, 180
and secularism, 152
and sexuality, 29, 127
and treaties, 26, 39, 42
Committee for the Equality of Women in Canada, 173n8
Communism, 6, 53-5, 78, 94, 96n13, 129, 132
community,
critical understanding of, 101-2
company union, 64-5
Confederation, 7, 31
Confédération des syndicats nationaux (CSN), 56
Confederation of Canadian Unions, 66
Confederation of Catholic Unions (CCU), 56
confrontation of abusers, 86-9
Congregational Union of Canada, 154
Congress of Industrial Organizations (CIO), 56
Connor, Mary, 165
consciousness raising groups, 80, 146, 157-9
Conservative Party,
Alberta, 37
of Canada, 53
Ontario, 6, 19-20n2
Quebec, 54
Co-operative Commonwealth Federation (CCF), 124, 129
Council of Canadian Unions, 66
Council on Homosexuality and Religion, 133

198 – Gender and Sexuality

craft unions, (see also labour movements) 52, 56
Cree Nation, 9, 29, 34, 37-8
Criminal Code of Canada, 138, 144, 155
cultural appropriation, 27-8
culture, 25, 44n7, 50-1, 104
  indigenous, 24-5, 27-8, 34-5, 37-9
  reification under multiculturalism, 101-2
  and religion, 149, 152-3, 172n4
  and sexuality, 124-7, 130, 136, 143, 144n5
  and social organization, 9

Daly, Mary, 154
David, Françoise, 117
Debs, Eugene, 66
defeat, 66-7
Department of Indian Affairs, 31-2, 37, 42
Depression, Great, 7, 45, 53, 56, 68n13
difference,
  and assumption of inferiority, 26
  and knowledge, 25-6, 27, 174
  political significance of, 18, 21n11, 98-102, 181
  problems of categorizing, 17-18, 98-100
  produced by capitalist violence, 49-51, 67n7
  social production of, 3-4, 101-2, 104-5
  and violence against women, 74-5, 103-6, 181
  as trap, 102
direct action
  instances of, 24, 63-5, 69, 85, 86-7, 128-29, 130
disability, 11, 22n18, 48, 72, 99-100, 106, 145n15, 182
domestic workers, 3, 106
Dominion Textile Company, 18, 45, 48, 58, 60-6, 181
  strike against, 61-6
Douglas, Tommy, 129
Duplessis, Maurice, 2, 45, 54-5, 60, 62, 64-6, 68n13
Dworkin, Andrea, 87, 96n3, 96n9

École Polytechnique, 116, 119

education system, (see also Plains Indian Cultural Survival School) 6-8, 13, 23, 44n6, 55, 79, 107, 174
  colonial, 3, 23-5, 30-35, 37, 40-2, 44n7, 44n10, 75, 155, 176, 180, 183
  heterosexism in, 134, 143, 145n14, 169-71
  indigenous challenges to, 3, 18, 23-4, 30-1, 36-43, 180, 183
  sexism in, 30, 33, 79-80
  theological, 151, 157-8, 161, 166, 169-71
  trans experience of, 145n14
Egan, Jim, 1
Emmanuel College, 157
Episcopal Divinity School (Boston), 170-1
epistemology, (see knowledge production)
equal marriage, (see gay and lesbian movements, marriage equality; marriage)
equal pay for equal work, 17, 77, 162
Fédération des femmes du Québec (FFQ), 45, 116-21, 122n8
feudalism, 49, 51
Finson, Shelley, 15, 18, 156, 171-2, 172n1
  Christianity and identity, 150-2
  introduction to, 146-7
  involvement in the Movement for Christian Feminism, 147, 160-3, 167
  involvement in the United Church task forces on sexism, 162-5
  involvement in the women's movement, 152, 157-65, 182
  pointers to online audio clips, 173n9, 173n12, 173n13
  struggles with heterosexism, 166-71
  in the United Church, 156-71
  and white privilege, 165-6
First World War, 52-4
French Revolution, 62, 128
Friends of Hagar, 146, 158-60, 173n9
Friends of Rape Relief Committee, 89-90
funding by the state, 37, 42, 78, 82-3, 85-6, 89-94, 103, 105-6, 109-12, 118, 142-3, 157
fundraising, 38, 42, 86, 89, 112, 142-3, 184

Gandhi, Indira, 97, 108, 111

gay and lesbian movements, 1-2, 18, 22n18, 86, 96n11, 123-4, 128-44, 144n1, 145n9, 145n13, 166, 168-71, 181-2
　ableism in, 132, 143
　and Christianity, 127, 133-4, 141, 147, 167-71
　demonstrations, 132-3
　marriage equality, 134-7
　media, 133-5
　other oppression in, 100
　racism in, 132, 143
　seeking inclusion in human rights codes, 139-42
　sexism in, 131-2, 143
gay men, (see also gay and lesbian movements; heterosexism; lesbians; queer people) 1, 8, 11-2, 15, 123-4, 127-30, 132, 136-43, 144n1, 145n11, 147, 168-71, 181-2
　emergence of gay identity, 128
　racialized, 127, 130, 132
　violence against, 96n2, 137-8
Gay Pride, (see Pride events)
Gays For Equality, (see also Campus Gay Club; Rainbow Resource Centre) 131-3, 139, 142
gender, this book's understanding of, (see also patriarchy/sexism; women; women's/feminist movements) 16-18, 43-4n2, 99
Giovanni's Room, 142
Good Fish Lake Reserve, 33
Gordon, Blair, 62
Grey, Josephine, 2, 18, 183

Halifax, 52, 146-7, 169
Hamilton, Ontario, 6, 78
Hassle Free Clinic, 157
health care, socialized, 8, 13, 129
heterosexism, (see also gay and lesbian movements; sexuality, social regulation) 86, 124-9, 130-4, 181-2, 184
　in access to benefits and services, 139-42, 143
　and Christianity, 148, 165-71
　defined, 126
　in the education system, 143, 145n14
　individual experience of, 168-9
　in the judicial system, 11-12, 18, 130, 138
　in state regulation of relationships, 18, 134-6, 139
　in urban planning, 123
　violent expressions of, 137-8
heterosexuality, 12, 136, 138, 145n6
　compulsory, 126
Hinduism, 11
history,
　in citizenship processes, 7, 13
　in communities/movements, 14-16
　conventional/official and its problems, 3, 6-8, 12-14, 16, 21n15, 24-5, 36, 43n1, 68n13, 180
　in educational institutions, 6-7, 13-4, 25, 43
　from below, 1, 3, 6, 10, 14-16, 18-9, 21n12, 21n14, 21n15, 39, 43, 173-4, 178-9, 182-5
　inevitable incompleteness, 19, 180, 182
　in the media, 7, 183
　nationalist, 13
　standpoint and, 12-13, 16, 21n12, 28, 179
　in unions, 14
homelessness, 47, 72, 130
homophile movement, (see also gay and lesbian movements) 1, 129, 131, 137-8
Homophile Association of London Ontario (HALO), 137-8
Houda-Pepin, Fatima, 117
Hudler, Richard, 137-8
Hudson Bay Company, 36
Human Resources Development Canada, 42
human rights codes, 135, 139-42, 144, 168
Illich, Ivan, 79
immigrants, 3, 7, 11, 34, 45, 52, 97, 99-102, 108-11, 117, 122n10, 156
　and mainstream women's movements, 75-7, 98-9, 102, 105-6, 116-21
　state regulation of, 75, 101-5, 115-6, 121
　violence against women who are, 72, 85, 103-6, 108-9, 113-5
　women's organizing, (see also Mulay, Shree; Siddiqui, Sadeqa; South Asian

Women's Community Centre) 77, 99, 102-3, 105-6, 115, 118-21, 181
immigration policy,
  heterosexism in, 139
  racism in, 3, 8, 13, 52-3, 101-5, 116-7, 118-9, 121n6, 122n10
  sexism in, 104-5, 118-9
incest, 72, 85
India, 97, 107-8, 111, 113
Indian agents, 31-2
Indian Institute of Technology, 107
Indian People's Association in North America (IPANA), 97, 107-9, 121n4
indigenous movements, (see also colonization) 2, 4, 13n18, 15, 17, 24, 27-9, 37-43, 44n3, 49, 76, 106, 151, 180, 183-4
indigenous peoples, (see also names of specific nations; colonization; indigenous movements) 3-4, 7, 11-2, 13n13, 15, 23, 27, 29, 31, 44n6, 48-9, 51-2, 148, 151, 154, 176, 180, 184
  before contact, 25-26, 51
  cultural genocide of, 13-4, 25-32, 37, 103
  elders, 23, 26, 34-5, 38-9
  "indigenous" versus "Aboriginal", 20n6
  knowledge systems, 25-30
  and land, 12, 25, 49
  as nations, 29-30
  pedagogy, 30
  queer, 127, 132
  slaves, 52
  treaties, 26
  urban, 3, 37, 43, 44n5
  women, 17-8, 23, 27, 29-30, 35-6, 38, 43-4n2, 44n3, 48, 72, 75-6, 106, 127, 166, 180, 183
  workers, 48, 52
  youth, 23, 30-40
industrial unions, (see also labour movements) 53, 56, 58
Industrial Workers of the World (IWW), 52
International Circle of Elders, 23
International Women's Day, 86
intersectionality, (see subheadings under specific oppressions; social relations, intertwined)
Iroquois Confederacy, (see also Mohawk Nation) 13, 31

Islam, 11, 103, 148, 150, 152
Jamaica, 146, 156, 166
Jewish people/Judaism, 11, 148, 153, 159
Jones, Lynn, 2, 183
judicial system, 2, 55, 112, 114, 137
  heterosexism in, 11-2, 125, 127-30, 138-4, 145n13
  racism in, 11-2, 22n18, 49, 75, 88, 30, 103-4, 127
  sexism in, 30, 50-1, 83-5, 88, 91-3, 103-4
  support for capital, 54, 59-64, 66
  and violence against women, 30, 72, 75, 83-5, 88, 91-3, 96n12, 103-4, 113, 126
justice, understandings of, 25-6

Kinesis, 89
Knights of Labor, 52, 68n12
knowledge production,
  as active process, 174-5
  in this book, 15-6, 19, 20n7, 21n15, 22n16, 21n18, 28, 172n2, 174-80, 183-4
  and colonization, 24-32, 37, 43n1, 44n7, 180
  dialogical, 2-3, 5n3, 174-5, 179
  and difference, 25-6, 98-102, 174-7
  experience in, 21n15, 174-8, 180
  and movements, 178-9, 182, 184, 185n3
  and the origins of capitalism, 51
  and racism, 100, 175-6
  and standpoint, 12-3, 16, 28, 71, 175-7, 185n4
  and violence against women, 71-75, 95n1, 181
kyriarchy 185n2

labour law, (see work, state regulation of)
labour movements, 2, 6, 8, 13, 14, 20-1n2, 46, 48-9, 52-4, 56-8, 77, 92, 181, 183
  Catholic Church and, 56, 62-4
  children in, 59-60
  conservatism in, 57, 66
  organizing, 48, 52-3, 56-61
  other oppression in/by, 100
  and queer issues, 141

racism in/by, 53
sexism in/by, 53, 57-9, 76, 92, 181
state repression of, 53-4, 60-6
strikes by, 45, 48, 52, 55-6, 61-67, 85, 90, 171, 174, 181, 184
in textile and garment industries, 55-6, 57-66
women in, 17-8, 45, 55-60, 67
Lachute, Quebec, 66
Lakeman, Lee 2, 15, 18-9, 181
introduction to, 69-71
involvement in Vancouver, 86-93
involvement in Woodstock, 80-3, 85
politicization, 78-80
pointers to online audio clips, 96n6, 96n8
reflections on struggle, 94-5
writing by, 84
land,
theft of, (see colonization)
understandings of, 12, 25
language,
and colonization, 12, 25-6, 32, 35, 38
and resistance, 38, 81, 153
barriers to services, 105
sexist, 99, 160, 162, 164-5
training, 106, 109, 114-5, 118
law, (see judicial system)
Léger, Paul-Émile, 63
Lesage, Jean, 66
lesbians, (see also gay men; gay and lesbian movements; heterosexism; queer people) 1, 8, 11, 15, 81, 99, 106, 126, 128, 130, 132-4, 136-7, 140, 143, 144n1, 166-7
in Christian contexts, 147, 151, 154, 167-71
emergence of lesbian identity, 128
experiences of sexism in queer movements, 131-2
violence against, 12, 72
Liberal Party,
of Canada, 129
Quebec, 54, 66, 117
London, England, 81, 87, 131
London, Ontario, 137-8, 160
Lubicon Nation, (see also Cree Nation) 38, 44n9
Lutheran Church, 160

MacPhee, Donna, 3, 15, 18, 180, 183
education-focused activism, 38-40, 42-3
introduction to, 23-4
as mentor, 39-40
pointers to online audio clips, 44n9, 44n10
Mallett, Kathy, 3, 18, 44n3, 183
Manitoba, 124
University of, 129, 131
first gay demonstration in, 134
governmental opposition to gay rights, 139-42
Manuel, George, 32, 37
marriage, 81, 114, 124-6, 134-7, 139-42, 143-4, 160
first widely publicized same-sex marriage in Canada, 134-5
masculinity, (see also patriarchy/sexism) 11, 29-30, 43n2, 48, 50-1, 53, 57-9, 68n9, 70-1, 73-5, 79, 83, 87-90, 96n2, 104-5, 107, 113, 115, 125-8, 131-2, 148, 155, 157-9, 161, 165
McClung, Nellie, 13, 155
McGill University, 45, 54-5, 97
media, 7, 12, 125, 165, 176, 182-3
grassroots, 134, 138, 145n10
and queer movements, 133-5, 138, 141
and other movements, 41, 91, 184
violence against women in, 71
Mennonite Church, 148
Mohawk Nation, (see also Iroquois Confederacy) 26, 38, 44n9, 154, 177
money, (see funding by the state; fundraising; poverty)
role in social organization, 4, 47, 49, 51-2, 125
Montreal, 18, 45, 55, 58, 60-4, 97, 107-9, 111-7, 181
Montreal Massacre, 116, 119, 122n7
Monture-Angus, Patricia, 26
Movement for Christian Feminism, 147, 160-3, 167, 173n12
Mulay, Shree, 15, 18, 45, 67n2, 181
anaylsis of Quebec sovereignty struggle, 122n10
introduction to, 97, 107
involvement in Fédération des femmes du Québec, 117-8

involvement in Indian People's Association in North America, 97, 107-9
involvement in National Action Committee on the Status of Women, 118-9
involvement in peace movement, 107
involvement in South Asian Women's Community Centre, 108-9, 111-5, 117-120
pointers to online audio clips, 121n4, 121n5
multiculturalism, 3, 101-2, 150
Multilateral Agreement on Investment (MAI), 6, 19-20n2
Muslims, (see "Islam")
mutual aid, 48, 68n12, 94, 148
Nanaimo, British Columbia, 91
National Action Committee on the Status of Women (NAC), 45, 67n4, 118-20, 162
National Gay Rights Coalition, 131
National Indian Brotherhood, 32, 37
national liberation movements, 77
neoliberalism, 1-2, 6, 19-20n2, 42, 44n11, 90-2, 152, 184
New Democratic Party (NDP),
British Columbia, 90, 93, 139
Manitoba, 124, 130, 139-41
Ontario, 139
New Left movements, (see also names of specific movements) 77-8, 99, 105-6, 107, 129-30, 157, 179
New York City, 120, 128, 130, 145n6
Nixon, Kimberley, 96n11
non-monogamy, 126, 136, 144n5
No One Is Illegal, 3, 121
North, Richard, 15, 18, 181
hunger strike 124, 140-1
introduction to 123-4
involvement in queer struggles 130-7, 139-42
marriage to Chris Vogel 134-7, 139
pointer to online audio clip 145n10
politicization 129-31
nurses, 85-6

Obonsawin, Roger, 3
One Big Union, 53

Ontario, 6, 8, 18, 19-20n2, 44n10, 53, 69, 78-9, 124, 137, 144n4, 168, 170, 175, 181
Ontario Days of Action, 6, 19-20n2
oppression, (see also names of specific oppressions) 10-12, 74, 98
dangers of simplistic categories, 16-17
impacts of, 12
intersections among, (see also social relations, intertwined) 11, 16-17, 43n1, 67n8, 95, 101-2, 177, 185n2
within movements, 17, 53, 57-9, 74-8, 96n11, 99-100, 105-6, 107, 131-2, 143, 181
organizational form, 40, 42, 48, 52-3, 82, 131
Oscar Wilde Memorial Society, 142
Oshawa, Ontario, 53
Owen Sound, Ontario, 160
owners of capital, 11-2, 47-9, 52, 54, 58, 62

Padlock Law, 54-5, 68n13
paganism, 148
Pakistan, 98, 109
Parent, Madeleine, 2, 15, 18, 46, 67n1, 67n3, 122n9, 180-1
introduction to, 45
involvement in labour movement, 45, 55-66, 68n14, 181
involvement in student movement, 54-6, 180
involvement in women's movement, 45, 66, 67n4, 117, 119, 181
pointers to online audio clips, 67n4, 68n14
targeted by judicial system, 60, 64, 66
Paris Commune, 68n16
Parti Quebecois, 117, 122n10
patriarchy/sexism, (see also women's/feminist movements) 43n1, 67n8, 70-1, 184
and capitalism, 50-1, 67n7, 67n8, 181
in Christian contexts, 148, 151-2, 153-5, 157-65, 173n14
and colonization, 24, 29-30, 50, 76
confronting perpetrators, 87-9
and financial dependence, 47, 50, 52-3, 70, 109-11, 115-6, 120, 177, 182, 184

in immigration, 104-5
individual experiences of, 9, 24, 33, 40, 75, 79-80, 81, 95, 107, 113-4, 115, 116
in the judicial system, 83-5, 103-4
in/by movements, 53, 57-9, 74-5, 77-8, 99-100, 107, 121n1, 131-2, 143, 181
and multiculturalism, 101-2, 104-5
and sexuality, 51, 96n3, 125-7
social organization of, 11, 99-102, 104-5, 177
and social services, 104-5, 115-6, 118
and violence against women, (see violence against women)
peace movements, 76-8, 107
  other oppression in, 100
  sexism in, 78, 107
Penner, Roland, 140-1
people of colour, (see racialized people, non-indigenous; women of colour)
Persons Case, 76
Plains Indian Cultural Survival School (PICSS), 24, 36-43, 44n8
  closing of, 42
  funding of, 42
  impacts of, 42-43
  indigenous culture in, 38-9
  intergenerational focus, 39-40
  naming of, 41
police, (see judicial system)
polyamory, (see non-monogamy)
Popert, Ken, 131
pornography, 86-7, 165
poverty, 2, 6, 11, 13, 18, 24, 47-8, 50-1, 59, 79-80, 96n2, 108, 110, 117-20, 130, 153, 156-7, 183
  and sexuality, 127
power, 3, 46
  defined, 10
  power-over, 10, 20n5, 21-2n15, 49, 175
  power-to-do, 10, 13, 20n5
  social organization of, (see also social relations) 11-12
Presbyterian Church, 147-8, 154, 160
Pride events, 86, 130, 133
primitive accumulation, 49-51, 67n7
privilege, (see also ally work) 3, 10-1, 14, 16-7, 43n1, 51, 71, 74, 90, 98, 100, 135, 144n1, 175
  class, (see also owners of capital) 90, 156
  defined, 10
  heterosexual, 125-6, 128-9, 136-9, 141-2
  masculine, (see masculinity)
  settler, 13-4, 24
  white, (see whiteness)
professionals, 83, 85, 90, 107-8, 129, 142

Quakers, 148
Quebec, 2, 18, 22n18, 38, 45, 54-60, 63, 66, 76-7, 109, 181
  Quiet Revolution 66
  sovereignty movement, 78, 117-8, 122n10
  state regulation of workplaces, 60-2, 64-5, 181
  women's movements (see Fédération des femmes du Québec; Mulay, Shree; Parent, Madeleine; Siddiqui, Sadeqa; South Asian Women's Community Centre)
Quebec City, 61, 117
queer, defined, 144n1
queer movements, (see gay and lesbian movements)
queer people, (see also gay men; lesbians) 1, 11, 22n18, 124, 126-30, 132, 135-8, 142, 144n1, 147, 181-2
  indigenous, 127, 132
  racialized, 130, 132
  violence against, 72, 96n2, 137-8
  youth, 145n14
Quiet Revolution, 66

racialization, definition, 68n10
racialized people, non-indigenous, (see also indigenous peoples; racism/white supremacy; women of colour) 8, 11, 49-50, 75-7, 79, 88, 90, 96n2, 96n7, 100-5, 112-3, 115, 118-9, 121, 121n6, 130, 147, 166, 171, 176
  as workers, 48, 52-3, 90, 90, 108
  organizing by, (see also anti-racist struggles; Mulay, Shree; Siddiqui, Sadeqa; South Asian Women's Community Centre; women of colour, organizing by) 53, 90, 105-6
  queer, 130, 132, 144n1

204 – Gender and Sexuality

racism/white supremacy, (see also anti-racist struggles; indigenous movements) 3, 11, 31, 68n10, 76, 103, 122n10, 147, 166, 176-7, 180, 182-4
   and Christianity, 150-2, 166, 169
   and education, 30-5, 37, 40-42, 75
   family as refuge from, 74, 104-5
   and immigration, 3, 8, 13, 52-3, 101-5, 116-7, 118-9, 121n6, 122n10
   individual experiences of, 23-4, 40, 79, 144n4, 183
   and the judicial system, 11-2, 75, 88, 103-4, 127
   and knowledge production, 15, 27, 100, 150, 175-6
   in movements, 53, 76, 93, 99-100, 105-6, 117-9, 121, 121n3, 132, 143
   and multiculturalism, 101-2
   and the origins of capitalism, 49-50, 67n7, 67n8, 181
   and secularism, 148, 150
   and sexuality, 126-7, 144n4
   social organization of, 11, 101-2, 104-5
   and social services, 104-6, 115-6, 118
   and violence against women, 29-30, 40, 72, 75, 95, 103-6, 108-10, 113-5, 121n6, 181, 183
Rainbow Resource Centre, 131, 142
Reagan, Ronald, 90
reification, 4, 46-9, 51, 181
religion, in general, (see names of specific religions and Christian denominations; Christianity) 50, 100, 147-52, 172n2
   understood individualistically, 149-50
   understood socially, 150-2, 182
replacement workers, (see scabs)
residential schools, 30-33, 155
   impacts of, 32
   resistance to, 30, 32
Resisting the State: Canadian History Through the Stories of Activists, 1-3, 6, 15, 18, 19n1, 19-20n2, 44n3, 44n5, 44n11, 96n4, 173n6, 178, 183, 185n1
Reuther, Rosemary Radford, 153
Riddington, Jillian, 81
Roach, Charles, 2
Roback, Lea, 55-6
Rowley, Kent, 57-8, 61, 64, 66
Royal Canadian (or Northwest) Mounted Police, (see also judicial system) 32, 54, 156
Royal Commission on the Status of Women, 77, 173n8
ruling relations, 185n2
Rumscheidt, Barbara, 151-2
Russian Revolution, 53
Ryerson Polytechnical Institute (now University), 78

Sabia, Laura, 157, 173n8
same-sex marriage, (see gay and lesbian movements, marriage equality; marriage)
Sanders, Doug, 1
Saskatchewan, 129
scabs, 58, 63, 68n15, 92
schools, (see education system; Plains Indian Cultural Survival School; residential schools)
Second World War, 45, 53-6, 128-9, 156
secularism, 100, 147-50, 172n2, 172n4
   critical understanding of, 152
settlers, (see also colonization) 11, 27-36, 40-41, 180
sexism, (see patriarchy/sexism)
sexuality, (see also gay and lesbian movements; heterosexism) 11, 22n18, 74, 81, 102, 127-9
   and Christianity, 148, 151, 154-5, 167-71, 173n14
   and colonization, 17, 29, 127
   and class, 127-8
   decriminalization of same-gender, 128-9
   social regulation of, 12, 29, 51, 124-8, 130, 132-44, 144n3, 145n6, 148, 154-5, 157, 167-71, 182
   and racism, 126-7
shame, 71, 125, 127, 136, 144n3, 161
Shepherd, Loraine MacKenzie, 169-70
Shore, Edith, 158
Showler, Isabel and Frank, 2
Shushwap Nation, 32
Siddiqui, Sadeqa, 15, 18, 181
   introduction to, 97-8
   involvement in the Fédération des femmes du Québec, 116-8, 120-1
   involvement in South Asian Women's

Community Centre, 97-8, 109-11, 113-21
  involvement in World March of Women, 119-20
  pointers to online audio clips, 122n8, 122n11
Sikhism, 148
slavery, 8, 13, 49-50, 52, 76, 106, 151
Smith, Andrea, 17, 29-30
Smith, Dorothy, 20n4, 185n2
Social Credit Party,
  British Columbia, 90-2
social gospel, 2, 76, 96n4, 154-5, 173n6
social relations, 4, 9-12, 19, 20n4, 21n15, 43-4n2, 72, 74, 98-102, 123, 173n4, 175-7
  defined, 11-12
  intertwined, 17, 20n7, 43n1, 67n6, 67n8, 95, 98, 124-7, 165, 176-7, 179-80, 182, 185n2
  and intimate settings, 74
  of making and doing, (see also capitalism) 46-51, 136, 152
  partial list of axes, 11
socialist movements, 48-9, 53, 76, 78, 95, 132
  sexism in, 78, 99
social services, (see also education system) 8, 13, 47, 81, 85, 89, 97-8, 131, 142
  colonial experiences of, 30, 35-6
  critical analysis of, 19, 79, 82-3, 92-5
  cuts to, 91-2
  heterosexism in, 143
  other oppressive experiences of, 12, 79
  racism and sexism in, 88, 92-3, 104-6, 115-6, 118
  by/for women of colour, 97-8, 106, 109-14, 115-6, 118, 121
solidarity, importance of, 48, 92, 102, 121
Solidarity (B.C. anti-cuts coalition), 92
Somers, Bruce, 1
South Asian Women's Community Centre (SAWCC), 97-8, 121n5, 121n8
  addressing economic dependence, 109-11
  addressing violence against women, 113-5
  challenging the state, 115-121
  engagement with mainstream women's movements, 116-121
  holistic approach, 109-10
  internal divisions, 111-2
  origins in Indian People's Association of North America, 108-9
Spanish Civil War, 6, 20n3
Spence, Doreen, 3, 15, 18, 180, 183
  education-focused activism, (see also Plains Indian Cultural Survival School) 36-42
  introduction to, 23
  resisting forced sterilization of indigenous girl, 35-6
  pointers to online audio clips, 44n4, 44n8
  as student, 33-5
St. Catherine's, Ontario, 6, 15
standpoint, 12-5, 21n12, 28, 175-7, 179, 185n4
Statistics Canada, 72-3
Status of Women (federal department), 160
sterilization, forced, 23, 35-6, 44n4
Stonewall Riots, 130-1, 143
strikes, (see labour movements, strikes)
student movements, 45, 54-6, 129-30, 180
  sexism in, 78
Supreme Court of Canada, 55, 141-2

Take Back the Night, 69, 86-7, 89, 96n8, 96n10
talkingradical.ca, 15, 44n4, 44n8, 44n9, 67n4, 68n14, 96n6, 96n8, 121n4, 121n5, 122n8, 122n11, 145n10, 173n9, 173n12, 173n13
temperance movements, 76
textile industry, (see also Dominion Textile Company) 55-7
Thatcher, Margaret, 90
Thobani, Sunera, 101, 104-5
Thompson, E. P., 3, 5n4, 21n14
Toronto, 35, 44n6, 76-9, 106, 120, 121n3, 128, 131-2, 138-9, 146-7, 156-7, 160, 169, 173n7
tradition, reification in multiculturalism, 101-2
trans people, 11, 15, 21n9, 22n18, 96n2, 96n11, 99, 121n2, 145n14, 182
Trotskyist organizations, (see also

206 – Gender and Sexuality

Communism; socialist movements) 132
Trudeau, Prime Minister Pierre, 78, 129
Tse-tung, Mao, 94, 96n13
Turtle Island, 14, 17, 21n13, 24-26, 29-31, 39, 43-4n2, 51, 76, 174, 177, 180-1
Two Row Wampum, 26-27

Union Nationale, 54, 68n13
unions, (see labour movments)
United Church of Canada, 18, 146-7, 151, 153-5, 157, 173n10
   and abortion, 155
   feminist struggle in, 147, 158-66, 182
   heterosexism and queer struggle in, 147, 167-71, 182
   Observer, 161-2, 165, 167-8
   opposition to empire, 153
   ordination of gay men and lesbians, 147, 168-70
   origins, 154
   patriarchy/sexism in, 155, 158-9, 161-5, 173n14
   and residential schools, 155
   and the social gospel, 154-5
   task forces on sexism, 147-8, 162-6
United Nations (U.N.), 120
United Nations Working Group on Indigenous Populations, 23
University of Manitoba, 129, 131
urban space, (see also specific cities) 3, 44n5, 123, 128

Valleyfield, Quebec, 55, 58, 62-6
Vancouver, 18-9, 69, 86-7, 89-93, 96n10, 131-2, 163, 181
Vancouver Rape Relief, 19, 69, 86-7, 89-95, 96n11
Velvet Fist, 157, 173n7
Vietnam War, 97, 107, 129
violence against men, (see also gay men, violence against) 96n2
violence against women, (see also women's/feminist movements) 2, 13, 17-9, 69, 71-5, 81-95, 96n2, 96n7, 96n9, 98, 119-21, 126-7, 165, 181, 183
   against disabled women, 72
   against indigenous women, 27, 29-30, 32, 40, 51, 72, 75, 96n7, 103
   against queer women, 72, 132

against racialized women, 51, 72, 75, 96n7, 100, 103-6, 108-10, 113-6, 121, 121n6, 181, 183
   direct action confrontations as response, 86-9
   gendered character, 72-3
   and the origins of capitalism, 50-51
   and the state/judicial system, 72, 75, 82-6, 88, 89, 90-4, 96n7, 103-5, 110-3, 114-6, 118-21, 181
   statistics, 72-3
   victim services response, 92-3
Vogel, Chris, 2, 15, 18, 181
   introduction to, 123-4
   involvement in queer struggles, 130-44
   movement fundraising, 142-3
   marriage to Richard North, 134-7, 139
   pointer to online audio clip, 145n10
   politicization, 129-30
Voice of Women, 77

War of 1812, 31
War on Terror, 152
Weitz, Don, 2
welfare system, (see also poverty) 47, 79, 115-6
   and sexuality, 125, 127
Welland Canal, 52
whiteness, (see also racism/white supremacy) 3, 7-8, 11-4, 17, 24-8, 34, 43n1, 44n7, 50, 53, 71, 100, 105, 126-7, 132, 144n4, 147-8, 150-2, 166, 175-6
Winnipeg, 18, 44n3, 123-4, 130-4, 137-9, 142, 181, 183
   General Strike 53-4
Winnipeg Gay Community Centre, (see also Campus Gay Club; Gays For Equality; Rainbow Resource Centre) 142
Wise, Tim, 43n1
witch hunt, 50-51, 68n9, 151
women (see also patriarchy/sexism; women's/feminist movements) 8, 11, 13, 50-51, 54-5, 74-5, 80
   Christian, 150-1, 153-5, 157-66, 169-70
   disabled, 72, 99
   indigenous, 15, 18, 23, 27, 29-30, 32, 43-4n2, 44n3, 48, 72, 75-6, 93, 106,

166, 180, 183
middle-class, 93, 54, 76-8, 90, 93, 99
poor and working-class, 50-3, 55-6, 58-67, 68n16, 72, 76-8, 80, 90, 93, 99, 106, 117-8, 120, 127, 151, 166, 181, 183
queer, (see lesbians)
racialized, (see women of colour)
and sexuality, 51, 125-7, 145n11
and violence, (see violence against women)
white, 11, 15, 17, 29, 48, 52-3, 76-8, 93, 99, 116, 144n4, 166
and work, 3, 47, 50, 52-3, 55-6, 58-60, 67, 70-1, 79, 106, 159
Women's Aid Project (London, England), 81
Women Against the Budget, 92
women's/feminist movements, 2, 7, 16-8, 20n3, 45, 76-8, 80-95, 98-9, 173n8, 181, 183
ableism in, 99
against capitalism, 17
in Christian contexts, 2, 146-7, 157-66, 173n11, 182
and consciousness raising groups, 80
indigenous, 17, 29-30, 76, 106, 180
participation by men, 82-3, 89-90, 115
by/with queer women, (see lesbians; gay and lesbian movements)
by/with (non-indigenous) racialized women, (see also women of colour) 76-7, 97-100, 102-3, 105-6, 108-21, 121n3, 181
racism in, 76, 99-100, 117-9, 121, 121n3, 121n6, 181
and the state, 18, 78, 82-6, 88, 89, 90-5, 96n7, 103, 105-6, 109, 112, 115-21
suffrage, 55, 76-7
and trans people, 96n11, 99
against violence, (see also violence against women) 18-9, 69, 71, 75, 81-95, 96n7, 103, 105-6, 108-21, 181, 183
by/with working-class women, 17-8, 45, 51, 53, 55-9, 63-5, 67, 76-7, 99, 106, 108, 181
Women's Health Collective, 92
Women's Inter-church Council, 160
women of colour, 11, 17, 45, 48, 70, 93, 99-102, 109-11, 127, 166, 181, 183
and mainstream women's movements, 75-7, 98-9, 102, 105-6, 116-21, 121n6
organizing by (see also Mulay, Shree; Siddiqui, Sadeqa; South Asian Women's Community Centre) 18, 75-7, 93, 99, 102-3, 105-6, 110, 115-121, 121n1, 181, 183
state regulation of 75, 101-5, 115-6, 121
violence against, 72, 75, 95, 103-6, 108-10, 113-5, 121n6, 181, 183
as waged workers, 70, 108
Woodstock, Ontario, 18, 69, 79-83, 85-6, 90, 95, 181
World March of Women, 119-20, 122n11
work, 46-51
caring/reproductive, 50, 70-1
children and, 59
gendered organization, 29, 48, 50-2, 55, 70, 108
racialized organization, 48, 51, 52, 108
state regulation of, 9, 53-5, 60-62, 64-5
workers, waged, 7-8, 11-3, 16, 47-9, 51-3, 68n11, 68n12, 90, 181
struggles by, (see labour movements)
women as, 17, 45, 50, 52-3, 55-67, 70, 77, 90, 99, 108, 110-1, 115-6, 181, 183
racialized, 52-3, 70, 108, 110-1, 115-6, 183
Warner, Tom, 130

Yakachuk, Barbara, 81
Young Women's Christian Association (YWCA), 76, 81, 156
youth, 11, 63, 146, 168
indigenous, 23, 30-40
queer, 142, 145n14
and work, 58-60

Zapatistas, 2, 4, 184-5